THE CRAFT OF HISTORY AND
THE STUDY OF THE NEW TESTAMENT

Resources for Biblical Study

Tom Thatcher, New Testament Editor

Number 60

THE CRAFT OF HISTORY AND
THE STUDY OF THE NEW TESTAMENT

THE CRAFT OF HISTORY AND
THE STUDY OF THE NEW TESTAMENT

Beth M. Sheppard

Society of Biblical Literature
Atlanta

THE CRAFT OF HISTORY AND
THE STUDY OF THE NEW TESTAMENT

Library of Congress Cataloging-in-Publication Data

Sheppard, Beth M., 1966–
    The craft of history and the study of the New Testament / Beth M. Sheppard.
        p. cm. — (Resources for biblical study ; number 60)
    Includes bibliographical references and index.
    ISBN 978-1-58983-665-5 (paper binding : alk. paper) — ISBN 978-1-58983-666-2 (electronic format)
    1. Bible. N.T.—Criticism and interpretation. I. Title. II. Series: Resources for biblical study ; no. 60.
    BS2350.S47 2012
    225.6—dc23   2012041817

Printed on acid-free, recycled paper conforming to
ANSI/NISO Z39.48-1992 (R1997) and ISO 9706:1994
standards for paper permanence.

For Andy

Contents

ABBREVIATIONS

ANF	*The Ante-Nicene Fathers: Translations of the Writings of the Fathers Down to A.D. 325.* Edited by Alexander Roberts and James Donaldson. 10 vols. 1885–1887.
ANRW	*Aufstieg und Niedergang der römischen Welt: Geschichte und Kultur Roms im Spiegel der neueren Forschung.* Part 2, *Principat.* Edited by Hildegard Temporini and Wolfgang Haase. Berlin: de Gruyter, 1972–.
Ant. rom	Dionysius of Halicarnassensis, *Antiquitates romanae*
BDAG	Danker, F. W., W. Bauer, W. F. Arndt, and F. W. Gingrich. *Greek-English Lexicon of the New Testament and Other Early Christian Literature.* 3rd ed. Chicago: University of Chicago Press, 1999.
BMW	The Bible in the Modern World
CBQ	*Catholic Biblical Quarterly*
ChrCent	*Christian Century*
ERT	*Evangelical Review of Theology*
ExpTim	*Expository Times*
Geogr.	Strabo, *Geography*
HeyJ	*Heythrop Journal*
Hist.	Herodotus, *Histories*
HTS	Harvard Theological Studies
JPsychohist	*Journal of Psychohistory*
JBL	*Journal of Biblical Literature*
JCH	*Journal of Contemporary History*
JETS	*Journal of the Evangelical Theological Society*
JR	*Journal of Religion*
JRASup	Journal of Roman Archaeology Supplement Series
JRelS	*Journal of Religious Studies*
JRS	*Journal of Roman Studies*
JSH	*Journal of Social History*
JSJSup	Supplements to the Journal for the Study of Judaism
JSNT	*Journal for the Study of the New Testament*

JSOT	Journal for the Study of the Old Testament
J.W.	Josephus, *Jewish War*
LCL	Loeb Classical Library
LHBOTS	Library of Hebrew Bible/Old Testament Studies
LLA	Library of the Liberal Arts
LNTS	Library of New Testament Studies
NovT	*Novum Testamentum*
NovTSup	Novum Testamentum Supplements
NTS	*New Testament Studies*
PEQ	*Palestine Exploration Quarterly*
PRSt	*Perspectives in Religious Studies*
PTMS	Princeton Theological Monograph Series
ResQ	*Restoration Quarterly*
RHR	*Radical History Review*
Sat.	Juvenal, *Satirae*
SBLDS	Society of Biblical Literature Dissertation Series
SBLRBS	Society of Biblical Literature Resources for Biblical Study
SBTS	Sources for Biblical and Theological Study
SNTSMS	Society of New Testament Studies Monograph Series
STDJ	Studies on the Texts of the Desert of Judah
TDNT	*Theological Dictionary of the New Testament.* Edited by G. Kittel and G. Friedrich. Translated by G. W. Bromiley. 10 Vols. Grand Rapids: Eerdmans, 1964–1976.
TS	*Theological Studies*
WW	*World and Word*

INTRODUCTION

History is the arena in which we explore the past. But not every historian will come to the same conclusions or find the same insights about a single episode that happened days, decades, or centuries ago. This is similar to a phenomenon in New Testament studies where interpreters who examine the same passage often have very different observations to make about it. Take the Last Supper, for example. When it comes to the final meal that Jesus shares with his disciples prior to his crucifixion, John's Gospel contains the most detail and stretches from chapter 13 through chapter 17. This part of the Gospel is known as the farewell discourse—or, more aptly, "discourses," since there are several topics of conversation that Jesus broaches with his disciples. On the surface, this extended farewell contains a number of poignant scenes, such as Jesus washing the disciple's feet, Jesus revealing that Judas would betray him, Jesus telling the disciples that he will be leaving them but will assign the Paraclete to remain in his stead, and Jesus praying to his Father on behalf of those who believe him.

So what have a few New Testament scholars who have an affinity for history been thinking about these passages? For his part, Robert Fortna is interested in determining what aspects of the Last Supper stem from an underlying tradition that the evangelist had at his disposal when pulling together the final version of the Gospel. To this end, he describes a source that included the events that lead up to Jesus' crucifixion, which he labels PQ, or the Passion Source. Fortna concludes, though, that chapter 13 has been rewritten by the author of the Fourth Gospel so extensively that it is impossible to separate out the strands that the evangelist himself contributed from those of this Passion Source.[1]

Instead of focusing on the history of how the Gospel was written, Ben Witherington goes in a different direction. He compares the Last Supper

---

1. Robert T. Fortna, *The Fourth Gospel and Its Predecessor* (Edinburgh: T&T Clark, 1988), 149.

with a Greco-Roman banquet. These meals often closed with a symposium, or period of training, entertainment, and dialogue. At points in his exposition of the meal and conversation as it is recorded by the author of the Fourth Gospel, Witherington includes mundane details about daily life in the first century. For example, when it comes to the image of Jesus as the vine (15:1–11), he notes that the vine was a prized plant because grapes could be grown inexpensively. Further, wine was a source of nourishment and strength for Mediterranean residents, who needed a reliable source of drink and sustenance in a climate that alternated between rainy seasons and summer droughts.[2]

The concept of the symposium also captures the attention of Bruce J. Malina and Richard Rohrbaugh. But they don't share Witherington's take on that institution. Rather than being fascinated with everyday details of meals and food in general, they are particularly attentive to the dynamics of group interactions and social norms. Thus they go so far as to include a sketch of banquet seating arrangements in their effort to illustrate which positions at a table were the most honorable and would be assigned to the persons of highest rank.[3] Their interest in group behavior is also apparent in their particular interpretation of the metaphor of the vine and the branches. They highlight the fact that the metaphor of a main vine with offshoots is used to encourage solidarity and foster close interpersonal bonds between Jesus' core group members. They also note that the stronger the bonds within a group might be, the greater its security from outsiders.[4]

Rather than focusing attention on nature of the banquet or the details of group interactions, Sandra Schneiders heads off on another new track when she launches an inquiry into the identity of a single guest at the meal, the Beloved Disciple (13:23). The key question that informs Schneiders's study is the query, "What if the Beloved Disciple happened to be female?"[5] This question allows Schneiders to highlight the vital role that women

---

2. Ben Witherington III, *John's Wisdom* (Louisville: Westminster John Knox, 1995), 232–33, 257.

3. Bruce J. Malina and Richard Rohrbaugh, *Social-Science Commentary on the Gospel of John* (Minneapolis: Fortress, 1998), 220.

4. Ibid., 233–34.

5. Sandra M. Schneiders, " 'Because of the Woman's Testimony…': Reexamining the Issue of Authorship in the Fourth Gospel," *NTS* 44 (1998): 527: "I do not think that the really crucial Beloved Disciple passages, particularly the scene at the Last Supper… absolutely require an exclusively male identification of the figure."

play in the Gospel and in the history of early Christianity, even though no woman is explicitly mentioned as being present in John's version of the Last Supper.

So Fortna, Witherington, Malina and Rohrbaugh, and Schneiders present four very different views of a single section of John's Gospel. Why are these authors' insights so dissimilar? In part it is because they have used widely divergent methods in how they go about doing the business of New Testament interpretation—methods rooted in the discipline of history. A method is the set of theories, philosophical presuppositions, and generally accepted techniques upon which a scholar relies when interpreting a text or pursing study of an individual or event from the past. The choice of method helps define what questions are asked, how evidence is treated when seeking to answer inquiries, and many other issues related to a given project.

To clarify, in the example of the Last Supper, the focus on the history of the formation of the Gospel text that was demonstrated by Fortna was a project driven by philological concerns about the authenticity and history of how the text came to be. For his part, Witherington's fascination with the details of the growing season of grapes puts him in sympathy with ethnohistorians, who assert that "ordinary things" from the past deserve as much attention as leaders, movers and shakers, wars, and other prominent aspects of the past.

Instead of focusing on everyday life, like growing grapes, a concern for group dynamics along with social norms and status aligns Malina and Rohrbaugh with the social historians. And, finally, Schneiders's desire to look beyond what the text actually says to discern what voices, groups, and factions are not prominent in the written records but nonetheless contributed to the growth of Christianity is similar to the techniques used by revisionist historians. So even though these scholars are New Testament interpreters, the methods that they are applying when delving into the Last Supper have their correlates in the methods used by historians who are studying subjects as diverse as the Middle Ages, world politics, or the U.S. Civil War.

We live in an era when the borders between disciplines are ever more permeable. Interdisciplinary studies programs in colleges and universities have been in vogue now for decades. Yet there is still much that we might learn from exchanges with those in the discipline of history.

For dialogue to be profitable, interlocutors must have a common vocabulary and at least a basic familiarity with the overarching conventions of each other's discipline. The initial chapters of this book provide a general introduction to the theoretical aspects of the field of history. In chapter 1, for instance, basic definitions for terms such as *historiography* and *philosophy of history* are offered. Philosophical concerns extend into chapter 2, which gives overviews of the role and nature of time, the various areas in which selectivity plays a part in historical projects, and the importance and nature of sources. Chapter 3 delves deeper into the theoretical aspects of the discipline of history and addresses issues such as how history should be used and the differences between analytical and speculative history. This section of the book is rounded out with a discussion of some of the primary stumbling blocks and fallacies to which historical studies are susceptible.

With the fifth chapter, gears shift a bit and we embark on a history of writing history. This subtle turn in orientation is still firmly rooted in the theoretical portion of the book, despite the fact that material will be presented in roughly chronological sequence. There is one caveat, though. Some methods that got their impetus in the early part of the twentieth century are still alive and well in the academy, and thus their ongoing application will be traced into the present time. In any event, as time progresses there are new approaches and even revivals of older styles of scholarship. This should not be surprising, given the ever-changing approaches that are wheeled out in our own field. After all, in biblical studies it is no secret that there are methods of interpretation that previous generations employed but that are no longer in vogue in modern times. For instance, the Pesher mode of interpretation, such as that used at Qumran, and allegorical interpretations, such as those employed in the Middle Ages and involving the fourfold interpretation of scripture, are no longer in fashion. Likewise, the field of professional history has not been static in its application of methods to the study of the past. So chapter 5 provides a survey of the main techniques employed by Western historians from ancient times to the early twentieth century. It begins with both ancient Jewish and Greco-Roman historiographies and culminates with an approach known as historicism, which was still prevalent at the beginning of the last century and lingered in biblical scholarship through the middle of the last century. A few words about a method known as New Historicism are also introduced.

The bulk of the twentieth century and the beginning of the twenty-first century gave rise to an explosion of historical methodologies. Marxist history, the *Annales* School, and other approaches came into existence and are still flourishing in the field. Chapter 6 introduces these and other tactics in the historian's methodological kit.

By the middle of the twentieth century, however, postmodernism rocked nearly every academic discipline, history included. The seventh chapter describes methods that developed when researchers sought to approach materials using different viewpoints and lenses, such as revisionist history, postcolonialism, and even imaginative history.

Methods, however, remain vaguely abstract without some examples that assist an historian to execute his or her project. The last three chapters of the book demonstrate the application of some of the theoretical aspects presented in the early chapters when employed in the analysis of biblical texts. The three studies—one on clothing in Luke, one on the Samaritan woman, and the final one focused on Paul's body analogy in 1 Corinthians—between them draw inspiration from three different types of history: economic, administrative or legal, and medical. While this trio of studies would be broadly described as social history, they might more precisely be identified as inspired by the work of the history of private life or cultural history, a methodological focus where minor details of everyday life are as interesting and as worthy of study as the political or military interests that are usually associated with events of historical significance. Beyond that, one study represents a revisionist slant in methodology and another incorporates a paragraph or two involving simplistic quantification methodology. One other point must be made about these essays. They all take seriously the Romanization of the provinces during the imperial period. It is important to say a word about this because only in the past few decades have Roman influences on the New Testament gained increasing attention. What is at heart here are a number of paradigm shifts that are affecting the way New Testament scholarship is executed.

History, by its nature, is about context. Events and people live not in solitary isolation but within the realities of larger movements, philosophies, wars, inventions, and so forth. Scholarship itself even follows trends and patterns. During the last half of the twentieth century, for instance, there were several significant works in the field of biblical studies that pointed out that Christianity was birthed in a Jewish milieu.[6] Although

---

6. Back in 2003, Gregory Riley expressed this clearly when he talked about an "Israel-alone" model of understanding Christianity, a model in which more attention was paid to Jewish antecedents of Christianity than those of the Greco-Roman world (*The River of God: A New History of Christian Origins* [San Francisco: Harper, 2003],

today we can easily concede that Jesus is addressed by the Jewish title *rabbi*, that he traveled to Jerusalem to observe and participate in Jewish festivals, and that the first disciples perceived of themselves both as Jewish and followers of Christ, at some periods in the history of biblical interpretation emphasizing the Jewishness of the New Testament would have been shocking. There was indeed an era in which scholars were preoccupied with the "uniqueness" and "specialness" of Christianity and consequently did not address the significance of the Jewish background of the New Testament. Similarly, until very recently there hadn't been much work done on how Roman culture impacted the way lives were lived in biblical times. Archeological discoveries of Roman settlements in Israel and new understandings of the role that an imperial power plays in colonized lands, however, are creating a burgeoning interest in Roman backgrounds of the New Testament. To put it another way, newer understandings of the process of Romanization reveal that the influences of an imperial power permeate every level of culture. Therefore "Roman" aspects are just as intertwined as Jewish, ancient Near Eastern, and others in the cultural heritage of the New Testament. The three essays represent this understanding.

Indeed, the potential for historical investigations of New Testament texts is both varied and inexhaustible. It is likely that biblical scholars, by making use of the full palette of methods and tools of the discipline of history and delving into the Roman contexts in which early Christianity was birthed, will enrich our understanding of the Bible for decades to come.

Before diving into the first or theoretical portion of the book, I would like to take the liberty of making a few comments. First, a work such as this that attempts to do justice to two disciplines often fails to satisfy specialist practitioners in both. At points where this presentation seems overly simplistic or, even worse, reductionist, the readers should be aware that this treatment is only meant to provide the preliminary scaffolding for a bridge that spans the two fields. Thus the reader is heartily encouraged to use the bibliography and footnotes to find avenues and resources for pursuing the subject further.

Second, writing is merely a portion of a conversation put on paper. Given that, much is owed to those who have been unseen partners in the discussion and those who have provided the support and space to allow

---

5). See also Beth M. Sheppard, "The Rise of Rome: The Emergence of a New Mode for Exploring the Fourth Gospel," *American Theological Library Association Summary of Proceedings* 57 (2003): 175–87.

this portion of the dialogue to come to fruition. To this end, I would like to thank President Phil Amerson and Vice President for Academic Affairs Lallene Rector of Garrett-Evangelical for granting me a sabbatical during the spring of 2011 to complete the manuscript. Tom Thatcher, the series editor, whom I first met several years ago at a Society of Biblical Literature conference, has always been a supportive colleague. Thank you very much for the encouragement, not to mention your close reading of the text and assistance in clarifying the nature of the readership for this book. Your help was invaluable, and this is a much better work due to your wisdom and insight. Conferences such as those offered by SBL and ATLA also provided me venues in which to give portions of this manuscript a trial run. I truly valued the feedback that I received at the individual sessions at which sections of chapters 6, 8, 9, and 10 were read. Kathleen Kordesh was very brave when she agreed to take on reading an early draft of this manuscript for obvious typos and making certain that I adhered to SBL's style requirements. She is a saint who literally corrected the same "full stop or comma?" issue in hundreds of footnotes and never complained about my inability to just learn the convention. Loren Hagen, who is one of the most well-read persons I know, graciously loaned me his personal copy of Dray—for more than a year! Thank you so much. This work would have had a totally different flavor without the books that you loaned to me. I would also like to express my deepest appreciation to Newland Smith, who came out of retirement to serve as interim library director during my absence and the other new members of the Garrett-Evangelical library staff—Portia, Lucy, Beth N., and J. Lauren—who took on extra duties while I was away and have been very encouraging throughout the project.

Finally, Andy. It has been almost twenty years now since our first conversations about historiography back when we were in England. Thank you for those discussions and all of the others in the intervening years. This book is for you.

PART 1
THEORY

1
A Meeting of Two Disciplines

New Testament studies is awash in methods, or interpretive approaches to the text. There is a wide array of standard "criticisms" or methodological techniques upon which students and scholars of the New Testament may draw: literary criticism, rhetorical criticism, and many others. Yet there are occasional eras of intellectual fervor that require biblical scholars to derive insights from disciplines beyond literature for the tools to analyze new breakthroughs. Given recent interest in the Roman world as a context for the New Testament[1]—a growing area of inquiry spurred on in part by archeological endeavors like the ongoing excavations of the Roman city of Sepphoris, which is located a mere four miles from Jesus' hometown of Nazareth, or the interest in discovering the impact of Romanization on the early church—New Testament scholars are once again turning to the discipline of history. This project is about the craft of history in the Western world and how the methods of that discipline might be used to enrich our understanding of the biblical text.

The general public has a passion for history in general and the Bible in particular. Popular perspective about the account of the human past is formed by coffee-table books, the History Channel, and occasional trips to museums. The Museum of World Treasures, located in Wichita, Kansas, for instance, is an institution that seeks to feed the fascination people have for the past. While the core collection on display at the museum began as a privately owned group of artifacts assembled by a local globetrotting physician, it is now a small nonprofit enterprise with an eclectic array of

---

1. An excellent introduction, now more than a decade old, that acknowledges the Hellenistic aspect of the New Testament but nonetheless understands the Roman context as well is James S. Jeffers, *The Greco-Roman World of the New Testament Era: Exploring the Background of Early Christianity* (Downers Grove, Ill.: InterVarsity Press, 1999).

exhibits. Visitors can see everything from Egyptian mummies to signed photos of Hollywood luminaries.

On the first floor, which features both a set of dramatically posed dinosaurs in battle and the Hall of Ancient Cultures, there is a small cubical glass exhibit case containing a rustic piece of wood. A discreet card identifies this display as a thorn from Christ's crown, the same headdress worn at his crucifixion. The visitor is treated to a view of briars twisted into a circle. Is this particular artifact *the* crown of thorns worn by Jesus (Mark 15:17)? The skeptic, no doubt, would wonder how this "historically significant object" would differ from the thorny wreath currently housed in a reliquary at Notre Dame Cathedral in Paris or why, if the Wichita crown is in large part a reproduction sporting a true thorn somewhere in its construction, this thorn is at a secular museum whose single curator of displays is an expert in early American pioneer forts.

That this torture device used during Jesus' execution would occupy space in a small museum located in the Bible Belt, though, is not surprising. The New Testament contains a record of the birth of Christianity, an event that may be subjected to historical inquiry. And what better place for history to be given visual expression than in a museum? The New Testament is a historical document by virtue of its age. It has a context that is nearly two millennia distant. As a consequence, historical investigations of the milieu in which it was written can shed light on the New Testament text and subject matter while, at the same time, the contents of the twenty-seven books of the canon themselves might be used as source documents for asking what happened in the first-century world. A biblical scholar who undertakes such a query would do well to borrow from the vast array of techniques practiced by conventional historians, lest he or she encounter methodological or theoretical quagmires.

1.1. Who Is a Historian?

Before embarking on the task of unpacking the nature of history and outlining the ways historians go about their tasks, however, there is a caveat about terminology. Who might be labeled a historian? Are biblical scholars who are trained to use historical methods historians? Are some New Testament academics historians if they nonetheless have colleagues in the discipline who are not?

The answers to these questions are complex. Because many biblical professionals who teach or research do so in conjunction with seminaries, schools of theology, departments of religion, chapter houses, and the like, one might hazard to guess that a large percentage received their formal academic training in the fields of biblical studies or religious studies rather than via college and university departments of history. Still others who work in the areas of history of religions and the history of ancient Christianity might have been exposed to courses in both religious and historical disciplines. In any event, it is not clear that academics whose educational backgrounds are exclusively in the field of history and who are currently at work in departments of history or classics would recognize those whose academic backgrounds differ from their own as historians. Rather, since the Bible is a library of prose and poetic documents—as opposed to other types of written artifacts, such as deeds, registers, wills, or inscriptions—it might be argued that biblical scholars are merely "literature people" who are using a few methods that are historical in nature to analyze the text.

This critique is justified to the extent that, in this day and age, those who research the New Testament are educated in a wide variety of interpretive techniques drawn from many cognate disciplines, not just history. When one studies the "witness motif" in the Fourth Gospel, for instance, an analysis of this recurring theme in the narrative would require the use of processes more akin to those associated with the field of literature. Studying the role of John the Baptist as a "witness" in order to trace trial protocols as they spread throughout the empire and using the *Digest*, part of the body of Roman civil law compiled by Justinian I, as a source, however, is more of a historical enterprise. So is an exploration of the extent to which the early Christian communities made use of Roman jurisprudence. By contrast, examining the *Digest* to gain insights into how the word *witness* is used in the Fourth Gospel or to clarify the setting of the Beloved Disciple's work would occupy a grey area between the disciplines of literature and history. Although this latter investigation involves the use of historical materials and methods to enhance comprehension of the text, it is the type of study that would be at home in literature departments. As a result, it is possible to classify it as a literary enterprise despite the use of historical techniques in its execution.

The distinction here is quite subtle—so much so that knowing how and when to apply the term *historian* may pose a conundrum. The situation is even more complicated when an individual researcher in biblical studies changes methods over the course of time, perhaps writing one monograph that is historical in nature and another down the line that utilizes a method drawn from another discipline, such as linguistics. If it is the case that "one is what one writes," the same biblical scholar may be a historian, a literary critic, an apologist, a social commentator, or any number of things. To be blunt, the scholar elects the particular hat that he or she will don with each new writing project.

One solution to this dilemma in terminology is to allow practitioners in biblical studies to self-identify. Paul Minear, for instance, describes himself as a "modern historian," a term he uses to differentiate himself and his methodological approach from those of the first and second century authors of the New Testament texts that are the subject of his study.[2] Another remedy is to devise vocabulary to distinguish between those trained in departments of history and those who were not.

Gerhard Maier, for his part, attempts to dodge the difficulties inherent in the use of *historian* by making use of the term *historiographer*. In his glossary, he describes a historiographer as one who "has been designated to write official history; one who is acquainted with the principles of historical research and with methods of recording history."[3] In essence he is attempting to employ the term *historiographer* to differentiate those who execute research related to the "secular" world, who investigate general topics of history like wars or the Enlightenment, from those who approach biblical texts from the perspective of theology.[4] In actuality, Maier also uses the terms *historiographer* and *secular historian* to designate anyone who approaches the Bible as a mere written artifact rather than as a sacred text.

One must be careful in setting up a dichotomy in which historians are "secular" practitioners while biblical scholars are part of religious faith communities. Any attempt to distinguish *historian* and *biblical scholar* according to belief systems is not a true distinction and does academics in both the fields of history and New Testament studies an injustice since pigeonholing scholars in this way inhibits dialogue and open exchange.

So, for the purposes of this study, it is recognized that some New Testament scholars are trained in the formal discipline of history; some are trained in exegeting texts for faith communities and take into account historical aspects of the New Testament documents. Some professional his-

---

2. Paul S. Minear, *The Bible and the Historian: Breaking the Silence about God in Biblical Studies* (Nashville: Abingdon, 2002), 17.

3. Gerhard Maier, *The End of the Historical-Critical Method* (trans. Edwin W. Leverenz and Rudolph F. Norden; St. Louis: Concordia, 1977), 107.

4. Ibid., 50–52.

torians who work in the history departments of secular colleges or institutions may view their work as an extension of their drive to deepen their belief, but others who study the early Christian era and use the Bible as a source may not. In short, academics in both categories—New Testament scholars and "professional historians"—come in both flavors: confessional and not. Every category has shades of grey. This book is intended for an audience composed of biblical scholars and graduate students taking courses in biblical studies. So, when the terms *historian* and *biblical scholar* are apparently contrasted, the intent is only to point out that, despite the commonalities of both fields, each does have its own unique professional vocabulary as well as a number of methodologies at its disposal that are currently not widely in use by colleagues in the cognate field. Beyond that, whether any particular individual might be identified as a historian depends on to what extent their work reflects the type of investigations typically associated with historians. So what exactly are the tasks that historians undertake?

1.2. What Historians Do

If history is the account of known events of the human past, and historiography is the study of the written record of that past, then the historian is the person who attempts to understand the past by asking questions. Mark T. Gilderhus, who has written a primer on the discipline of history, describes the three successive phases of queries in a simplistic model for historical investigations:[5]

- ► Phase 1: What happened? How did people behave? What did they do?
- ► Phase 2: Why did these things occur? What motivated the principals to behave the way that they did?
- ► Phase 3: How did things turn out? For good or ill? What is the lasting significance or influence of the event or individual?

The historian's primary task may be boiled down to one word: "interpretation." A historian's job is to look at the records and material remains

---

5. Mark. T. Gilderhus, *History and Historians: A Historical Introduction* (6th ed.; Upper Saddle River, N.J.: Pearson/Prentice-Hall, 2007), 9–10.

relating to a person, event, or phenomenon and describe what happened by creating from the available information a plausible narrative synthesis that includes an explanation and analysis of the subject being studied. Bare facts, lists, or raw data that do not include interpretation are not in themselves histories but may form the artifacts upon which histories may be written.

In New Testament studies there are documents that serve simultaneously as histories created by the early Christians and sources upon which modern monographs that deal with the period of the first centuries may be formulated by today's scholars. For instance, the canonical Gospels are history to the extent that they do weave an account of Jesus' sayings and actions into stories that seek to highlight the import of Jesus' life for their readers. These four Gospels are markedly different in flavor from another ancient text, the Gospel of Thomas, which eschews canonical sequencing of events and storyline to present a collection of 114 proverbs, aphorisms, and utterances of Jesus. As John Kloppenborg and his colleagues comment when describing the dissimilarity between the canonical texts and the document found at Nag Hammadi in the 1940s, "For all practical purposes, the Gospel of Thomas is a gospel without narrative—a 'sayings gospel.' "[6] In the arena of the discipline of history, then, "Gospel" or not, Thomas is no more a history than are the registers and inscriptions of the Assyrians and Babylonians or the chronicle written by Eusebius. In fact, all of these other types of records may actually be slightly more historical in tone than the gnostic Gospel because they are chronological and display a rudimentary historical consciousness.[7] But this does not mean that the Gospel of Thomas should be discarded. It is, instead, a document that today's scholars may use to help reconstruct "what happened" almost two millennia ago.

Generally, with the rare exception of a historian being present at an event itself, "what happened" or, alternately, "who done it" must be determined from intermediary sources. The source evidence employed may include documents, oral testimony, ruins, statistical analysis, pottery shards, tombstone inscriptions, and a host of other realia to help substantiate the circumstances about the person, event, or phenomenon being studied. Different historians, using different presuppositions or methods, may

6. John S. Kloppenborg et al., *Q-Thomas Reader* (Sonoma, Calif.: Polebridge, 1990), 84.

7. Gilderhus, *History and Historians*, 14.

analyze the same evidence but still provide divergent pictures of a single event or person. Why is this the case? Shouldn't the same data produce the same results? Not necessarily. Instead, one scholar may emphasize some bits of the available information more than other pieces, while the next historian may decide that a piece of evidence discarded by others as super-fluous may in fact be a key element in the composition of the portrait of the past. The fact that one can never absolutely know what happened in the past is why, in the U.S. court system, convictions are made based on the premise that there is no *reasonable doubt* that the event occurred as the prosecution described it; *absolute certainty* is not the standard.

The variety of ways in which a historian may interpret an event is clearly evident in the subgenre of history that is called biography, a genre in which careful scholars such as Charles Talbert and Richard A. Burridge maintain the canonical Gospels should be categorized.[8] The ability for one event to spawn many interpretations may be illustrated by a modern exam-ple. There have been dozens and dozens of biographies written on Prin-cess Diana. One can imagine a scenario where a particular author might focus on her role as mother, while another might emphasize her work for charity. A third may determine that Diana's economic status prior to her marriage was an influential factor in how she executed her role as princess, yet even another biographer may conclude that the pressures of the public expectations of being a princess drove her actions. Still one more writer might examine Diana's impact on hairstyles or fashion. The point here is that no single biography and no single historian will ever create the sole

---

8. Richard A. Burridge, *What Are the Gospels? A Comparison with Graeco-Roman Biography* (Cambridge: Cambridge University Press, 1992). Charles H. Talbert, *What Is a Gospel? The Genre of the Canonical Gospels* (Macon, Ga.: Mercer University Press, 1985). In his very brief article, Darryl Palmer also makes the odd claim that "[t]he Gospels are properly biography rather than historiography" but the book of Acts is "best classified as a historical monograph." At the very least, Palmer's use of "histori-ography" within this formulation is overly simplistic, at worst, misguided. Specifically, to divorce biography from history is not easy or clear cut. As Ralph Waldo Emerson observes, "There is properly no history; only biography" (*Essays: First Series*, 1841). And just as there is a scholarly tradition that regards biography as a literary preserve, there is an equally strong strand of thought among historians such as Thomas Carlyle (d. 1885) in which biography is viewed as a subgenre of history. Palmer does not even acknowledge this debate ("Historiographical Literature," *Dictionary of Biblical Criti-cism and Interpretation*, 163). Palmer's concerns will be discussed in more detail in chapter 5.

complete portrait of the individual who was Lady Diana Spencer, became the wife of a British prince, and died in a car crash in France. Just as there are multiple accounts of the life of this British royal, there is more than ample room for four canonical Gospels and a host of modern lives of Jesus. There will always be room for additional, valid biographical portraits that employ, as it were, different brush strokes, different pigments, or a slightly different sense of composition.

1.3. The Nature of History

If history, then, involves interpretation, we might wonder how one could ever know the truth about an event or person from the past. Which biography of Diana is the *right* one? One must be careful to realize that there is a difference between "truth" and "The Truth," the first being a plausible depiction of an event or person based on synthesizing data and the second being the totality of all there is to know about the actual event or individual. In order to explain the difference, an analogy between art and history was advanced by Thomas Macaulay, a preeminent historian during the industrial revolution.[9] Macaulay notes that for history to be "perfectly and absolutely true it ought to record *all* the slightest particulars of the slightest" occurrence. But this is not possible, just as "no picture is exactly like the original."[10]

Say one sets out to paint a dog named Oswald. There are facts that must be discovered. Was Oswald an Irish setter or a poodle? Was he sleeping on his back or his side? Was he snoring and running in his sleep? As more facts are known, one can add more detail to the portrait, yet the portrait still is not Oswald himself. As Macaulay observes, no history can present us with the whole truth.

One may ultimately discover more facts and be able to render a three-dimensional, realistically sized sculpture of Oswald in repose, though even then not all there is to be known about Oswald will be apparent. What was his personality? Was he drowsy because he ate too much kibble? Had he just been on a long romp in the yard and became exhausted?

---

9. The essay is reproduced in Fritz Stern, *The Varieties of History: From Voltaire to the Present* (New York: Meridian, 1956), 72–89 and appeared originally in *Miscellaneous Works* (ed. Lady Trevelyan; New York: Harper Brothers, 1899), 1:153–98.

10. Stern, *The Varieties of History*, 76.

The more one learns about Oswald the dog, the more questions arise. So one can never ultimately know, at least in this life, every last detail, motivation, cause, economic circumstance, or subtlety related to an event or person. There are only interpretations about the available facts and the never-ending search for newer facts. In essence, the author or editor of the final version of the Fourth Gospel is aware of this when, at the conclusion of the account of the actions of Jesus, he comments, "But there are also many other things which Jesus did; were every one of them to be written, I suppose that the world itself could not contain the books that would be written" (John 21:25).[11]

That is not to say that every historical interpretation is truth with a small *t* and should be accepted at face value. As described above, the task of the historian is to provide an *accurate* interpretation based on the extant evidence; to the extent that the evidence is sound, the history is valid. Some histories are better than others because they have taken into account a wider array of facts or a new fact that has just come to light. Some may even be flawed with barely a shred of truth in them because the facts upon which they are based are erroneous.

In New Testament studies, for instance, there are occasionally works that are published but based on faulty evidence. The flawed studies that were produced in the wake of the 2002 discovery of a burial box known as the James Ossuary are a prime example. An ossuary is a small limestone container designed to hold the bones of the deceased after the body has decomposed, and this particular twenty-inch-long chest was inscribed with the words "James, son of Joseph, brother of Jesus." Subsequent to the publication of several articles and books on the subject, however, a team of chemists and geologists examined the patina on the box, and it is now thought by many to be a forgery. With the fallout of the scandal, the scholarly works that focused on this piece of evidence have dubious value.

Nevertheless, in studies where no taint of forgery is involved in the evidence employed, to the extent that a historian takes account of facts and seeks to offer a cogent and accurate explanation of how those pieces of evidence may be combined, his or her account or portrait of the event is "true." Furthermore, even this truth is regarded as relative by today's historians. As Gilderhus points out, "different times and places literally saw

---

11. Unless otherwise specified, all biblical citations are from the Revised Standard Version (RSV).

and experienced the world differently.... It may also be that very divergent conceptions of truth and believability have separated the present from the past."[12] John Knox echoed this sentiment during the middle of the last century in a concise work on Jesus Christ: "We cannot help seeing Jesus, if we try to see him at all, through our own eyes, and our eyes must in the nature of the case distort him. Our eyes are modern Western eyes; Jesus was an ancient Jew."[13]

In short, truth for historians is not absolute "Truth" and even historians are sometimes subject to human failings. For instance, in the era associated with World War II, historical writing in Europe was caught up in a trend that involved the production of "national histories." These works were commissioned and sometimes even authorized by those who were in power. For astute thinkers living in this time period—like Barth, who was skeptical about the discipline[14]—history may have been virtually indistinguishable from propaganda, and consequently the output of historians would be of questionable value or, at worst, even represent a warping of the truth.

This doubt about the value of history for reporting facts in a fair-minded way might be applied to other phases and eras of historiography as well. For instance, Flavius Josephus, one of the principle sources for the first- and second-century era, declares himself to be a reporter of events who counterbalances the errors in prior records. Indeed, according to the introduction to his *History of the Jewish War against the Romans,* after he condemns previous attempts to recount the events of the rebellion of the Jews as having "collected from hearsay casual and contradictory stories," the Jewish historian announces his intention to set the record straight. He writes,

> I—Josephus, son of Matthias, a Hebrew by race, a native of Jerusalem and a priest, who at the opening of the war myself fought against the Romans and in the sequel was perforce an onlooker—propose to provide the subjects of the Roman Empire with a narrative of the facts, by translating into Greek the account which I previously composed in my vernacular tongue and sent to the barbarians in the interior.[15]

---

12. Gilderhus, *History and Historians,* 5–6.

13. John Knox, *Jesus Lord and Christ* (New York: Harper & Brothers, 1958), 9.

14. As mentioned by Carl Braaten, *New Directions in Theology Today II: History and Hermeneutics* (Philadelphia: Westminster, 1966), 24–25.

15. Josephus, *J.W.* 1.1 (Thackeray, LCL).

Yet despite these lofty claims, historians today regard many portions of Josephus's works as unreliable at best and, at worst, intentionally distorted to serve his own purposes. John Curran expresses the low esteem with which the first-century historian's works are held by noting that Josephus is given the "lowest status as a recorder of historical data from his own times."[16]

Although there have indeed been time periods when the methods and works of historiography have not represented the discipline's most stellar moments and that might lead one to question the contributions the discipline might make, every field has both moments of which to be proud and those that are less savory. One should not throw out the baby with the bathwater. Carl Braaten, a Lutheran theologian, recognizes the value of the historical enterprise for Christianity. He writes,

> The category of history is undoubtedly indispensable for a theology based on God's reconciling activity in Christ. The act of reconciliation is a climactic historical event, with definite historical presuppositions in Yahweh's covenant with Israel and equally definite historical results in the election of the church. To the extent that the redemption through Christ is taken seriously, history must be given its due.[17]

To give history its due, as Braaten advises, requires a firm grasp of the discipline. Understanding concepts and terminology is key to that enterprise, and thus understanding the concepts of historiography and philosophy of history as well as biblical studies' own historical criticism is worthwhile.

1.4. DEFINING TERMS

1.4.1. HISTORIOGRAPHY

In university and college settings, senior history majors and graduate students are often required to take at least one course focused on historiography. So what exactly is that? Scholars in the discipline of history use the term *historiography* for their ongoing discussions about the "history

---

16. John Curran, "Flavius Josephus in Rome," in *Flavius Josephus: Interpretation and History* (ed. Jack Pastor, Pnina Stern, and Menahem Mor; JSJSup 146; Leiden: Brill, 2011), 65.

17. Braaten, *New Directions*, 16–17.

of writing history." In short, historians use the word *historiography* where New Testament scholars use the word *criticism*, roughly as a synonym for *method* when referring to concepts like rhetorical criticism—in which the figures, symbols, structures, and arguments of a text are analyzed to assess how they might persuade readers—or literary criticism, which is a mode of interpretation by which one looks at how an author has structured a composition and employed vocabulary to highlight themes and motifs as well as other matters. It is a cipher for the various approaches that have been put in place to do the business of history from the past to the current era. The reader who is familiar with the various modes or methods of doing history is able to read a work written by a historian and identify the author's technique, presuppositions, and philosophical orientation. It is no different from a visitor to an art museum having the knowledge to differentiate between works representing realism, pointillism, cubism, or some other method of painting.

Every "history-based text," whether produced in the larger field of history or our own discipline of biblical studies, can be placed on the historiographical continuum by those who have had an introduction to the methods of history. So a popular book commonly available in the history sections of chain and online bookstores, like the physician Siddhartha Mukherjee's *The Emperor of All Maladies: A Biography of Cancer*,[18] employs particular methods and conventions that will allow current and future scholars to situate that book in its own niche in the broader enterprise of writing history. Likewise, a historically based work in New Testament scholarship, like Francis Watson's *Paul, Judaism, and the Gentiles*,[19] may be categorized according to its particular historiographical context despite the fact that his interlocutors are biblical scholars. Both of these works straddle two disciplinary worlds by virtue of using historical methodologies and approaches to subject matter irrespective of whether the authors hold professional credentials in history or some other field, like medicine or biblical studies.

Before proceeding, however, there is one more caveat to offer about terminology. So far, we have been using the word *historiography* in its broadest sense. In New Testament studies, however, the term is sometimes

---

18. Siddharta Mukherjee, *The Emperor of All Maladies: A Biography of Cancer* (New York: Scribner, 2010).

19. Francis Watson, *Paul, Judaism, and the Gentiles: Beyond the New Perspective* (rev. and exp. ed.; Grand Rapids: Eerdmans, 2007).

understood in a more limited fashion. To be specific, at times it is marshaled to refer almost exclusively to attempts to situate individual New Testament documents in the Greco-Roman world by comparing and contrasting them with various genres and techniques used by those ancient historians who were contemporary with or who may have influenced the biblical authors. This tends to obscure the idea that modern histories of the New Testament, like Watson's, which was mentioned above, also are subject to historiographical analysis.[20]

Rather than trying to differentiate historiography in a broad or narrow sense, it is easier to understand historiography as the ongoing narrative of the techniques and mechanics of doing history into which one may place writings from any era that record and interpret the past, be they writings focused on individuals, groups, movements, or other human events. Watson's work and that of the author of Acts are both history and both may be studied from the perspective of historiography.

Textbooks that deal with the subject of historiography often take a chronological approach to discussing the various methods with which historians in diverse locations and situations have approached their craft. But that is not the only approach to analyzing and discussing the methods and presuppositions that drive historians. An alternate tactic is to create categories for describing works of history and their theoretical underpinnings. The inclination to organize material in this way is associated with the task of philosophy.

1.4.2. PHILOSOPHY OF HISTORY

Philosophy of history is an area of study that is closely related to historiography. Sometimes when historians speak of philosophy of history, it is treated as a field unto itself. At other times it is considered within the realm of historiography. While historiography is more closely aligned with methodological considerations, philosophy of history involves deeper theoretical aspects of the discipline and may include attempts to develop classification schemes under which various methods may be understood.

Within this more theoretical sphere, questions addressed could include: How does one evaluate and analyze lessons learned from the past?

---

20. The limited use is evident in Palmer "Historiographical Literature," 163. Palmer does not address the history of historical writing about the New Testament from earliest times until today.

How does one organize knowledge about the past? What is the difference between a primary source and a secondary source? May the same piece of evidence be at one and the same time a primary source and a secondary source? Is time linear, cyclical, spiral, layered, chaotic, progressive, or in some other configuration? Is it okay to convey one's interpretation of history by telling a story, or are charts, graphs, and statistics more helpful? Is a chronicle a history or merely a resource that may be used by a historian in interpreting some of the events listed in it? Are there operating presuppositions that must be taken into account either on the part of the historian or with regard to the evidence that is being investigated? Together, historiography and philosophy of history compose the realm in which historians ask how one does the business of history, and these fundamental aspects of the discipline of history will be the focus of chapters two and three. But first, since it is one of the key methods that is practiced in New Testament interpretation, it is important to define historical criticism's approach to unpacking texts and describe how it relates to the types of methods used by those formally trained in historiography.

1.4.3. HISTORICAL CRITICISM

For many the ultimate objective of biblical interpretation is exegesis—the extraction of theological, moral, or other meaning for application in the "contemporary church and the world."[21] To accomplish this task, one collection of methods that may be employed is historical criticism.

Historical criticism is a catchall designation frequently found in textbooks on method in biblical studies for a family of approaches utilized to analyze ancient texts. For those interested in exploring the first century and its people, places, and events in general, the more narrow term *social-science history* is used. It is the designation for historical-critical studies that investigate the customs, group dynamics, economic circumstances, political maneuverings, and other elements that characterized the world in which Jesus and the early Christians lived.

Not every historical critic, however, is preoccupied with matters related to social-science history questions. Instead, some historical critics concentrate on how New Testament documents were formed, written,

---

21. Gordon D. Fee, *New Testament Exegesis* (rev. ed.; Louisville: Westminster John Knox, 1993), 27.

constructed, and transmitted. For instance, because we do not have the autograph or the original manuscript of any canonical document that was either written in the author's own hand or dictated to a research assistant or amanuensis (the technical name for an ancient secretary), textual criticism is the subcategory of historical criticism that compares the various copies that later scribes produced to determine where these copies might exhibit differences, or variants. Then a number of standards are applied to determine which version represents what was likely in the original.

Another historical-critical method that is centered on the text rather than the Mediterranean context is source criticism. To oversimplify, this is the attempt to trace the oral or written resources upon which an author might have relied while composing a text. Sadly, unlike modern authors, ancient writers did not use footnotes, so a number of techniques have been developed to ferret out this information. Related to source criticism, redaction criticism tries to unearth how an individual author may have emphasized some stories rather than others or provided a particular narrative framework for some material to specifically target the particular needs and circumstances of the original audience or congregation by which the document was intended to be read. There are other criticisms that also address issues of the formation, construction, and nature of early texts, but space does not permit going into each and every one of them.

John H. Hayes and Carl R. Holladay have written an introduction to exegesis in which they offer a helpful shorthand for differentiating between social-science oriented historical-critical endeavors and text-focused historical-critical investigations like those undertaken by textual, redaction, and source critics. They talk about history *in* the text verses history *of* the text.[22] Speaking generally, those focused on looking at the history *in* the text tend to accept writings of the New Testament period "as they are" (in received form) or "as they have been reconstructed" (a critical edition) for their point of departure when launching into broader questions about context, cause and effect, and so forth. As Robert Hull charmingly puts it, these scholars have the impression "that the experts have 'delivered the goods' and that we can simply rely on the text they have given us."[23]

---

22. John H. Hayes and Carl R. Holladay, *Biblical Exegesis: A Beginner's Handbook* (3rd ed.; Louisville: Westminster John Knox, 2007), 56–57.

23. Robert F. Hull Jr., *The Story of the New Testament Text: Movers, Materials, Motives, Methods, and Models* (SBLRBS 58; Atlanta: Society of Biblical Literature, 2010), 3.

Conversely, those preoccupied with the history *of* the text engage in techniques like source criticism and textual criticism, which explore variants and other aspects of the manuscript, first. For them, the text isn't a given but the object of history.

Whether one is speaking of history "in" or "of" the text, one must be careful to understand that students taking historiography courses in a history department would not be learning the terms *historical criticism* or *social-science history*.[24] To be clear, the basic, popular historiography textbooks authored by Georg Iggers and Ernst Breisach do not contain these concepts. They are terms deeply embedded in the field of New Testament studies, but not in history.[25] In fact, *social-science history* as it is used by biblical scholars is an umbrella term under which one finds gathered a variety of methods that, for historians, were specifically developed to correct weakness of or present alternate techniques to each other. Knowing this, historiographers might be more reluctant than New Testament scholars to put them all together under one descriptor since that would mute their distinctive characteristics.

Essentially, a biblical scholar or student who engages in historical criticism is not using the same vocabulary, methods, or philosophical understandings about the past that would characterize the field of history. Certainly there is some overlap, but they remain two separate fields.

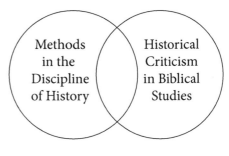

Methods in the Discipline of History

Historical Criticism in Biblical Studies

So, if "history" as understood by historians and "historical criticism" as described by practitioners in our own field are two different but overlapping things, what does each sphere in the diagram contain? In a

---

24. The closest one might come is "social history," which, as will be demonstrated in a later chapter, is a much narrower area of study that what biblical scholars intend by "social-science" criticism.

25. Ernst Breisach, *Historiography: Ancient, Medieval and Modern* (3rd ed.; Chicago: University of Chicago Press); George G. Iggers, *Historiography in the Twentieth Century: From Scientific Objectivity to the Postmodern Challenge* (Middletown, Conn.: Wesleyan University Press, 2005). The journal *Social Science History* would closely correlate to the term *social-science history* in biblical studies. It is an interdisciplinary journal that publishes articles that reflect the intersection of history and other disciplines within the social sciences.

nutshell, the history sphere contains many methods—some of which are unfamiliar to New Testament scholars, some of which are known but are underutilized, and some that are staples in the New Testament scholar's bag of tricks. It also includes modes of investigation that could never be employed in our field. As much as one might wish, for instance, one can never travel backward in time with a MP3 recorder in order to collect oral history from the recipients of the Pastoral Epistles! Likewise, "world history," which is represented by multivolume works and encyclopedias because it attempts to be comprehensive, is beyond the scope of the student or scholar of the New Testament era, who is generally focused on lands within the Roman Empire occupied by the early Christians and thus has no overt need to consider the history of places like Antarctica or other periods of world history more generally.

To illustrate how broad the field of history really is, one might note that historians will use terms like *Whig history, microhistory,* and *total history,* among others, when they are talking about methods. These terms, however, may not be commonly heard in the hallways where those who engage in biblical studies gather. Some of these aspects of historiography would be quite valuable, however. For example, Whig history had a particular methodological flaw that we must be careful not to replicate in our work with the Bible. And microhistory, for its part, is the study of a very tiny and well-defined slice of the past and something akin to what biblical scholars do when they are writing a monograph on a single pericope rather than an entire book of the New Testament. To a great extent, then, within the wider sphere of history, there are methods, discussions, and theoretical elements that would be beneficial for graduate students and professionals in biblical studies to know and perhaps even use. This is why the terminology and methods employed by historians will be unpacked in the following chapters.

But we mustn't neglect the circle in our diagram represented by historical criticism. What does it include that does not preoccupy historians? Well, in current decades many departments of history have no longer concentrated on the type of exercises that are related to textual criticism, source criticism, and other endeavors that explore history "of the text." [26] Given

---

26. At the history department of American University, none of the areas that are listed as "supporting disciplines" in the graphic on page 28 appear in the course listings or course descriptions on the departmental webpage for history, though students are offered courses in methodology entitled the "Historian's Craft," "Oral History,"

that the task of historians is to formulate stories about what happened, why it happened, and how the past is meaning-ful, these criticisms—along with the history of language, which is called philology—are considered to be the activities of disciplines sup-porting or auxiliary to his-tory in the same way that archaeology and paleog-raphy (the study of handwriting) are. In fact, Mark Gilderhus does not even distinguish between text criticism, source criticism, and the history of lan-guage but lumps all three under the term *philology*.[27]

Methods in the Discipline of History

Historical Criticism in Biblical Studies

- Source Criticism
- Textual Criticism

Supporting Disciplines Box

- Lexicography
- Paleography
- History of Lang-uages/Philology

So, to reiterate, as far as the New Testament discipline is concerned, both source criticism and textual criticism would be included in the sphere of historical criticism, even though they are methods derived from philology. From the perspective of historians, however, many works that are related to philology, whether in its broader sense or more restricted definition as the history of language, would not qualify strictly as history but are part of an auxiliary discipline.[28] Thus, at the risk of oversimplifying, our diagram may be modified as shown above.

---

and "Historians and the Living Past" (American University, "History PhD" [cited 1 April 2011]; online: http://www.american.edu/cas/history/phd-requirements.cfm and http://www.american.edu/cas/history/PHD-HIST.cfm).

27. Gilderhus, *History and Historians*, 32–33. Terminology is slippery, and there appears to be no agreed-upon standard. Biblical scholars James Alfred Loader and Oda Wischmeyer, contrary to Gilderhus, limit the "philological" method to textual criticism, grammar, semantics, and the study of realia while viewing the "reconstruc-tions of the original texts in their historical contexts," including form criticism and source criticism as a later development ("Twentieth Century Interpretation," *Diction-ary of Biblical Criticism and Interpretation*, 377).

28. One must be cautious about oversimplifying. Robert F. Hull, a text critic in New Testament studies, observes that text critics in the last two decades in particular have been expanding their area of interest to include the social history of early Chris-tianity. See Hull, *Story of the New Testament Text*, 155. He comments that, in biblical

The rectangle in this rendering illustrates that, while to some extent biblical studies *may* subsume all or some portions of the supporting disciplines listed in the square part of the graphic, the field of history relates to them only tangentially.

The disjunction between the role that textual criticism and source criticism play as they are understood in biblical scholarship, and the values placed on those philological methods in the discipline of history at large, becomes clearer when one considers a lament offered by the scholars in the Department of History at the University of Massachusetts about their own discipline. The scholars there are working on developing critical texts of significant Chinese works as part of the "Warring States Project." They write,

> The science of philology was developed to solve the problem of getting back to the obscured originals. Thus arose what is sometimes called "source criticism." Its home area was texts in Greek and Latin…The partnership of philology and history, in the criticism and the interpretation of the source documents for earlier times, became the standard view during the 19th century. It is embodied in the classic manual of Langlois and Seignobos (1894, and still in print), and in later works down to the middle of the 20th century. That way of thinking, however, has not continued strong. At present, text philology is not generally recognized as a concern of historians, and it is taught, if at all, only in Departments of "Classics" and Schools of Theology, where Greek in particular is still a working language.[29]

So if there is anything to be learned from this exposition of what history is and the differences between historical criticism, historiography, and philosophy of history, it is that—despite some overlap and common interests between the disciplines of history and New Testament studies—there is still much that we might learn from each other in order to encourage greater dialogue and cross-fertilization of ideas between the two realms. To that end, the next chapters will focus on the philosophy of

---

studies, students are at least exposed to textual criticism in the curriculum, even if they are not required to master it (2).

29. The Warring States Project, "The Discipline of History. Postmodernism Is Not the Only Problem" [cited 1 April 2011]; online: http://www.umass.edu/wsp/methodology/difficulties/discipline.html.

history and unpack some of the more theoretical elements related to the craft of history.

2

THEORETICAL UNDERPINNINGS

The classic 1970s rock song "Fly Like an Eagle," by Steve Miller Band, includes the phrase, "Time keeps on slipping, slipping, slipping, into the future." The message is uncomplicated. According to the lyrics, the present, past, and future are not necessarily distinct periods but somehow merge into one another. One might even say that they overlap or begin to melt into one another. The upshot? Time should be used wisely. One might choose to "fly like an eagle" up out of the mire of the past and help to feed, clothe, and house children and others who are in need. Oddly enough, the rock star's perception of time is not innovative. Even some early Christians held to a model of ages melding into one another: they asserted that God's kingdom, traditionally associated with the future, was instead breaking into the present. In Matthew's Gospel, for instance, Jesus is able to cast out demons because the kingdom of God had begun (Matt 12:28).

Just as was the case with the early Gospel writers, something with which all historians must still wrestle is the nature of time itself. And, oddly enough, there are different ways to perceive it. The theory that the past and present overlie each other a bit—as expressed in the 1970s song lyrics and in Matthew's Gospel—is just one of many options. And issues about time are just the tip of the philosophical iceberg. There are other questions with which a historian must come to grips before embarking on a project as well. Some of these involve selectivity. For instance, each finished history text is flavored not only by the historian's understanding of how the past relates to the present and future but also by the individual topic chosen for investigation. In addition, there are decisions to make about the primary force or forces that drive history or promote change. For instance, is change propelled by economic forces, social pressure, politics, or something else? Even the determinations a historian makes about how and what sources are to be used help to make each book of history different. In sum, even if five different historians were to write a history about the Roman use of crosses in crucifixion, the individual philosophical understandings with which the historians are working would result in five very dissimilar works. If this is true today, so too has it been since historians first began to commit their investigations to writing. Thus it is no wonder that there are four different canonical Gospels!

The philosophical elements relating to time, selectivity, and sources provide the basic building blocks for historical writing, and each will be unpacked in turn.

2.1. The Role of Time

As depicted in the New Testament, Christianity stands out as a system that envisions both an end of history (the cross) and an end of time (the cataclysmic final days depicted in Revelation). In other words, the cross is the decisive event that determines our destiny, and the Apocalypse provides a vision for its realization. Time, however, is a many-faceted thing. Most frequently in our everyday experience, events from the past are mapped out as dates and points on a timeline that visually represents happenings in a linear fashion. Every child who has ever been enrolled in an elementary school has seen timelines like these on classroom walls or in social-studies textbooks. To some extent, then, a linear concept of time is more familiar to most of us than the melting-together formulation presented by the Steve Miller Band or the early evangelists. But the versions have something in common. They perceive of time as moving inexorably forward. For the classic rocker, the future just seems to get here sooner than it does when dates and points plod along on a schoolroom graphic.

In actuality, while a historian may conceive of time as an advancing progression, as is inherent both in timeline and overlapping models, that is not necessarily the way it must always be understood. Time may also be cyclical or even chaotic. Cyclical patterns such as those present in the changing of seasons or the repetitive sequence of night following day may have been the inspiration for some of the earliest concepts of time among prehistoric people. Philosopher of history Mark Gilderhus maintains that, even as late as the era of classical Greek culture, the prominent notion of history was one in which time was understood as essentially recurring.[1]

---

1. Gilderhus, *History and Historians*, 13, 16.

Even though there are three basic concepts of how events relate to one another—linear, cyclical, and chaotic—some theorists think that this formulation is too simplistic. Indeed, it is possible to combine two or more understandings of time into ever more complex versions of how events from the past relate to events either closer or more distant to one another or even to the period in which a historian is living and writing. Hegelian dialectic, for example, with its repetitive sequence of thesis, antithesis, and synthesis, is at first glance a cyclical philosophy that underlies some forms of history, including Marxist history. Actually, though, the dialectic also has a progressive element, so it might be portrayed more like a spiral, a shape of the sort that is found in the construction of a spring as opposed to a closed circle that would characterize a purely cyclical model. Others may conceive of time more as a zigzag, with time rocketing forward but having periods of decline or devolution that backtrack.

We have already mentioned that some early Christians thought that different eras of time had an overlapping characteristic. When the entire Judeo-Christian tradition is taken as a whole, though, the impression might be that time is almost exclusively linear. Indeed, the canonical biblical text follows a progression from the point of the beginning of time at creation through the period of God's self revelation to the Jews, onward to the spread of the gospel to the larger world, and ultimately to a prediction of the end of the world in Revelation. Nonetheless, as has been hinted at by mention of Matthew's concept of the kingdom, Christian historians have held a wide array of conceptions of time.

Within a more limited section of the biblical text itself, for instance, the Deuteronomistic historian promotes a cyclical understanding of how events unfold in the book of Judges. According to that author, the Israelites fall into apostasy by worshiping foreign gods, and as a result these foreign nations overpower God's people. Eventually, a judge is provided by Yahweh with the result that the people repent and are temporarily delivered until the judge dies and they resume their pursuit of foreign deities. This, of course, puts them at the beginning of the cycle again. Despite its repetitive nature, however, this cycle is also a part of a providential history for, as John Van Seters notes, even the role that the conquering nations play in this cycle is part of the divine plan.[2]

---

2. John Van Seters, *In Search of History: Historiography in the Ancient World and the Origins of Biblical History* (New Haven: Yale University Press, 1983), 342.

Leaving the Bible, Reinhold Niebuhr is the prime example of a Christian modern historian who has a view of time that is not linear. Instead of time marching inexorably forward in a straight line, the theologian posits what may best be described as a chaos model. In Niebuhr's system, events are contingent, unforeseen, and driven by the mechanism of original sin, a condition that will be resolved only at last judgment.[3] If one were to try to sketch this, one might draw a funnel in which isolated events randomly bump into each other but nonetheless all pass through last judgment eventually. So for Niebuhr there is chaos, but even the period of disarray is moving toward an end.

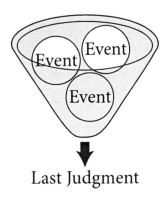

Last Judgment

Paul Minear unpacks still another conception of time when he describes the author of Revelation as engaging in a layered understanding where all epochs might be seen at once.[4] Indeed, the idea that events from different periods are omnipresent for the author of Revelation is clear when Minear mentions, "Time did not separate the pharaohs from the Roman emperors but brought them together." To understand what Minear is getting at, one might imagine a cake with alternating layers of chocolate cake and vanilla frosting. These are assembled each in its own sequence in time, but when the cake is cut, the layers are all revealed simultaneously.

It is easy to think of another example from a field more closely related to history: archaeology. Certainly Minear's version of time would also resemble the various strata on an archeological keyhole excavation where different events in a city's past are concurrently apparent to an archeologist, who then makes a choice to read the layers in a particular sequence as long as the layers have not been disturbed after deposition.

2.2. Selectivity

In addition to a historian's conception of time, the act of having to make choices related to the study one intends to undertake is itself of interest to

---

3. William H. Dray, *Philosophy of History*, (Englewood Cliffs, N.J.: Prentice-Hall, 1964), 62, 100–110.

4. Paul Minear, *The Bible and the Historian: Breaking the Silence about God in Biblical Studies*, (Nashville: Abingdon, 2002), 63.

theoreticians. This is because the selections one makes about topic, scope, method, the type of history (economic, women's, cultural, political, etc.), and even the sources upon which one will rely, all affect the finished piece of written history. Marcion (d. 160 c.e.), an excommunicated Christian who founded a heretical movement in the early church, provides a dramatic example. In electing to discard the works of the Old Testament, the birth narrative of Luke, the other Gospels, and the Pastoral Epistles, he revealed much about his view of the past. First, in breaking away from the God depicted in the texts of Judaism, this innovative thinker demonstrated that any history that preceded Jesus' actions in Galilee was irrelevant because God's love had replaced the law. Then, by eliminating the infancy narrative, the heretic's gnostic bias against the material world was evident. There is nothing messier and more rooted in our physical humanness than birth! But Marcion wasn't done there. Through dropping the Pastoral Epistles on the grounds that their Pauline authorship was dubious, Marcion exposed something of his view of the validity of the source material upon which he wished to draw. In brief, Marcion's very act of selecting material was integrally related to his view of how history should be used and what sources provided the most accurate foundation for his work. Although his choices ultimately put him at cross-purposes with the orthodox theological position, the theoretical moves he was making in relation to evaluating sources and presenting a critical view of past events are legitimate ones for a historian to make. Discarding the infancy narrative on the basis that one doesn't care for it, however, would contravene generally accepted practices of impartiality and is the point that would lead most historians to question the validity of Marcion's work.[5] Nonetheless, the example clearly demonstrates that actions related to selectivity are an integral ingredient in philosophy of history.

Now, selectivity is actually a pretty complex area of the philosophy of history, not because it is hard to grasp the idea that historians must make choices relative to their projects but because there are so many points

---

5. Marcion's writings are not extant but are known through the comments of his opponents. The point that is being made here is not that Marcion was a professional historian by trade; he was a well-off businessman in the shipping industry. Nonetheless, Marcion's interaction with the canonical biblical documents reflects at least the rudimentary philosophical engagement with material remains that is common to historians at the preliminary stages of planning and writing a project.

at which a historian is forced to do so. Let's begin by looking at what is involved in simply picking a broad topic upon which to write.

2.2.1. Settling on a Topic

There are essentially three aspects of the action of selection that come into play when deciding on the specific subject matter to treat in a historical study. The first is the historian's personal interest and curiosity about a topic. The second is the bias revealed in the act of selecting the area of focus, and the third is the obligation to decide on a subject that may be relevant to present-day situations and concerns or that is thought to be of instrumental importance because the episode or person was a catalyst for subsequent actions or events.

Regarding the first element of raw interest or curiosity, unless the topic is assigned by an editor or supervising professor, the historian must choose the subject matter upon which to write. This involves a personal affective element and, as Fritz Stern boldly puts it, can result in the project being either scintillating or drudgery for the researcher.[6]

The act of choosing at first light seems to be value neutral since the historian will simply elect to write on subject A or B or C. But in actuality an author's predispositions relating to the subject matter come into play. Generally the researcher is not choosing blindly but has some knowledge of the topic or has formed preconceived notions about it. Why, for instance, might C be chosen over B or A? These predispositions are essentially a mild form of researcher bias. This bias, whether subtle or not, is the second element that influences the choice of a topic.

The idea that the very act of selection of a topic reveals partiality that sometimes may affect accounts of events in extreme ways is clearly illustrated by an anecdote recounted by K. L. Noll. He remarks that, while attending school in one of the cities that served as a Confederate capital during the American Civil War, he discovered that battle accounts were plentiful and did not necessarily agree with each other. Noll wryly concluded, "Rarely were the facts denied, but usually they were selectively remembered and creatively packaged, and always the interpretation conformed to the ideological identity of the teller."[7] The tendency to warp,

---

6. Stern, *Varieties of History*, 25.
7. K. L. Noll, "The Evolution of Genre in the Book of Kings: The Story of Sennacherib and Hezekiah as Example" in *The Function of Ancient Historiography in Biblical*

either consciously or inadvertently, the material we elect to tackle as historians is perhaps why some biblical scholars reveal the possible influences that might have affected their choices up front in their books. Margaret Davies provides a beautiful example of this practice. She writes,

> Every commentary highlights some matters while obscuring others through its interpretive strategies. My commentary will be no exception, so let me tell the reader to which interpretive communities I belong. I am a British, female academic, a member of the Anglican Church, but not of its evangelical wing, a member of the Labour Party and of several civil liberty groups.[8]

More often than not, the author does not disclose these sorts of personal details in a manuscript. Yet astute readers can often identify something about a historian based on the author's place of employment as reported on the book jacket, the ideology of the press that publishes the work, the theological outlooks of the individuals who provide endorsements on the back cover, and even the overarching themes revealed in the larger body of the historian's previous publications during his or her career.

If there is any comfort to be taken at all given the issue of selection bias, it may be found in the fact that, when it comes to "selection," bias is not limited to the field of history. Even a scientist who devotes a career to the study of cancer or to the eating habits of a particular beetle is not immune from exhibiting slants in relation to the selected topic. Further, awareness of the act of ascribing value to a topic simply due to a historian's choice to study it is not something that is new or a realization of the postmodern era. The historian Friedrich Meinecke described the inevitability of bias in the act of selection in 1928, when he warns that value judgments are "there between the lines" in historians' manuscripts.[9]

In addition to outright curiosity and subtle bias, relevance is the third issue that plays a role in topic selection. Something from the past may be relevant either because it was a key event or instrument for the occurrence

---

and Cognate Studies (ed. Patricia G. Kirkpatrick and Timothy Goltz; LHBOTS 489; New York: T&T Clark, 2008), 30.

8. Margaret Davies, *Matthew* (Sheffield: JSOT Press, 1993), 15. Davies's commentary is actually focused on literary rather than historical interpretation, yet the impulse for her self-revelatory comments is the same.

9. Friedrich Meinecke, "Values and Causalities in History," in Stern, *Varieties of History*, 273.

of other events or because it has consequence for the present day.[10] As William Dray, a philosopher of history, puts it, one is not just studying the past but the significant past.[11] Regarding this last point, the historian James Harvey Robinson was critical of those who follow blindly along with writing histories based on what was selected in prior eras.[12] For Robinson, history shouldn't just function like a knickknack that sits on a mantle and occasionally gets dusted off. It should focus on the events from the past that have meaning for the present generation. He means that historians are not to be like lemmings and only focus on tried and true topics but must be willing to explore new, relevant areas and subject matter in their investigations.

In addition to determining a topic, there are other places where selectivity affects the work of a historian. One such area involves setting the parameters for the spatio-temporal scope of the project.

2.2.2. SCOPE

Almost as crucial to a historian's work as the selection of topic is establishing the scope of the research to be undertaken. At the whim of the historian, subject matter may be limited or expanded by any number of factors, not the least of which are location and date. If there were a continuum of how big or small a chunk of the past a historian might choose to study, then the two extremes might be represented by world history and microhistory.

World history, in a nutshell, would seek to present an overview or compendium of all cultures, a daunting undertaking for a single individual, given the diversity of the past in all regions of the globe and our ever-expanding knowledge of what took place. A way to limit the scope a bit would be to choose to present a work of universal history that addresses a

---

10. This is beautifully expressed by Martha Howell and Walter Prevenier, who write, "historians do not discover a past as much as they create it; they choose the events and people that they think constitute the past, and they decide what about them is important to know.... [H]istorians always create a past by writing it" (*From Reliable Sources: An Introduction to Historical Methods* [Ithaca, N.Y.: Cornell University Press, 2001], 1).

11. Dray, *Philosophy of History*, 28.

12. James Harvey Robinson, "The New History," in Stern, *Varieties of History*, 257–60.

segment of the entirety of the human history but has a sense of how that slice of the past relates to the wider thrust of history as a cogent whole. Treatments of this type attempt to elucidate the shared destiny common to all eras of history, from prehistorical societies through ancient civilizations, the Bronze Age, the Iron Age, the classical world, and so forth right up through the modern era, contemporary era, and the present day. Francis Fukuyama provides an excellent description of universal history. He points out that an early example was written by Augustine (354–430 C.E.), a theologian and bishop in North Africa who "had no interest in the particular histories of the Greeks or the Jew as such; what mattered was the redemption of man as man, an event that would constitute the working out of God's will on earth. All nations were but branches of a more general humanity, whose fate could be understood in terms of God's plan for mankind."[13] To some extent, a universal history perspective pervades the Christian canon when read as a whole. Genesis begins with the work of God related to the protoplasts, Adam and Eve, who represent the advent of humanity. The destiny of human beings is then traced by focusing not on the world population but upon the Abrahamic line. The New Testament documents indicate continuity with this tradition in the form of Luke's genealogy of Jesus (3:23–38). And John, too, fits into the paradigm of this universal history because he clearly views Jesus not only as the means of salvation for the Jews but also as "Savior of the world" (4:42).

On the opposite side of the scope of a study from universal history is microhistory, which focuses on a tiny sliver of the past. It can be limited to an obscure place, a single event, or even a family or individual. A colleague of mine once tried his hand at writing corporate histories for individual businesses located in Kansas. Limited, as each was, to a single business in a single state, these might be considered microhistories. In biblical studies an excellent example of a microhistory is an analysis that has been conducted by Antoinette Clark Wire on the female prophets in Corinth. As Wire states in her introduction,

> The purpose of this study is to reconstruct as accurate a picture as possible of the women prophets in the church of first-century Corinth. I am interested in their behavior, daily, and occasional, their position in society and the church, and their values and theology. Broad studies

---

13. Francis Fukuyama, *The End of History and the Last Man* (New York: Free Press, 2006), 56. On universal history, see also chapter 5 in general.

are available on women in the Greco-Roman world and women in the ancient church, recently even on women in the Pauline churches. But these wide-angle views are more suggestive than conclusive because the specific texts they depend on have not been analyzed with reconstructing the women's lives in mind.[14]

While some historians might deem Wire's method in her book more linguistic than historical since she creates her portrait using Paul's rhetoric, nonetheless her conscious effort to limit the scale of her project to create a sketch of a handful of women in a single city during the Pauline era enables one to describe the work as microhistory.

Although Wire and Fukuyama demonstrate the extremes of breadth and restriction of subject matter, historical treatments may fall anywhere on the continuum, and historians may carve their material for study into manageable portions in a variety of ways. Some historians, for instance, hold specialties based on location (European historians, Russianists, American historians, local historians, and so forth). Others might identify with time periods (modernists, early modernists, classicists, etc.). There are combinations that add even more specificity. For instance, one might be a European historian focused on the contemporary period. To some extent, too, these labels are all relative. While an American scholar writing on the works of John Duns Scotus (1266–1308 C.E.), a medieval friar and theologian, might be labeled as a Europeanist by colleagues in the United States, in a department of history in Great Britain he or she might be classified as a local historian since Scotus hailed from Scotland. Despite being to some extent relative, however, the labels do serve the useful function of allowing scholars with similar research interests to seek each other out at conferences and other venues that promote scholarly dialogue.

The drive for specialization and selectivity in subject matter is not unique to the discipline of history. In New Testament studies, for instance, there are generalists, of course. But there are also those who are Matthean, Johannine, Pauline, and many other different kinds of specialists. Specialists in any field are natural outgrowths of two factors: differences in source material that may require a specific base of knowledge, languages, or tools to access the primary materials and the ever-burgeoning pools of secondary literature that oblige a scholar to expend considerable time

---

14. Antoinette Clark Wire, *The Corinthian Women Prophets: A Reconstruction through Paul's Rhetoric* (Minneapolis: Fortress, 1990), 1.

and effort to simply keep abreast of new developments and publications in the specialty. To illustrate the later point, I myself specialize in studying the Fourth Gospel. In the days before I had access to a well-stocked theological library, I made an attempt to purchase every monograph on John published each year. After no more than four years of this practice, I literally ran out of room on my shelves and hit almost 100 monographs and commentaries on the work of the Beloved Disciple. Even though I was collecting just a small fraction of the books available in the field of New Testament on a single topic, the output on such a narrow subject proves the need for some scholars to limit their studies to a very restricted specialization just to keep current.

Some of this conversation about selecting material for study and specialization may seem like common sense. And it is. In any event, selecting and limiting the material for a subject is a major consideration in executing a historical investigation. What is selected for study with regard to location or time period—whether microhistory, universal history, or something in between—may affect other theoretical aspects of the project, such as overall approach and use of sources. Before talking about sources, however, there are two more factors that influence selectivity: a historian's perception of what constitutes the driving force behind historical change and his or her methodology.

2.2.3. The "Types" of History

In 2000 Elisabeth Schüssler Fiorenza penned a history about the "history of contemporary research" relating to the historical Jesus. The second half of her title, *The Politics of Interpretation*, provides a clear indication of her thesis—that much scholarship was driven by the politics of the era, including the "resurgence of the religious Right."[15] Essentially she revealed that many works focused on the historical Jesus reflected an ideology of political conservativism, a form of research bias. Now, the fact that Schüssler Fiorenza chose to link biblical interpretation and politics may seem odd, but this juxtaposition merely demonstrates Schüssler Fiorenza's grasp of the fact that history contains "standard mechanisms" that are thought to bring about change. Politics is one of these. Those who write political his-

---

15. Elisabeth Schüssler Fiorenza, *Jesus and the Politics of Interpretation* (New York: Continuum, 2000), 4.

tory, or who might be known as political historians, are keen to track down the influence of politics on any given historical event regardless of whether the event is religious our secular. Despite the vaunted separation of church and state in the United States, politics transcends national ideologies, and the church itself is a very politically driven and motivated institution.

Other historians might eschew politics to focus their writings instead on economic forces, legal developments, military maneuverings, or other factors which influence the course of history. For instance, if one holds that money makes the world go around, one may be inclined to trace how issues like supply and demand, availability of labor, trade agreements, the education of a labor force, work ethics, barter systems, the rise and fall of various industries, and many other economic elements influenced events in the past. Marxist historians, as we will see in a later chapter, are a species of economic historian since they focus on the role of labor as a means of producing goods and labor's interactions with those in power who control the capital.

Sometimes these fundamental or driving forces in history are found in lists that identify the "types of history." So, in addition to political history and economic history, there is legal history, military history, medical history, and so forth. Some other types of history might include women's history, ecclesiological and religious history, social history, cultural history, and intellectual history—even then, the list is not comprehensive. In the final chapters of this book, medical history, economic history, cultural history, and women's history are all reflected as applications of history. It is also the case that several factors may be combined. While Schüssler Fiorenza identifies politics as the main catalyst for momentum in historical-Jesus research, her work also incorporates more than a dash of women's history in its recognition of the problem of Jesus' maleness in feminist Christological discourses.[16] Furthermore, an individual scholar might shift between types of history during the course of his or her career, penning for instance an economic history, a political history, and even an intellectual history about the same time period and subject matter. Of course, a historian might elect to specialize in producing a certain type of historical study consistently.

Although Schüssler Fiorenza's main topic was the "history of historical Jesus scholarship" in the contemporary time period, one might also

---

16. Ibid., 9.

choose to employ political history, feminist history, or, for that matter, a combination of both as the main interpretive lens for any given event in the early Christian era. The various types of history are just another set of tools from which a historian might select in executing a historical analysis of any past person, happening, or phenomenon.

2.2.4. METHODS

When scholars seek to clarify the method, or the technique, of gaining knowledge that will be used in the history they are undertaking to write, it is not unusual for them to specify the type of history that will be the overarching principle in the study. Michael H. Crosby, for instance, authored a work in 1988 in which he sought to "discover the possible underlying link or fusion between religion and economics"[17] through a word study based on Matthew's use of *house*. While the nexus of religion and economics represents two types of history, that is not the entire story about the method he used. Generally, a historian also decides to approach the topic from a descriptive angle, focusing on what took place, or an explanatory perspective, hypothesizing why or how something occurred. And if that isn't enough, an author must also determine whether to use a qualitative or quantitative method. Crosby, for instance, produced a qualitative study that is descriptive and that identifies justice as the foundational concept "providing the ethos and ethics for Matthew's households."[18] The difference between qualitative and quantitative studies is generally easy to discern.

Quantitative methods involve the creation of a data set consisting of a number of cases with particular characteristics or variables, each of which has its own value and may be analyzed statistically. Thus, the questions asked in these sorts of studies in relation to a given institution, policy, group or movement are "how large? how long? how often? how representative?"[19] Because of its numeric nature, studies that use this method often present data in table format. Quantitative studies tend to be relatively rare in biblical studies, perhaps due to the nature of the surviving documents from the era. This is because inductive quantitative studies rely on sampling,

---

17. Michael H. Crosby, *House of Disciples: Church, Economics, and Justice in Matthew* (Maryknoll, N.Y.: Orbis, 1988), 5.

18. Ibid., 230.

19. John Chapham, "Economic History as a Discipline," in Stern, *Varieties of History*, 309.

and there is always the niggling question of how accurately a very small number of existing documents can represent the larger population at the time period being studied. Despite the fact that qualitative studies tend to be the most commonly represented method in our discipline, there is indeed an almost wide-open field for those who wish to try their hands at statistically based reconstructions and models based on comparative data from other cultures of the period. By contrast, qualitative studies like Crosby's will not be peppered with charts, graphs, and statistics. Instead, qualitative studies attempt to discover the meaning that people bring to words, actions, and events and present it in a coherent narrative.

Essentially, then, any given approach to "doing history" must consider the nature of time, the scope of the project, the type or types of historically based mechanisms that will propel the study, and ultimately whether the method will be qualitative or quantitative. In short, there are myriad decisions for a historian to make even before starting to examine the evidence presented by the sources. History, however, would not be possible as a discipline without the raw materials that the evidence supplies to researchers.

2.3. Sources

To a large extent, the discipline of history came into its own when those interested in the past began to use sources or evidence to flesh out their storytelling about both their origins and what they deemed to be significant events in former times. Indeed, the use of sources is one of the hallmarks differentiating history from the genres of fable and myth. In modern primers of historiography, Herodotus (ca. 484–430/420 b.c.e.) is often credited as the "father of history." This description of the ancient Greek historian is apt because of his use of sources. For his chosen topic he investigated the causes of the Greek-Persian Wars, which took place in the first half of the fifth century b.c.e., and he crafted his account of events based on his own observations, tales from eyewitnesses, and records of the state. At one point he even conducted interviews with the Delphians and the Milesians in order to hear their sides of the story.[20]

Yet Herodotus was not the only ancient figure from the fifth and sixth centuries b.c.e. to use supporting materials to undergird assertions. This point was made by John Van Seters, who identified the Deuteronomistic

---

20. Herodotus, *Hist.* 1.19–21 (Goodley, LCL).

Historian of the Hebrew Bible as the Father of History's analogue.[21] In drawing out his source-related comparison between Herodotus and the Deuteronomist, Van Seters observes that, just as is the case with his Greek counterpart, the author of documents including Joshua to 2 Kings took the initiative to gather his own sources. Indeed, this historian made use of not only oral stories but also records and royal chronicles[22] such as the "Book of the Chronicles of the Kings of Judah," a written record mentioned in 2 Kgs 14:18.

Moving forward in time several centuries, sources were also in use during the New Testament's composition by those who sought to preserve an account of events in written form. Luke, for instance, mentions narratives that were based on the recollections of eyewitnesses (Luke 1:1–2) and in recounting the trial of Paul even crafts a letter reminiscent of one sent by Claudius Lysias to Felix, governor of the province (Acts 23:25–30). Despite the use of such supporting materials, however, it is not clear that ancient historians spent much time weighing the worth of the evidence they used in their histories.

In more recent centuries, perceptions about the merit of any individual source underwent a paradigm shift that helped to distinguish the modern enterprise of writing history from that of the ancient world or the Middle Ages. While Herodotus or Luke might have taken records at face value or even as authorities that need not be questioned or verified, beginning with the Renaissance thinkers were a bit more cautious. In the fifteenth century, for instance, Lorenzo Valla used philology—specifically his knowledge of Latin and its development over time—to prove that a document known as the *Donation of Constantine*, assumed to be from the fourth century, was in fact a forgery because it relied upon vocabulary and Latin not current until the eighth century. In essence, from that point of time onward, the process of not only using evidence but also authenticating sources became vital to historical methodology.

In the nineteenth century at the University of Berlin and under the direction of Leopold Von Ranke, seminars on *Quellenkritik* (source criticism) gave students exposure not only to how sound a source might be but also provided criteria to judge which sources were to be preferred over others. Thus it became fashionable to distinguish between primary and

---

21. Dating is based on the last episode recorded in the book of Kings, the exile of 586 B.C.E.

22. Van Seters, *In Search of History*, 17.

secondary sources. Von Ranke maintained that eyewitness reports and documents created most contemporary with the events being investigated were better to consult when writing history than accounts created much later than the time period of the event in question, or secondary sources. Primary sources are the types of materials that we might find in archives, in museums, or at digs.

Need a clearer example of which is which? With regard to the New Testament, for instance, the twenty-seven books in the canon would serve as primary sources about early Christianity, while commentaries would provide an example of secondary resources.[23] Sometimes "primary sources" can be further broken down into the categories of "direct" and "indirect." A direct source, to illustrate, might be a bill of sale for a ship that sailed on the Sea of Galilee. An indirect, but still primary, source might be a list that details the number of fish in the daily catches, from which the historian would make inferences about the skills of the fishermen on the boat or the number of fair-weather days that allowed them to ply their trade.

During von Ranke's period, hand in hand with determining the sources to employ and how germane they might be for a project, textual criticism was also utilized. A close cousin to philology, the object of textual criticism was to identify corruptions to manuscripts as a result of the process of time and transmission so that scholars had access to the most "correct" form of a given document.[24] Eventually, both textual criticism and source criticism came to be applied to the early Christian writings, including the New Testament, and have taken their place as the philological strand of historical-criticism that has already been outlined in chapter 1. Even if these methods no longer have center stage in the field of history today, they are at least considered support activities.

At the same time that work was being completed in textual criticism, progress was also being made in New Testament lexicography, the historical study of New Testament terms. This field, which is more properly

---

23. Sometimes a source may be a primary source for one project yet serve as a secondary resource for another. For instance, the Synoptic Gospels may serve as a primary source for studying the character of late first-century Christianity but as a secondary source for writing a life of Jesus (if they were not written by eyewitnesses).

24. For beginning students, Arthur G. Patzia's *The Making of the New Testament: Origin, Collection, Text and Canon* (2nd ed.; Downers Grove, Ill.: InterVarsity Press, 2011) provides an excellent, short introduction to textual criticism, complete with charts and a few plates in chapters 6 and 7.

a subdiscipline of linguistics than history, nonetheless produces tools for historians. Like source and textual criticism, it also has verification at its heart because lexicons assist translators in applying the most "appropriate" or "correct" equivalent when translating or transferring meaning between languages separated from one another by culture and time.

Many of the works from the last century in the arena of lexicography have achieved the status of classic reference works and are still invaluable today. One example is the ubiquitous *Theological Dictionary of the New Testament* (*TDNT*)[25] edited by Gerhard Kittel and Gerhard Friedrich. Despite being a collaborative work with 160 contributors,[26] this collection of historical essays is not the final word on the language of the New Testament. James Barr has written an erudite evaluation of how linguistic "evidence" is handled in biblical translation and is very clear that lexicons such as the *TDNT* are as much historical interpretations as they are mere dictionaries. This is due in part to the fact that translators and lexicographers make word selections based on their own preconceived theological predilections.[27]

This criticism applies equally as well to other respected works that have perdured for at least a century now. For instance, there have been many editions, revisions, and translations of the *Griechisch-deutsches Wörterbuch zu des Neuen Testaments und der übringen urchristlichen Literature* by Erwin Preuschen (1910), to which Walter Bauer also later added his insights in 1928.[28] One of the keys to this particular lexicon's usefulness was an ever-broadening consideration of sources in definitions. Bauer, for instance, searched for parallels to the language of the Greek New Testament in a wide variety of literature extending to the Byzantine era. The first English translation, which went by the title *A Greek-English Lexicon of the New Testament and Other Early Christian Literature*, was produced by William Arndt and F. Wilbur Gingrich, who added words from Papias. The tendency to consider additional sources extended into the second English edition in 1979, where Frederick Danker joined the

---

25. The Geoffrey Bromiley English reprint edition (*TDNT*), set in ten volumes, is readily available via Eerdmans in Grand Rapids, Michigan.

26. A list is available in the index compiled by Ronald E. Pitkin and available as the tenth volume in the *TDNT* set.

27. James Barr, *The Semantics of Biblical Language* (London: SCM, 1961), especially 206–62.

28. Bauer's contribution to the project began in 1925.

project and contributed further references from papyri, inscriptions, texts from Qumran, and, most recently, coverage of intertestamental resources and the early Christian apologists. While historians might not deem the lexicon "history" proper to the extent that it isn't a narrative account of the past, there are historical elements related to the project and it is not obvious that those who worked on the English edition did not, at least to some extent, consider themselves historians. Certainly, in his introductory essay to the third edition, Danker is clear that language is culture bound and necessitates sensitivity to "socio-cultural perspectives relating to non-verbal linguistic components."[29] One of Danker's colleagues on the 1957 and 1979 editions of the project, F. Wilbur Gingrich, was even more forthcoming on the intimate relationship between lexicography, an auxiliary science of history, and the discipline of history itself.

As undergraduate students who majored in Greek, one of my classmates and I once had the privilege of spending an afternoon with Gingrich. He was in his late eighties at the time of our visit but was a sprightly host. He was generously complimentary of his coworkers on the project but did express disappointment with the University of Chicago Press, which had retained copyright of the *Lexicon* on the grounds that they thought there would not be a big market for the book—at least that was his take on the situation. Gingrich wryly noted the irony that the press thought that it would need the royalties to pay the production costs and urged myself and another student guest to always remember to obtain copyright of any works we might write because one can never really judge market demand.

Words of wisdom aside, the most fascinating aspect of the meeting was a tour of Gingrich's home office, which he was gracious to show us. The room was stacked floor to ceiling with shoeboxes filled with index cards, one for each entry in his section of the lexicon. He pulled out a few cards to show us the sort of notes that he had compiled. He chuckled and told my friend and me that even at that juncture he was still occasionally making additions to cards as he was reading classical literature.

At one point during the visit, my classmate asked Gingrich how many cards were used for the Greek word καὶ ("and"). This prompted our sagacious host to spend a few moments explaining the difference between a concordance project, where every instance of a word might be collected, and a lexicon, which requires "selection." Furthermore, he told us that

---

29. BDAG, ix.

the interesting thing about lexicography was seeing how the meaning of words change over time, or how specifically Christian vocabulary could influence the vocabulary of later time periods.[30] One thing was very clear from this visit. Gingrich was not a mere compiler of word lists but viewed himself as a historian in his own right who was delighted that his work was useful in helping students like us to access the New Testament in its original language.

Whether considered to be auxiliary to the discipline of history or subsumed under the auspices of historical criticism,[31] the areas of study known as textual criticism, source criticism, and lexicography are vital for the process of verifying and translating first-century sources. Sources, however, when used as evidence, do not all bear the same weight. It has already been mentioned that von Ranke gave preference to eyewitness accounts, the same sort of material upon which both Herodotus and the author of the Gospel of Luke drew. Yet the high merit of eyewitnesses is not something to be taken for granted.

2.3.1. The Value of Eyewitnesses

In the section above I recounted a personal anecdote that involved a visit with F. Wilbur Gingrich. The decision to break from an analytical mode of discourse into prose that was a bit more informal was intentional because the episode is an example of eyewitness testimony and may be used to illustrate some of the difficulties inherent with this type of source material. For example, since Gingrich is now deceased, how does one know that the account of my visit with him is true? How might one "weigh the evidence"? An extreme skeptic might doubt that the visit took place at all and want proof of that, too.

To get at the heart of what did or did not happen, a historian might contact the alumni office and learn that I did attend Albright College and would notice the name of the F. Wilbur Gingrich Library. This might indicate that, just as I was once on campus to earn a degree, there is a connection between Gingrich and the campus as well. But that does not prove that our paths crossed. A look at the campus yearbook would confirm that I majored in Greek and thereby increase the possibility that I

---

30. See also F. Wilbur Gingrich, "New Testament Lexicography and the Future," *JR* 25 (1945): 179–82.

31. Please refer to the graphic and discussion in chapter 1.

might have encountered an emeritus professor who and previously taught that subject, but that wouldn't be guaranteed. The probability that the incident took place would improve further if the historian had access to my personal library and noticed that Gingrich inscribed and dated my well-worn copy of the second edition of the lexicon. But even then the historian would have to verify that the handwriting was truly Gingrich's and also track down whether or not the visit took place on campus or in Gingrich's home as the account of the episode suggested. Then there is the question of how reliable the version of the conversation might be.

If it is likely that the visit did take place, for example, how certain might anyone be that Gingrich did indeed express frustration about the royalty arrangement with the press? Doubt might be raised about this point, especially since Danker records in the third edition of the lexicon that the University of Chicago had already been in dialogue with Bauer to secure rights of publication prior to Gingrich becoming involved with the project in the 1950s and that initial funding for the translation of the German lexicon was provided by the Missouri Synod of the Lutheran Church.[32] These facts imply that a stipend was involved in lieu of royalties. If I were available to be interviewed by the historian who was trying to find out the "truth" about the event given this slight discrepancy between Gingrich's version and Danker's, and if I repeated the details of my conversation with Gingrich again just as I did above, that might be considered consistent testimony and might lend the story a ring of credibility.

But if the conversation is accurate, how does one explain the seeming inconsistency between my own conversation with Gingrich and the account of the project's inception recorded by Danker? One might, for instance, question whether my memory of a conversation that took place more than two decades ago is accurate. I may have been an eyewitness, but one who is now temporally removed from the event to the point where details would blur and be misremembered. As a solution, the historian might be extremely lucky and track down the "other student" mentioned in the anecdote to provide additional confirmation of what took place.

A detractor playing devil's advocate might take another tack and question the accuracy of the account based on the age of the participants in the conversation. Gingrich was, of course, nearing ninety and I was in my late teens. How credible are witnesses who are that old and that young,

---

32. BDAG, vi, vii.

respectively? The historian might want to discount the testimony at this point, but it might also be possible to find others who knew us at that time period and might attest to the sharpness of our memories or produce my academic transcripts and Gingrich's publications and lend credence to our ability to remember the episode as recalled.[33]

Another explanation for the seeming disjunction between Danker's description of the role of the press and Gingrich's might be that Gingrich had not been clear about the arrangements that the press had made with Bauer regarding permission to translate and the source of the project funding, while Danker had access to records and documentation at the press to which Gingrich did not.

What this example indicates about this piece of eyewitness testimony are the following two points: (1) Knowing without a shadow of doubt what actually took place and what was said or why in a small home in Reading, Pennsylvania, in May in the late 1980s can only be ascertained with differing degrees of probability and never with 100% certitude. (2) Eyewitness testimony, when there is lack of an MP3 recording of the conversation or an authenticated transcript, may only be deemed credible based, in part, on the following: (a) knowledge of the character and abilities of the person providing testimony; (b) proximity of the eyewitness in time to when the event occurred; (c) repetition and consistency of the testimony when solicited multiple times; and (d) evidence from other sources, either other eyewitnesses, written documentation or even physical remains (i.e., the library with Gingrich's name on it) may be marshaled to lend veracity to the story. What is very clear is that, while ancient historiographers and even von Ranke may have put a premium on eyewitness testimony, as Allan Megill notes and the example of my personal conversation with Gingrich demonstrates, "Our modern view of memory is more chastened."[34] To this end, historians like R. G. Collingwood insisted that eyewitness testimony should always be confirmed by material traces.[35] And, where other types of evidence are not extant, historians may approach eyewitness accounts

---

33. Howell and Prevenier add several other issues that might impact the trustworthiness of an observer, including politics, pressure, the need to shade details related to job or other connections, and even the vanity of the observer (*From Reliable Sources*, 68).

34. Allan Megill, "Memory," in *Encyclopedia of Historians and Historical Writing*, vol. 2 (ed. Kelly Boyd; New York: Routledge, 1999), 798.

35. Ibid.

with a great amount of caution. Without a way to test the trustworthiness of eyewitness evidence, it is impossible to separate fact from fiction.

This skepticism about eyewitness testimony represents a philosophical shift from the classical and medieval periods to today's understanding of how sources are to be weighed, and it may seem to put the modern historian of the New Testament era in a bind, especially given that the Gospels are presented as early "testimony" about the key event in Christian history.[36]

Broadly speaking, the field of New Testament studies has the daunting task of dealing with not one issue but two. Of course, the first is whether or not the eyewitness testimony of the Gospels is believable, given modern skepticism about reliability of this form of evidence. And the second is whether or not the Gospels could actually have been written by eyewitnesses or by authors who at least had contact with those who lived during the events they record. Questions always arise about the education level and life spans of the potential witnesses relative to the dates of the texts' composition. As Timothy Paul Jones inelegantly frames at least part of the discussion, "How dumb were the disciples?"[37]

Regarding the first issue, Richard Baukham develops a list of factors that, when present, help clarify how well an event will be recalled by witnesses.[38] For instance, memory is sharper when the event is unique, important to the witness, and something with which the witness is emotionally involved. How the witness recounts the event to others also holds clues as to the credibility of the testimony. To be specific, more accurate memories tend to include vivid imagery and irrelevant details that support the theory that the memory is a "copy" of the original event rather than a reconstructed recollection. Also, memories that are frequently rehearsed or recalled by the witness appear to have a greater degree of correctness.[39]

---

36. That is not to say that eyewitnesses are not always to be preferred in modern historiography. In fact, they are preferred when they deal with facts known by most contemporaries and were in a position to accurately report what transpired. So a TV news broadcast about a tornado will seek out and interview an eyewitness, but the fact that the tornado occurred will be a generally known occurrence. See Howell and Prevenier, *From Reliable Sources*, 70–71.

37. Timothy Paul Jones, *Misquoting Truth: A Guide to the Fallacies of Bart Ehrman's* Misquoting Jesus (Downers Grove, Ill.: InterVarsity Press, 2007), 113.

38. Richard Bauckham, *Jesus and the Eyewitnesses: The Gospels as Eyewitness Testimony* (Grand Rapids: Eerdmans, 2006), 9.

39. Ibid., 330–34.

As for the questions of who the authors of the Gospels were and whether they did participate in the events they record firsthand, the issues have been endlessly debated. At core is the concern about whether or not a second- or thirdhand "witness" or source is as reliable as an individual who reports an account seen firsthand, and whether an anonymous document is as credible as one for whom authorship is unquestioned. To be blunt, it is unlikely that the question of who penned the Gospels will ever be resolved. But, as Bauckham points out, it is entirely possible that eyewitness testimony was incorporated—that the Gospels were written in living memory of the events that were recounted rather than following a long period of oral transmission.[40] Furthermore, it is not the case that an anonymous document or one for which authorship is not known is any less reliable than one whose authorship is well established. After all, even though I wrote the prior account of my own conversation with Gingrich, some may choose to doubt its veracity, as has been demonstrated.

In any case, whether eyewitness testimony is preferred or regarded with unease, it—like any other piece of evidence or even when combined with other types of sources—will never provide immediate access to the past. It is, though, one means by which the past may be mediated to us with either greater or lesser degrees of probability and accuracy. When dealing with source material, the relative value of eyewitness materials is only one issue with which biblical scholars must wrestle. There is also the problem of how to weigh the merit of "sacred books" in relation to other types of evidence.

2.3.2. INSPIRED SOURCES

Clearly, there is a huge elephant in the room at the marriage of the disciplines of history and biblical studies: an inspired source. Although not every New Testament scholar who uses the New Testament in writing histories of the first century is a Christian or accepts the twenty-seven books of the New Testament as sacred texts, many scholars in the discipline of New Testament studies do. By contrast, when historians are writing histories of subjects as diverse as the American Civil War or the transmission of AIDS in Africa, the documents, texts, and relics that are consulted about

---

40. Ibid., 7, 472.

the war or the devastating epidemic are not generally considered by the researchers to be the word of God.

The bias inherent in ascribing sacred status to texts can lead to extreme reactions. In an attempt to avoid undue weight in considering the biblical text when writing monographs on the first century world, classicists may eschew the use of New Testament documents all together. Their counterparts in the discipline of biblical studies, by contrast, may at times overemphasize the twenty-seven books of the New Testament or some portion thereof, such as the Gospels, to the exclusion of other Greco-Roman documents. Yet it is becoming ever more popular for scholars on both sides of the divide to consider sources more broadly. Some examples are worth noting.

First, Bruce W. Winter, in his work *Roman Wives, Roman Widows: The Appearance of New Women and the Pauline Communities*,[41] shows that the boundaries between classical studies and New Testament studies are fairly fluid. "The Index of Scripture and Other Ancient Sources" at the end of his text[42] includes a wide array of classical literature in both Greek and Latin from an extensive range of genres. Everything from Plutarch to Martial is represented. That a classical scholar would give credence to a book, like Winter's, that mixes resources drawn from Christianity's sacred writings and these documents written by pagan authors is proven by the fact that *Roman Wives, Roman Widows* sports a cover endorsement by Beryl Rawson, an emerita professor of ancient history at Australian National University. While today there is more dialogue between ancient historians and New Testament scholars and an increased willingness by both to use both divinely inspired and uninspired texts, that has not always been the case.

Keith Bradley, a classicist, may be used as an example of a scholar who just two decades ago was unaware of the potential that New Testament documents might hold as source materials for the Ancient World. To illustrate, in his book *Discovering the Roman Family*,[43] he does not make use of any evidence from New Testament texts, likely because he conceived of them "scripture" rather than classical documents. Even when discussing

---

41. Bruce W. Winter, *Roman Wives, Roman Widows: The Appearance of New Women and the Pauline Churches* (Grand Rapids: Eerdmans, 2003).

42. Ibid., 231–36.

43. Keith R. Bradley, *Discovering the Roman Family: Studies in Roman Social History* (Oxford: Oxford University Press, 1991).

men's roles in child care in the provinces, he overlooks the rich father-son motifs in the Fourth Gospel and even a Pauline metaphor in which the apostle himself acts as a nursemaid to provide milk-like theological content for infant believers (1 Cor 3:20). Rather, Bradley shows a marked preference for inscriptions, along with the works of the Roman Emperor Justinian (482–565 C.E.); the orator and statesman Cicero (106–43 B.C.E.); and the great Latin poets Ovid (43 B.C.E.–17 C.E.) and Martial (d. 101 or 104 C.E.). He even bends to employ Josephus, the first-century Jewish historian.[44] But not a single New Testament character or passage is mentioned.

But bias in itself, while value laden, needn't be cause for dismissing works that either do or don't make use of sacred texts. In fact, the idea that the Christian canon is a sacred text may provide the impetus for talented, bright scholars to select first-century history as their subject of study. That is valuable for the field as a whole. And, in any event, professional courtesy dictates that individual scholars may nonetheless exchange ideas and interact as colleagues regardless of their positions relative to the divinely inspired status of some sources.

At a bare minimum, both sides can at least agree that the histories and scholarly works that stem from using the books of the New Testament as sources are not themselves accorded the status of being the word of God. In other words, the use of sacred texts does not result in "inspired" interpretations. Even monographs subject to the *magisterium*, or teaching authority of the Catholic Church, and bearing the designations *Nihil Obstat* and *Imprimatur* are not infallible. The certification only confirms that there will be "no ill effect on the faith and morals of Christ's faithful"[45] if they are read. Plenty of room remains for disagreement and dialogue regarding their content and methods.

2.3.3. CANONS OF SOURCES: ANOTHER ASPECT OF SELECTION

One advantage that a discussion about some quarters of scholarship viewing the New Testament books as sacred documents brings to light is the fact that every discipline is formed of communities of scholars who agree

---

44. See, for instance, the notes provided by Bradley, *Discovering the Roman Family*, 29–36, 65 n. 4.

45. Code of Canon Law, 1983, "Title IV: The Means of Social Communication" 823.1; online: http://www.ourladyswarriors.org/canon/c0822-0832.htm.

on certain conventions relating to sources, be they centered on the word of God or not. Regarding his own discipline of philosophy, for instance, Richard Rorty laments that his field has created canons not only about what questions are most appropriate for the study of philosophy but also concerning which writers of the past are to be included in survey histories about philosophy's roots.[46] Certainly, the works of Aristotle (384–322 B.C.E.), Hegel (1770–1831 C.E.), and Kant (1724–1804 C.E.) are not generally considered to be "sacred texts," but these philosophers number among those who are regularly included in such histories while other, lesser-known figures are skipped or treated skimpily.

Rorty reminds colleagues in his own discipline of the need to "respect the right of others to create alternative canons" that include new or unfamiliar names.[47] He subtly warns that a discipline that always makes recourse to the same stable of sources may become fossilized. Along these same lines, individual scholars should beware having stock resource favorites that are frequently consulted. To be certain, scholarly discussion is enlivened with the use of new sources.

There are multiple ways to expand collections of "go-to" resources. In biblical studies, for instance, occasional discoveries of manuscript caches in the desert—such as the Nag Hammadi find or the Dead Sea Scrolls, both of which occurred during the last century—provided new primary sources that stimulated many fruitful conversations about the background of New Testament characters, traditions, and theology.[48]

Although the discovery of new manuscripts creates a good deal of enthusiasm and new scholarly output for a discipline, when dealing with the New Testament era, the number of primary sources that survived and to which historians have access is still relatively limited. Standards like the writings of Josephus, who was a contemporary of the writers of the New Testament documents and recorded the destruction of the temple in the 70s C.E., have been used since the earliest times. Nevertheless, advances

---

46. Richard Rorty, "The Historiography of Philosophy: Four Genres," in *Philosophy in History* (ed. Richard Rorty, J. B. Schneewind, and Quentin Skinner; Cambridge: Cambridge University Press, 1984), 58–59.

47. Ibid., 67.

48. Krister Stendahl, ed., *The Scrolls and the New Testament* (London: SCM, 1957), represents an early example. For more recent texts, see George J. Brooke, *The Dead Sea Scrolls and the New Testament* (Minneapolis: Fortress, 2005); and Florentino García Martínez, ed., *Qumran and the New Testament* (Leiden: Brill, 2009).

and new historical insights may still be made using the existing sources in two ways: either old sources might be read in new light or sources that have been previously overlooked or not generally included in the standard "canon of sources" might be brought to bear.

An example of advancing scholarship by using the same sources differently may be found in the work of J. Christiaan Beker, a Pauline scholar whose publications during the 1980s brought him much notoriety. In the early 1990s I was enrolled in a doctoral-level seminar class taught by Beker. One day a student asked Beker for his opinion on a particular passage from Romans, appealing to Beker on the grounds that he was an authority on Paul. The request, or how it was phrased, really stopped Beker in his tracks. Slouched in a chair with his elbow propped on the table, Beker told us the story of how his so-called fame as an authority in biblical studies came to be. He said that the key to his work was the distinction between "coherency" and "contingency." Of course we all knew this. Although his own texts were not assigned reading for his own class because Beker felt that we got his opinion in seminar and should read detractors, we all had read his most famous book on our own anyway.[49] At any rate, Beker continued his story by telling us that these two concepts were all based on a dream. One night in the wee hours, he woke up with the words *coherency* and *contingency* dancing in his head. When he couldn't fall back to sleep, eventually it struck him that the word *contingency* referred to the individual contexts and settings of each of Paul's letters, yet there was nonetheless a coherent core that marked Paul's basic understanding of the content of the faith. This differed from some of the prior scholarly attempts at understanding Paul's writings where the particular, situational settings of the letters were ignored or obscured in favor of constructing a systematic Pauline doctrine. Beker shook his head. He was incredulous we were ascribing great wisdom to him when there wasn't anything more to it—no secret to his success other than a simple dream.

Beker's tale actually was a multifaceted teaching tool. On the one hand, it was a lesson to a class of prospective PhDs on balancing humility and self-confidence. Sometimes it isn't the most complex theory that advances scholarship but one that is essentially simple. And anyone, even lowly students, had as much facility to make a significant contribution to

---

49. J. Christiaan Beker, *Paul the Apostle: The Triumph of God in Life and Thought* (Philadelphia: Fortress, 1980), 11–19.

scholarship as an esteemed professor. On the other hand, it was a lesson about sources. Rather than following the herd and using the Pauline Letters exactly as others had before him, Beker simply looked at old sources in a new way. As he explained at one point in his writings, his choice of Galatians and Romans for exploring the contextual nature of Paul's theological thinking "may seem surprising because these letters are often used together to exhibit Paul's systematic doctrinal thought."[50] Standard sources may always be read in new light.

In addition to furthering knowledge in a field by reading comfortable and familiar primary materials in new ways, as the example from Beker demonstrated, the second means of advancing scholarship in a discipline when no new manuscript discoveries are in the offing is to see what might be offered by valuable sources that have not been traditional standbys. In short, one has to venture outside and away from the canon of what is comfortable and well worn.

The word *traditional* is apt because it implies set expectations and ways of doing things within a defined scholarly profession. The academy, although it idealizes those who break new ground, is a community in its own right and has traditions of scholarship that codify how particular sources are used. In the case of the field of history, the practice of limiting the sources used was so common that in 1873 the classicist Barthold Georg Niebuhr, whose main work was a history of Rome, excoriated his predecessors, exclaiming, "Some restrict themselves to the collection of truncated fragments of reports from antiquity without attempting to solve their underlying riddles; they resist the impulse to strain their view in order to see the form of the whole to which the pieces belonged. Such a lifeless compilation of fragments is of no use."[51] In essence, Niebuhr was urging others to make use of new sources for the study of Roman history rather than to just blindly accept the work of Livy (59 B.C.E.–17 C.E.), a Roman historian, merely because that had been the authoritative source in the field for centuries.

Almost fifty years later, James Harvey Robinson, an American historian who was mentioned earlier in this chapter for chastising those who only wrote about tried and true subject matter, was also critical of the limited way in which his peers were using sources. He derided history schol-

---

50. Ibid, 37.
51. Translated by and quoted in Stern, *Varieties of History*, 48.

ars of his day because they were "victims of tradition in dealing with the past. They exhibit but little appreciation of the vast resources upon which they might draw, and unconsciously follow, for the most part, an established routine in their selection of facts."[52] To be blunt, not only were the same sources being used over and over again but even a limited number of passages within the "standard" sources were being used. For those of us in biblical studies, who are familiar with pastors who routinely read the full range of lectionary texts as part of Sunday's liturgy yet nonetheless always manage to preach on the same book of the Bible or from the same genre of biblical documents, we would say in regard to Robinson's comments that the discipline of history had formed "a canon within the canon" of possible resources. To be succinct, even one's use of sources, either from a deep or shallow pool, involves an element of selectivity. So we have circled around again to an issue that was presented earlier in the chapter.

Selectivity (whether it relates to choosing a topic or the other elements mentioned in this chapter such as determining the driving forces behind change), a historian's understanding of time, and the nature and use of sources are all building blocks that have been combined in various ways across the centuries by those who have engaged in writing history. They are aspects of projects that anyone who wrestles with a topic that focuses on an event, individual, or institution associated with the past must come to grips, whether writing about Winston Churchill's role as the prime minister of the United Kingdom in World War II, the historical Jesus, or some other topic. Philosophers of history, though, are also interested in high-level decisions that writers may not always be conscious of making. These include what the writer understands the overarching function of history to be and whether or not history is leading somewhere, however that goal might be envisioned.

---

52. Quoted in ibid., 259.

3

BASIC PHILOSOPHICAL MATTERS

In our modern era, not all history is judged to be "good" history. In the last chapter, mention was made of works that were less than satisfying as valid accounts of the past. Some were based on archaeological pieces of evidence that were subsequently identified as forgeries; others were national histories of the World War II era in which the account of events was deliberately skewed to promote the agendas of those who commissioned the works; and finally there was brief mention of the questionable veracity of the work of Josephus, who is now considered to have conflated fact and fiction. This would all seem to lend credence to the wry adage by Samuel Butler, "God cannot alter the past, though historians can." Nonetheless, when history is done well and is not abused, it is deemed to be a constructive resource for civil society. As Pearl S. Buck said, "If you want to understand today, you have to search yesterday." This brings us to the subject of the typical uses to which history may be put.

3.1. THE USES OF HISTORY

Philosophers have a predilection to create systems and categories to describe knowledge, and in 1874 Friedrich Nietzsche tried his hand at listing the advantages that history might provide for life. He identified three uses of history. In the first, which he terms "monumental," the past provides examples of great teachers and comforters whom others might emulate in their own aspirations toward excellence. This use of history is not unfamiliar to the church and is evidenced in the traditions of the martyrs, the saints, and even in the What Would Jesus Do? movement—a phenomenon first associated with the work of Charles Sheldon and in the 1990s popularized across college campuses, where enthusiastic students signified a desire to adhere to the ethical behaviors demonstrated by Jesus through wearing bracelets decorated with the initials WWJD.

The second use of history that is identified by Nietzsche is "antiquarian." In this category, individuals esteem the past and wish to reproduce the experiences of earlier times for new generations. Nietzsche himself is rather lukewarm in his regard for this function of history. He describes it as a process where "all that is small and limited, moldy and obsolete, gains a worth and inviolability of its own."[1] In other words, everything from the romanticized era is held equally dear even if, in the eyes of the original participants from the past, certain aspects were incidental or valued differently relative to one another. The philosopher voices a further concern that staunch adherence to antiquarianism may be divisive in a community, creating a scenario in which there are in- and out-groups among subsets of members who hold the idealized time period in greater and lesser degrees of respect. Nietzsche also had a low opinion of antiquarianism because overemphasizing the past can lead to stifling action or constructive impulses that would propel progress.[2] Instead of developing an obsession with the past, a healthy view of history would look at times gone by in order to both understand the present and stimulate longing for what might be accomplished in the future.[3]

A New Testament scholar who might be said to model the antiquarian outlook in a way that does not fall into the trap identified by Nietzsche is F. F. Bruce. In the introduction to his book *Paul: Apostle of the Heart Set Free*, Bruce reveals how much he idolizes Paul in true antiquarian fashion, with the quixotic assertion that he has written his text *amore Pauli*. He gushes, "For half a century and more I have been a student and teacher of ancient literature, and to no other writer, ancient or modern, have I devoted so much time and attention as to Paul. Nor can I think of any other writer, ancient or modern, whose study is so richly rewarding as his." Bruce then goes on to offer an encomium to Paul, praising the "attractive warmth" of Paul's personality, and the "dynamism" with which he spread the gospel.[4]

---

1. Friedrich Nietzsche, *The Use and Abuse of History* (trans. Adrian Collins; Indianapolis: Bobbs-Merrill, 1957), 18.

2. Ibid., 42 . Nietzsche believed this was the case with Germany in the time in which he was writing.

3. Ibid., 10.

4. F. F. Bruce, *Paul: Apostle of the Heart Set Free* (Grand Rapids: Eerdmans, 1977), 11.

Further, Bruce conforms almost perfectly to the antiquarian paradigm when he assures his readers that the purpose for writing, "is to share with others something of the rich reward which I myself have reaped from the study of Paul."[5]

Despite idealizing this figure from the past and wanting to highlight the distinction in which Paul might be held for future generations, much as Nietzsche indicates antiquarians are wont to do with events and figures from bygone eras, Bruce's final pages indicate that he does not set out to stifle a reader's initiative to apply Pauline precepts to the modern era in whatever way he or she will. Instead, he presents a closing chapter in which he categorizes various figures and movements who drew on Pauline insights to promote the furtherance of civil society in very different ways. These include Martin Luther (1483–1546), who helped to lead the Reformation; John Wesley (1703–1791) a prominent preacher in the evangelical revival and founder of Methodism; and Karl Barth (1886–1969), an influential Protestant theologian. The old does not prescribe for the new but provides a building block that may be appropriated in many novel ways.

A third use of history is the "critical" function of history. One must be cautious here. While academics are familiar with the term *critical* and use it as shorthand way to designate "exercising analytical thought processes," for Nietzsche the term has the nuance of *judgmental*, as in "Samantha is critical of her friend's weight." The two different connotations should not be confused. A biblical critic simply employs established tools to investigate a text or an episode in New Testament history. But "offering negative assessments" in a way that condemns an event is not part of the task. By contrast, for Nietzsche, there is a certain service history provides when it *is* critical. In this scenario, practitioners of history desire deliverance from a past that they judge and denounce.[6] Now, Nietzsche himself doesn't promote the use of critical history as he defines it. More accurately, he worries that those who use history this way will ultimately forget that they are products of that very past. By cutting all ties, they are in danger of throwing out the baby with the bathwater. In a way, preserving the link to the past is one of the reasons why the early Christian church adopted both the Old and New Testaments rather than following an alternate model such as

---

5. Ibid.
6. Nietzsche, *Use and Abuse of History*, 21.

that of Marcion, who did not value Christianity's Jewish antecedents and hence dispensed with the Hebrew Scriptures.

In the larger scope of church history, the Reformation might be cited as an instance of Nietzsche's "critical" use of history. The judgment that Protestant scholars in the sixteenth century levied against the history and praxis of the church of their day resulted in schism. In our own field, one would be hard pressed to find examples of biblical scholars who would go so far as to reprimand and break so completely with their predecessors. An example might be Emanuel Swedenborg, who penned a commentary on Genesis where he described his contemporary Christian world at large as "deeply ignorant" of scriptural and heavenly matters because individuals focused too exclusively on the letter, or literal meaning, of the text.[7] Swedenborg perceived that he was doing something new, different, and that represented a radical departure from the Christian tradition of scriptural interpretation which preceded him. A full break with the past came with the formation of the Swedenborgian Church subsequent to his death.

Not every historian severs ties with the past. Another service history provides is to highlight events from prior time periods to encourage changes of behavior in the present day. For instance, E. P. Sanders's presentation of Palestinian Judaism at the time of Paul in *Paul and Palestinian Judaism* required him to argue against the positions held by some academic colleagues and support others in an attempt to correct misunderstandings of rabbinic Judaism that were pervasive in New Testament scholarship.[8] In this work Sanders isn't breaking with past traditions. He is merely trying, ever so gently, to steer scholarship in new directions through the presentation of evidence drawn from rabbinic writing and lucid arguments. He states his modest objective in his conclusion: "I hope only to have presented a study which will be helpful for understanding."[9] Sanders is, conversely, clear about what he is *not* attempting to accomplish. He is not taking a stab at reaching a "theological judgment about the inferiority or superiority of either Paul or Judaism."[10] To be concise, Sanders is essentially employing history to provide a means for human beings to acquire knowledge that will allow them to achieve transcendence over the

---

7. Emanuel Swedenborg, §§1–2 of "Genesis," in *Secrets of Heaven* (trans. Lisa Hyatt Cooper; West Chester, Pa.: Swedenborg Foundation, 2008).

8. E. P. Sanders, *Paul and Palestinian Judaism* (Minneapolis: Fortress, 1992), xiii.

9. Ibid., 552.

10. Ibid.

past. This allows individuals and societies at large to minimize mistakes or to maximize successes.

A fifth goal of history was described by Mark Gilderhus and is the impulse to arbitrate morality or provide an ethical sanction by "holding malefactors accountable for their misdeeds." [11] It may be clearly illuminated by referring to an example not from biblical historians but from those writing history of the World War II era. Modern historians that shed light on and consequently condemn the atrocities committed by Hitler and members of the Nazi party in the 1930s and 1940s are exercising the right to serve as the moral conscience of society through their writings. Although Gilderhus expresses the negative side of this task in his formulation, there is also a positive. Historians may, either tacitly or overtly, convey approval of past actors or events. And, to some extent, the wider public depends on these judgments because of the greater degree of familiarity a historian has with the subject matter being analyzed than does the novice. When a New Testament scholar provides evaluative comments, either praising or disparaging episodes from the past such as the role of the Jews at Jesus' crucifixion, gnostic theology, or even the imprisonment of Paul by the Romans, he or she is encouraging readers in their turn to either condemn or applaud these actors, events, or movements from the past and is acting well within the bounds of Gilderhus's understanding of this function of history.

Gilderhus, though, describes yet another purpose that history serves—its ability to assist in foreshadowing or predicting the future. In this scenario, precedents and trends are analyzed to decrease the perception of the randomness of events that have not yet unfolded. In essence, it is precisely this use of history that the apostle Paul marshals in his argument about the relevance of the death of Christ for believers in 1 Cor 15:1–31. He reasons that—since Christ's death and resurrection is, in his view, a historical fact given that it is based on reports of Christ's appearances to Cephas, the Twelve, and five hundred eyewitnesses—there is precedent for the hope that the dead in general will be raised. It is not a hope that is futile because resurrection is something that has at least happened once in the past.

In addition to these six uses of history there are two more interesting, if not necessarily noble, tasks associated with history. One was described by Sir Lewis Namier in an essay entitled "History," which he penned in

---

11. Gilderhus, *History and Historians*, 4–5.

1952. Put simply, one of the chief values of history is entertainment. As Namier opines, "it is written and read for its own sake; it answers a need in human nature and a curiosity; it pleases."[12] Richard Rorty adds the other use: it may be employed to treat figures from the past as dialogue partners in order to achieve self-justification.[13] At its most complex, the use of the past for self-justification is represented in the field of law. Indeed, when arguing a case, lawyers search diligently through past trial records and verdicts to find earlier examples of legal decisions that mirror the present situation and the desired outcomes for which the lawyer is arguing in the current trial.

In our own field, monographs that include footnotes that reference other individuals who hold opinions akin to ours or who have advanced arguments similar to the ones we are trying to make provide another example of drawing on the past—in this case, prior scholarship—to justify a position. Consulting the reference pages of any scholarly text in New Testament studies should turn up ample examples since this technique of argumentation is regarded as both worthwhile and indispensible in the academy.

Likewise, the prophecy-fulfillment motif in Matthew where one encounters the frequent formula "this was to fulfill what was spoken" (e.g., 1:22; 2:15) is an example of an ancient author using the words of the past to add authority to the points he himself was trying to convey about the actions recorded in his narrative. In short, there is nothing new or surprising about the idea of utilizing history to justify thoughts or actions that are contemporary with a historian.

Less virtuous than appealing to others to support one's own points is the danger of history devolving into straw-man argumentation. This is when an episode or line of reasoning from the past is either distorted or taken out of context in order to make one's own assertions appear more worthwhile by contrast. Generally regarded as an informal fallacy because it misrepresents the original position that is being disputed, this type of "abuse" of the past has its correlate in sermon preparation, where it is described as "eisegesis," taking a passage out of its literary context in order to prove the main thesis in Sunday's homily. In New Testament history texts, this undesirable practice would be represented by any works that seek to promote

---

12. Lewis Namier, "History," in Stern, *Varieties of History*, 372.
13. See Rorty, "Historiography of Philosophy," 49–75.

the superiority of Christianity to other Mediterranean religions through exaggerating their more salacious points or misrepresenting them, such as when Justin Martyr (ca. 100–165 C.E.), the Christian apologist, outright accuses the Jews of crucifying Jesus[14] and overlooking the fact that the disciples themselves were Jews. This abuse of history was in turn actually used against early Christians by their opponents who took descriptions of the Eucharist out of context and accused followers of Christ of engaging in cannibalism.[15] That historians of any stripe are not immune from the occasional temptation to employ history in ways that are a bit shady is not cause to abandon the historical project or its methodologies altogether. As D. A. Carson points out, "The Bible contains a lot of historical data and where finite, fallen human beings struggle with history, there will historians' fallacies be found."[16]

The final function associated with history is more ephemeral than those previously mentioned. It is the ability of history to take on a religious, quasi-prophetic, or even spiritual bent. In fact, the resemblance between clergy executing a prophetic role and duties ascribed to historians is so striking that Fritz Stern is able to draw a simile between them when he writes, "just as the historian was getting ready to become an academic monk, shut up in his study with his sources, the world about him sought him as a preacher" whose mission was to help reveal the meaning of human experiences via knowledge of the past.[17]

Not only is it possible to envision a historian playing a prophetic role in society, as Stern asserts, but the subject matter too can be revelatory. If one is to be so bold, one may say that the act of researching and interpreting history can be a spiritual exercise. Certainly some historians pursue their studies since they are inspired to do so, not unlike the individual who experiences general revelation through walking in the woods or seeing God's handiwork in nature. In essence, God's presence may be felt in history. Friedrich Meinecke, a historian, expressed this sentiment in 1928:

---

14. Justin Martyr, "Dialogue with Trypho" (*ANF* 1:xvi–xvii).

15. Note the language in John 6:53–56. The charge is confirmed by Irenaeus (*ANF* 1:570, frag. 14). On how the charge of cannibalism was used in both Greek and Roman rhetoric as a label applied to dissidents, see J. Albert Harrell, "Cannibalistic Language in the Fourth Gospel and Greco-Roman Polemics of Factionalism: John 6:53–56," *JBL* 127 (2008): 133–58.

16. D. A. Carson, *Exegetical Fallacies* (2nd ed.; Grand Rapids: Baker, 1996), 125.

17. Stern, *Varieties of History*, 12.

History, too, is divine service in the broadest sense. One wishes to see the spiritual goals one feels to be one's own confirmed by revelation in the world. One seeks to become conscious of the strength and continuity of the stream of spiritual life which wells up within the individual self, to find the faith by which man came to revere the powers that have brought our existence from a state of servitude to nature to the freedom of the spirit. However one conceives divinity, he will look for it in history.[18]

Likewise, Johann Gustav Droysen, writing in the nineteenth century, foreshadowed this exalted understanding of the nature of history and even directly quotes the New Testament itself when he creates another simile for the study of history: "History is humanity's knowledge of itself, its certainty about itself. It is not 'the light and the truth,' but a search therefore, a sermon thereupon, a consecration thereto. It is like John the Baptist, 'not the light but sent to bear witness of that light.'"[19]

Truly, any discipline can offer a spiritual or revelatory experience, from the sublime in music to the soaring and majestic in art, to the truly humbling triumph of spirit and will that a patient might reveal to a caregiver. With regard to history, Christianity need not be jealous of what it may deem to be its prerogatives but instead can embrace the techniques and craft of history in pursuit of its own goals and objectives.

3.2. The Two Philosophical Traditions of History

One feature common both to Christianity as a religion and history as a field is a fascination with the future. In the section above, we saw that one aim that might be held by historians is to identify trends from the past that will allow one to prepare for the vicissitudes of the time to come. This could be as simple as watching economic formulas to anticipate a recession or knowing with a fair degree of certainty that a storm with torrential rain that swirls over Kansas will eventually head to Illinois if particular wind patterns prevail. Sometimes, though, historians are preoccupied with the future on a grand scale. They give in to the urge to identify the penultimate event, social system, ideal, or some other factor toward which all of

---

18. Meinecke, "Values and Causalities in History," in Stern, *Varieties of History*, 274.

19. Johann Gustav Droysen, "The Principles of History," in Stern, *Varieties of History*, 144.

human history is striving or that gives history significance. Some histories that take a stab at hypothesizing about the meaning that history has for humanity even have a teleological flavor and indicate when the ideal has been or will be reached in the flow of time.

Views of history that offer some utopian or other vision for the future or try to discover deeper meanings in the course of history are known as speculative histories. Historians in this mode are speculating or conjecturing as to what a particular city, group, nation, civilization, or the human race will, or will not, achieve in the future. By contrast, histories that decline to theorize about what is possible and are cautious about reflecting on deeper imports in history are described as following the analytical or critical style of history. To put it more clearly, analytical history, rather than being concerned about the ultimate consequences of human actions in time, focuses primarily on questions related to the mechanics of how history is known. Thus its center of attention is on logic and epistemology. As a function of this orientation the analytical philosophy of history explores issues such as how history might be verified, causality, a historian's own objectivity, and so forth.

Now it is not necessarily the case that an author of a given historical monograph will clearly specify whether or not it is being written in the speculative or analytical tradition. Generally the reader must be astute to ferret out the basic philosophical approach taken in a given work, knowing that both lines of inquiry will use reason, will construct interpretations of the past based on sources. They both will seek to present the past, if not impartially, at least in a balanced way so that both the principal actors and their detractors are represented honestly, as will both supporting and contrary evidence. There are, thankfully, some markers that help readers distinguish between the two philosophical traditions of history. First, let's concentrate on fleshing out some key characteristics related to the analytical side of the house.

3.2.1. Elements of Analytical History

William Dray, in his philosophy of history,[20] focuses on two basic philosophical camps within the analytical strain of history: positivists and idealists. Positivists are influenced by Auguste Compte and view history as

---

20. Dray, *Philosophy of History*, 2.

a wholly scientific subject just as biology, psychology and other fields are "scientific." As a scientist uses the scientific method, the historian too looks for general rules and principles that guide history. An early twentieth-century New Testament researcher, Charles Jefferson, clearly revealed that he approached the task of exploring the character of Jesus from a positivist position by writing,

> To begin with the character of Jesus is to adopt the scientific method of study. The scientist of to-day insists upon studying phenomena. What he wants is data, and from these he will draw his conclusions. No scientist can begin his work unless put in possession of definite and concrete facts…Not only is this the scientific method, it is also the New Testament method. It was just in this manner that the disciples came to know Jesus. They did not begin with the mystery of his person…They began simply by coming near him, looking at him with their eyes, listening to him with their ears.[21]

The strong clue about Jefferson's positivist viewpoint is inherent in the terms he selected: *scientific method*, *data*, and *concrete facts*. Today positivists do not dominate the field of history to quite the extent that they did during the first half of the nineteenth century and, unfortunately, determining who is or isn't a positivist among New Testament scholars is not as easy a matter as looking for key words like *science* in a historian's text. Rather, the challenge is to study carefully whether or not the historian recognizes that facts require interpretation (a tenet of idealists) or whether, following the positivists, the facts gained through sense experience produce authentic knowledge that is deduced from the facts and lead to deductions that may be verified and replicated.

In a position that diverges from that of positivists, one finds idealists, among whose cadre of analytical historians Dray counts himself. Idealists are not convinced that history conforms to general or empirical laws that may be detected through scientific inquiry. They are skeptical that history is a science primarily due to the fact that history addresses events that are unique and unrepeatable while, in hard sciences, repetition and replication are assumed. To break this down into more simple terms, an illustration may be helpful. In the scientific method, a dandelion is yellow.

---

21. Charles Edward Jefferson, *The Character of Jesus* (New York: Crowell, 1908), 4–5.

And, barring genetic alteration of the seeds, any dandelion planted will yield a yellow flower, a phenomenon that can be observed over and over again with each new crop. That *a dandelion will produce a yellow flower*, therefore, is the general rule that may be deduced from initial observation and verified by subsequent study of the plant. For the idealists, the scientific method is not adequate to the task of history, since there was only one Jesus, one Paul, one Roman destruction of the temple in Jerusalem, and so forth. If every event is unique, then the scientific method won't work because there is no chance of repeated observation and replicated experimentation. Consequently, it is not possible to formulate a "general" rule like the one about the color of dandelions for any given event from the past. For the idealist there is a determinism in positivist formulations that the evidence cannot support.

John J. Collins provides an example of an analytical history of Jewish messianism written from the idealist perspective in his *The Scepter and the Star*.[22] Although comparing and contrasting messianism in Judaism and Christianity, which one might assume would be a natural exercise in looking for patterns, Collins eschews a positivist perspective because he does not approach his subject matter from the standpoint that there are general rules, models, or principles that characterize Jewish messianism. In fact, Collins is even reluctant to accept the conclusions of earlier scholars who identified "patterns" of messianic belief in the intertestamental period.[23] Instead, he highlights a trend in scholarship that plays up the diversity in Judaism's understanding of messianism.[24] Essentially, different Jewish communities in different times and locations understood the concept in diverse ways.

In the concluding paragraphs of his work, Collins subtly reveals his idealism even further. Although recognizing "common ground" between Christian and Jewish messianism, he nonetheless sees the unique character of each. He writes, "Christian messianism drew heavily on some of the minor strands [of messianism] and eventually developed them into a doctrine of Christology that was remote from its Jewish origins."[25] In short, if idealism resists the idea that episodes and ideas in history con-

---

22. John J. Collins, *The Scepter and the Star: Messianism in Light of the Dead Sea Scrolls* (2nd ed.; Grand Rapids: Eerdmans, 2010).
23. Ibid., 4.
24. Ibid., 5.
25. Ibid., 237.

form to set principles, then Collins's recognition that Christianity has unique aspects, such as the fact that "Only in the case of Jesus ... do we have a clear example of a messiah who was believed to have come down from heaven and expected to come again as eschatological judge,"[26] marks him as an idealist.

3.2.2. TRAITS OF SPECULATIVE HISTORY

If Collins's and Jefferson's works, different though they might be in approach, are still both on the analytical side of the house, how might one identify a speculative history? Mark Gilderhus provides helpful guidance in this endeavor by listing three overarching schemes into which speculative histories may fall.[27]

First, some historians are able to predict the future because they identify repeated designs or precedents in history that are cyclical; discover the archetype, and either the next cycle or the next phase should become apparent. Based on the past experience of the pattern, then, the speculative historian will infer the meaning or significance both for current events and possibly for those of the future. Note that there is a difference, albeit a subtle one, between a positivist, as described previously, and a speculative historian. While both are dealing with patterns, the positivist is looking for a pattern more in the sense that one would a look for a rule and would not ascribe a deeper meaning or future implication to the repeated element, as would the speculative historian. A second type of speculative history may be described as providential since the divine will, however that is conceived, provides guidance for the future. Modern historians may have methodological difficulties with providential histories. As Gilderhus puts it, it is one thing to say God acts in history and quite another to determine with precision where and when.[28]

Finally, there are speculative histories that turn on the theory that metaphysical or natural driving forces promote change and give history an element of predictability. These are "progressive" speculative histories. One example identified by Dray is the "world spirit," a metaphysical agent that supplies the final basis of meaning for Hegel.[29] Other forces that inform

---

26. Ibid.
27. Gilderhus, *History and Historians*, 53.
28. Ibid., 30.
29. Dray, *Philosophy of History*, 61

speculative histories include social Darwinism, which supposes that inferior institutions, nations, concepts, races, and other elements within the span of history will become obsolete while fitter ones will prevail; a Hegelian dialectic that suggests that two ideas or entities in conflict will be resolved in a way that transcends the original competing ideas or elements through the process of sublation; or even globalization, which appears to be an economically and technologically influenced catalyst that is compelling change in ways that may have preconceived outcomes. This is just a small sampling of systems that can be marshaled to undergird progressive speculative histories but hopefully they are somewhat familiar ones.

To an extent, some purists view speculative histories in a less favorable light than analytical histories. Dray himself scathingly observes, "Perhaps because an understanding of history matters so much to most of us, however, or because in a predominantly Judaic-Christian culture the expectation that history should be 'meaningful' is so strong, speculative philosophy of history has still not quite achieved the fossil status often attributed to cosmology."[30] This is indeed an unflattering assessment of the value of speculative history and perhaps overstates the influence of the Judeo-Christian tradition. Naturally, Christianity's conception that God is active in history does fit the providential model of speculative history. Yet this type of outlook is not exclusive to the Abrahamic religious traditions. Even the Greek historian Herodotus assigned the deities a role in human affairs while simultaneously recognizing the contribution made by human will.[31] Therefore, one must not make the mistake of assuming that Christians alone write speculative histories, that most speculative histories are based in providential mechanisms, or that they envision ultimate outcomes in line with Judeo-Christian theological concerns and interests. Francis Fukuyama, for instance, writes a speculative history in which he posits that the culmination of history is in liberal democracy.[32] Marxist historians envision that history will reach its pinnacle with a communist utopia. Both of these are speculative projects rooted in political philosophies that are completely independent from theocratic views.

Speaking of Fukuyama, another aspect of speculative histories is that they may turn on very specific understandings of when the predicted climactic episodes of history come to pass. To that extent, speculative histo-

---

30. Ibid., 2.
31. Ibid., 17.
32. Fukuyama, *End of History*.

ries are sometimes teleological, as has already been mentioned in passing. Fukuyama actually entitles his work *The End of History*. The culmination for Fukuyama is not some sort of millenarian prediction of the "last days," like that of the cataclysmic annihilation of the world as set forth in Revelation or the end of time, but rather the emergence of a decisive form of government beyond which no further development or progress is necessary or possible. Writing in the context of the conclusion of the Cold War and collapse of the Soviet Union, he concluded that liberal democracy, long practiced by this time in many Western countries, was the ideal or "end" system of government.

The end of history for Fukuyama was not the end of time. Time, though, along with determining the scope of one's project, and one's understanding of sources is an integral ingredient in the theoretical makeup of the discipline of history at large, as we have seen. Successful history projects, however, not only are grounded in these fundamental theories but also evidence clean argumentation that avoids pitfalls of logic that may creep into studies of the past. These are sometimes called historical fallacies and are the ingredients that will form the subject matter of the next chapter.

But first, a final caveat about speculative and analytical history: methodological choices concerning whether or not to use speculative or analytical approaches are independent of faith convictions. To be clear, a New Testament thinker can select either an analytical or speculative system when writing history, regardless of his or her religious affinities. Historical methods are merely tools that allow scholars to structure and convey their thoughts and ideas about the material that they are studying.

4
STUMBLING BLOCKS IN HISTORIES

The well-crafted history project is easily recognizable because it evidences a sound understanding of methodology, but it is but also a work where the author has successfully dodged some of the common errors of argumentation that tend to vex historians. Although there are many types of fallacies, both formal and informal, a few errors are persistently spotted in explorations of the past, and readers of history are well served by being able to recognize them. Problems stemming from chronology or cause and effect, for instance, are endemic to the field. The object of this chapter is to highlight some of the typical snags to which those who write history are particularly vulnerable so that those reading an article or history monograph will know when something funny is going on in the argumentation. It is not possible to cover the subject comprehensively in a single chapter, and thus reading David Hackett Fischer's older, but much more thorough treatment *Historians' Fallacies: Toward a Logic of Historical Thought*[1] is highly encouraged.

Four categories have been developed to aid in the exposition of the types of problems that historians might encounter. Those labeled "logical traps" tend to involve troubles that historians run into when depicting how events from the past relate to one another causally. Under the topic "errors of fact," issues that crop up about how evidence is handled by historians will take center stage. The third category shifts focus onto the historian him- or herself and highlights errors of perspective, or bias, that researchers bring to projects. Finally, a few comments about flaws that creep into basic project design will be discussed.

---

1. David Hackett Fischer, *Historians' Fallacies: Toward a Logic of Historical Thought* (New York: Harper & Row, 1970).

Although it might be easy to dismiss the fallacies that follow as pitfalls only suffered by history students, it is important to acknowledge that senior scholars as well, both in professional history and New Testament studies, are not immune to writing works with these typical weaknesses. In fact, several of the examples that have been chosen in the exposition below will clearly demonstrate this point. But the inclusion of any given scholar does not mean that he or she is to be blacklisted. After all, the perfect history doesn't exist, and not all flaws are fatal. Often a logical error in one portion of a work may not negate great contributions to the field of knowledge in other sections of the book. Further, if a defect is pervasive, you may notice that sometimes an author simply acknowledges the work's inherent weaknesses and reminds his or her readers of the limited or tentative nature of the resulting conclusions. Often, this is enough to redeem a very interesting and worthwhile piece of scholarship.

4.1. LOGICAL TRAPS

The way arguments are structured may weaken a thesis about an event from the past. Circular argumentation, or begging the question, for example, assumes the truth of what is being proven and may offer a premise that never actually substantiates the claim. An example is *Unicorns are happy animals because there is no such thing as an unhappy horse with one horn*. Putting the problem that unicorns are mythical beasts aside, the causal part of the sentence really is just a restatement of the definition of *unicorn* instead of actual confirmation of the state of happiness.

Rather than listing a myriad of fallacies, however, it is better to concentrate on explicating a few. Because historians set out to identify why something occurred, several difficulties in reasoning found in their works may be described as errors of causation. One such fallacy is reductionism. This is the tendency to assert that either all of the causes for an event are known or that a fairly complex event was precipitated by just a few things, like asserting that *the* cause of the American Civil War was a dispute over slavery. In other words, it is easy for those writing history to fall into the trap of oversimplification. Although simplicity sounds like it should be a good thing, artifacts and events are complex and arise out of multifaceted situations that are never as straightforward as they may seem. Carl R. Trueman cautions that a historian can never do justice to all the elements that precipitate an event, but the nature of writing requires the historian to select one or just a few in order to produce a manuscript with narrative coherence. The challenge, in the act of selecting, is to continue to remain open to the existence of other causes.[2]

Another type of error related to causation involves sequences of events, or chronology. This is termed *false cause* or, more formally, the fallacy of *post hoc ergo propter hoc* (things that happen after this happen because of this). Just because one event occurs in time before another does not mean that the later event was dependent on or a result of the earlier one. A variation of this fallacy involves imputing false correlations between two separate events. For instance, in an insightful work about the history of religions school, Jonathan Z. Smith demonstrated that it was a common apologetic technique in older scholarship for Protestant scholars to use false cause to link the mystery cults to Catholicism. Their goal was to impute corruption to Catholicism while asserting the genetic uniqueness of Protestantism.[3]

Before leaving the topic of logical errors to look at mistakes related to verification of facts and taking facts out of context, there are three additional errors of logic that deserve brief mention. The first is known as the fallacy of hasty generalization. Despite being associated primarily with statistical analysis, this type of logical flaw is one where a broad conclusion is based on a very small sample. When hasty generalizations pop up in studies that are primarily qualitative, they may be found lurking behind words like *some, many,* or *the majority.*

The fallacy of division, or imputing all of the characteristics of something in its entirety to each of its parts, is the next sibling in this family of fallacies. We can see it at play in an innocent comment made by one of my students: "The Gospels had to be written down in the mid-first century because everyone died young in the ancient world." While it was true that infant mortality rates brought down the average life span of persons living in antiquity, that does not mean that the Beloved Disciple could not have achieved the octogenarian milepost. One cannot reason from a quality possessed by the group (average life span) to that of any single member. Even Eusebius (ca. 263–339 C.E.), the church historian, reached his eighth decade.

---

2. Carl R. Trueman, *Histories and Fallacies: Problems Faced in the Writing of History* (Wheaton, Ill.: Crossway, 2010), 147.

3. Jonathan Z. Smith, *Drudgery Divine: On the Comparison of Early Christianities and the Religions of Late Antiquity* (Chicago: University of Chicago Press, 1990); see 9–15 for examples.

The final fallacy to be treated in this section is the "fallacy of composition." This fallacy is similar to that of the hasty generalization because it makes an inference from something small to something large—only instead of occurring in statistics, it turns on the idea that the characteristics of one member of a group extend to all. So in a way it is also the converse of the fallacy of division. The fallacy of composition can be illustrated by an example from my personal experience. I once took an exegesis class in which I was the only female student. We were engaged in some lively dialogue on the persnickety passage about women and veiling in 1 Cor 11:5–16. When the conversation started lagging, however, the professor turned to me in attempt to inject new life into the discussion and asked, "What is the women's take on this passage?" Hmm. Well, I could speak for myself, but in no way was I willing to cede that my opinions represented those of my entire gender. In a similar fashion, although Cicero was an orator, not every Roman was; just because Tacitus wrote histories didn't mean that all senators did so; and even though a few disciples were fishermen, not all of them were.

4.2. Errors of Fact

Apart from history's dalliance with imaginative or counterfactual exercises, which are known to be fictitious scenarios intentionally created to shed light on the actual event in history from which the parallel versions are derived, any given study is only accurate to the extent that the facts upon which it is based are valid. In Johannine studies, for instance, a treatment related to the story of the woman caught in adultery (John 7:53–8:11) and its historical significance for John's community may end up on a collision course with the recycle bin if the researcher doesn't discover early on in the project that the manuscript evidence about this particular pericope is troublesome. Indeed, the presence of noteworthy variants for this passage indicates the possibility that the story was not original to the Fourth Gospel or may have been part of Luke's material instead of John's.

There are several issues related to the accuracy of facts and their verification that will be handled at the outset in the discussion below, and then attention will turn more closely to hazards related to the original context of a fact and how a piece of data that is separated from its original setting might not be legitimately used to substantiate points about another situation entirely.

4.2.1. FACTUAL ACCURACY AND VERIFICATION

Pursuit of every discipline begins with mastering fundamentals, be it learning scales in music or memorizing a periodic table in chemistry class. When it comes to the history of Christianity and the early Roman Empire, no shortcut exists for becoming adept with the relevant research languages of Hebrew, Greek, Latin and Aramaic so that the accuracy of sources can be verified. There may also be a need to learn others, like Coptic, if a planned research project requires it. Now, the goal isn't for every historian to become an accomplished linguist but rather for the researcher to have sufficient proficiency to access solid critical editions, if they exist, or even the relevant manuscripts or inscriptions themselves. Being able to read the content of primary sources without the mediation of an interpreter prevents basic errors. For instance, it enables historians to avoid making an assertion about an ancient author's use of a certain concept only to find our later that the underlying word upon which translations are based is a synonym and that the particular ancient author's work is actually irrelevant to the present researcher's hypothesis.

In a way, knowing the original languages helps one skirt thorny difficulties and is a keystone in verification—making certain that one's translation is the right one. There are three other aspects of verification that can make or break how solid a work of history turns out to be.

First, the greater quantity of strong, *applicable* primary evidence that one can locate, the more persuasive an argument tends to be. Now, it is not always possible for historians to uncover every last bit of existing evidence, but sometimes overlooking entire types of literature or a complete corpus may prove troubling for audience or readers. I once attended a conference session in which a paper about burial rites and rituals in Second Temple Judaism and early Christianity was read. It was many years ago but, while I do not recall who was giving the paper, the content of the presentation remains vivid. I still wonder why, of the many examples that were discussed, the author didn't consider a single text from the Apocrypha. At a minimum, the book of Tobit begins with the protagonist incurring corpse defilement after burying a murdered family retainer during a religious feast (Tobit 2:3–9) and would have helped the author to make his point.

A second important consideration in the treatment of proof is that historians should account for evidence that offers an opposing viewpoint or is contrary to the assertion that he or she wishes to substantiate. If the author ignores detracting evidence, eventually someone will find it and present it as support for disproving the thesis. Strong works of history are recognizable because the author acknowledges problematic data up front and come to grips with that data rather than to allowing the study to remain vulnerable on that front.

This being said, sometimes researchers have a difficult time finding resources that undergird a hypothesis. In the absence of evidence or in the presence of only weak evidence, confident historians refrain from filling the gap with incidental or unrelated material. David Hackett Fischer warns about the use of pseudofacts, including any argument that has "a chameleonlike state which changes its color with its context and which might variously be used to prove the proposition that X is the case or that not-X is the case, as the author wishes."[4] It is also important to recognize that those writing history should avoid what are sometimes known as "arguments from silence." Just because an ancient author does not explicitly testify about something does not mean that he or she was not aware of an event. Nor is it necessarily the case that the ancient author's silence means he or she was complicit in the event or gave it approbation. Fischer states the bald reality, "'there is no evidence of X' means precisely what it says—no evidence."[5] It is not a legitimate logical move to draw conclusions when no proof exists.

Although so far we have pointed out that the best historians take precautions not to overlook information, are scrupulous in verifying translations, and avoid some common tactical errors that occur when unable to uncover any applicable evidence, it is not remiss to say a few words about inaccurate or flat-out erroneous data. Sadly, it isn't just the case that misinformation enters the arena of professional discourse because scholars are working with materials from the classical world that turn out to be fakes and forgeries. To be sure, this is one source of skewed data that creep into scholarly publications. Unscrupulous purveyors of artifacts and manuscripts are astonishingly clever at outwitting the scientists who verify antiquities. The James Ossuary, which ultimately proved to be a forged burial box that supposedly contained the bones of Jesus' brother, was a marvelous hoax that fooled even radiocarbon-dating technology. Apparently, an older patina with carbon of the right age can be added to

---

4. Fischer, *Historians and Fallacies*, 44.
5. Ibid., 47.

objects during their handling, as may have been done with this particular "relic."[6]

Even though the occasional bogus manuscript or counterfeit ancient *objet d'art* grabs headlines, a more persistent and slightly insidious problem occurs when historical inaccuracies of various sorts from older generations of scholars enter the scholarly stream and become codified in the literature. This may happen, one may imagine, when an esteemed scholar publishes materials that subsequent historians show to be a bit off the mark or when new archaeological evidence is found that disproves an older theory. Yet, because of respected scholars' reputations, newer researchers often continue to appeal to erudite scholars' works and persist in citing what has become misinformation. A prime example of this involves occasional undergraduate papers that rely on general Internet resources that are easily accessed because they were published prior to 1923 and are in public domain but are terribly out of date because they were written several decades prior to the discoveries of the Dead Sea Scrolls and the Nag Hammadi library. Nevertheless, Fischer shines a ray of hope. He observes that this problem of relying on the interpretations of older scholars in historical scholarship is not unusual among fledgling historians and contends that, as students in history departments gain maturity, "they tend to become more assertive in their own right. But the habit is not easily broken."[7]

4.2.2. Context

Although the scholars who uncritically accept assertions made prior to the Dead Sea discovery *ad verecundiam* are guilty of a type of fallacy related to the level of care needed for verifying and collecting evidence because they do not check or confirm the facts upon which older generations built their arguments, sometimes historians demonstrate another sort of problem related to how they handle facts. Specifically, they may betray a disregard for the original context of the data marshaled to substantiate assertions. The three basic type of errors related to context involve anachronism, assumptions about the universality of data, and what we in New Testament studies would recognize as "prooftexting." Let's take anachronism first.

---

6. Paul Craddock, *Scientific Investigation of Copies, Fakes and Forgeries* (Oxford: Butterworth-Heinemann, 2009), 14.

7. Fischer, *Historians' Fallacies*, 287.

Fischer has a clear grasp that people "in various places and times ... have not merely thought different things. They have thought them differently."[8] So, when Rudolph Bultmann, a well-known Johannine scholar, compares seventh-century gnostic texts with the late first-century Fourth Gospel,[9] his conclusions are vulnerable and may be contested by other researchers. As John Ashton states about Bultmann's view of the link between Gnosticism and John's Gospel,

> Here I simply want to be the point that whether we speak of Gnosticism in general or of Mandaean Gnosticism in particular, we do not really know whether it was sufficiently fully-formed by the end of the first century AD to have exercised the kind of influence ... called for by Bultmann's theory. That there were ideas in the air which were at some time incorporated into the full myth (e.g. the dualism of the Qumran texts) is certain; but much more is required if Bultmann's theory is to work.[10]

The problem related to the anachronistic use of texts in classical studies is not a simple matter of making sure that data and sources from one era are not transposed into another given the "publication" dates of the primary sources. The matter is complicated because several important, but later, sources are composite works in which earlier traditions were collected and compiled. The Mishnah, for instance, closed at the end of the second century. Even though by and large it reflects Jewish thought from the middle of the second century, the opinions of a few sages who were active at the time of the destruction of the temple in 70 C.E. are also represented. This phenomenon of incorporating earlier material into later works is a characteristic of legal codes and is also reflected in the *Corpus Iuris* of Justinian. Although it was compiled in the sixth century, the works in this Roman legal collection reflect precedents and rulings that extend back for centuries. Needless to say, both the Roman and Jewish legal texts

---

8. Ibid., 203.

9. Rudolf Bultmann, *The Gospel of John: A Commentary* (trans. R. Beasley-Murray et al.; Philadelphia: Westminster, 1971).

10. John Ashton, *Understanding the Fourth Gospel* (Oxford: Clarendon, 1991), 60. John Dominic Crossan also has been criticized for the anachronistic use of sources in his study of the historical Jesus. See Bernard Brandon Scott, "To Impose is Not to Discover: Methodology in John Dominic Crossan's *Historical Jesus*," in *Jesus and Faith: A Conversation on the Work of John Dominic Crossan* (ed. Jeffrey Carlson and Robert A. Ludwig; Maryknoll, N.Y.: Orbis, 1994), 26.

are invaluable witnesses to the milieu in which Christianity arose, but they must be used with extreme caution.

Just as it is possible to transpose resources from one time period to another, an additional difficulty related to yanking a source out of its original context involves geographic dislocations rather than temporal displacements. Granted, Hellenization and Romanization did provide at least a veneer of homogeneity in the Mediterranean region, and the ubiquitous nature of Greek and Latin might lead one to assume that any source from a selected time period might be applicable to any area of the empire for those same years, but that is not necessarily the case. It is important not to overlook or underrepresent the cultural diversity that characterized disparate locations. In other words, the data a historian uses may be not universal but specific to time and place. But that isn't all. Individual facts may also be dependent on the literary context provided by the documents in which they are found.

One of the first things students learn in biblical studies is the danger of prooftexting. Prooftexting, or eisegesis, involves excising a verse or passage of scripture from its literary context in order to support the point one wishes to make—in a sermon or elsewhere—regardless of whether or not the resulting interpretation of the passage would be sustainable if the larger context of the verse is taken into consideration. Prooftexting is a pernicious problem that plagues not only biblical studies but also the field of history. Anyone can prooftext from any ancient source, not just the Bible![11] Perhaps one of the reasons that misrepresenting the positions of ancient authors by creatively excerpting bits and bobs from their writings out of context is a prevalent problem is due to the use or, we should say, *misuse* of sourcebooks. Sourcebooks tend to be compilations of sample passages, often arranged topically, that are drawn from the vast literature of the classical world. Their goal is to assist students and scholars in understanding various aspects of ancient life or to point researchers to primary literature. Sometimes these begin their lives as collections of supplemental readings to support courses taught by the authors. This was the case with Ramsay MacMullen and Eugene N. Lane's *Paganism and Christianity, 100–425 C.E.: A Sourcebook.*[12] At other times they are intended to function

---

11. Taking words and concepts out of their contexts was a practice used by others in the history of religions school. See J. Z. Smith, *Drudgery Divine*, 25.

12. Ramsay MacMullen and Eugene N. Lane, eds., *Paganism and Christianity 100–425 C.E.: A Sourcebook* (Minneapolis: Fortress, 1992), ix.

more like concordances. Sometimes the excerpts in these resources run to several pages; at others, only a line or two is quoted. There is nothing inherently wrongheaded about sourcebooks of either type. The difficulty arises when a researcher, in need of a quote to substantiate his or her own thesis, pulls information from the sourcebook and eschews reading the original resource from which it was extracted in its entirety.

4.3. Errors of Perspective

Nearly every year during Advent, I begin receiving Christmas cards. My favorites are the ones upon which the artists depict Joseph leading Mary along on a donkey as they trudge through a snowstorm amid knee-high drifts. They are obviously on their way to Bethlehem to register for the census (Luke 2:1). Generally these cards are very lovely. And the senders were quite thoughtful—doubly so since, in my own rush to grade exams at term's end, I seem never to be organized enough to return the courtesy. But there is something about these cards that is a bit absurd. Irrespective of the fact that we don't know exactly when Jesus was born and its placement in the winter months is merely a common convention, I have actually been in Bethlehem in midwinter and was able to wear a T-shirt during the day and get away with a light jacket at night. While it is possible for Jerusalem and Bethlehem to receive a slight skiff of snow on occasion, it is in no way probable that Mary and Joseph were battling a Canadian-style blizzard of the type depicted in the renderings, no matter what time of year they were traveling.[13] It is easy to conclude that the artists of these cards, who likely hail from more northern climates, are not illustrating an accurate historical situation based on the climate of Judea but are projecting their own perceptions about the climate in their own home countries back onto a historical event that was set in the Mediterranean region. Now, there is nothing malicious in the artists' skewing of historical data. Quite the opposite. As Margaret MacMillan describes it, "We edit our memories over the years

---

13. Reporters in Jerusalem described the January 2008 snow in which there was one inch of accumulation as a "rare" snowfall. See Martin Patience, "Rare Snowfall Blankets Jerusalem" [cited 30 January 2008]; online: http://news.bbc.co.uk/2/hi/middle_east/7217429.stm. Another snowfall that hit Jerusalem in December of 2010 is described as "light" and one that "quickly disappeared after dawn." See Tzvi Ben Gedalyahu, "Light Snow Covers Jerusalem, 8 Inches of Rain in North" [cited 13 July 2011]; online: http://www.israelnationalnews.com/News/News.aspx/141113.

partly out of a natural human instinct to make our own roles more attractive or important."[14] The use of snow on these seasonal greetings allows the recipients of these cards who happen to reside in cold, frozen lands to feel as though they too are connected with the story and the events that took place in the first century—events that are integral to the Christian faith.

Although artistic license permits this sort of "geographic-centrism" based sleight of hand for Christmas cards, in the field of history a bias that obscures or even contradicts basic facts is viewed with dismay. It is true that a researcher can never escape all bias in his or her research. Nonetheless, we must be attuned to the reality that we view the world through lenses tinged by ethnocentrism, culture-centrism, and many other "centrisms" that we may never fully transcend. This may hopefully assist us to identify a few mistaken, perception-based assumptions that might creep into the histories that we happen to read.

Although blinders related to perception can result in research errors because basic facts are not examined but presumed, a more detrimental problem occurs when the context of the researchers predispose interpretations that are one-sided or misleading and are marshaled serve some sort of apologetic purpose. In extreme forms, this can even involve intentionally suppressing facts in order to obtain a result that agrees with one's own ideology. Margaret Macmillan cites an example from China in which the journal *Freezing Point* was shut down by government authorities after carrying an article that asserted that history in the Chinese public schools was being taught in ways that justified "the use of political power and even violence to keep people on the right path."[15]

In the United States, a subtler perception-based problem that is referred to as "triumphalism" crept into accounts about the dissolution of the Soviet Union and the ending of the Cold War. The historian Ellen Schrecker recognized that many of the histories written by Americans in that period attributed the failure of communism to "the technological dynamism of the American economy, and the moral and cultural superiority of the American system that simply (but peacefully) overwhelmed the backward tyrants of Moscow."[16] In glorifying the United States, these

14. Margaret MacMillan, *Dangerous Games: The Uses and Abuses of History* (New York: Modern Library, 2008), 46.

15. Ibid., 121.

16. Ellen Schrecker, "Introduction: Cold War Triumphalism and the Real Cold

triumphalist accounts rarely credited the denizens of Eastern Europe themselves with having a hand in events.

Triumphalism can sneak into any historical study, and scholars in the field of religion should be especially alert. For instance, one must take care not to crow about the accomplishments about Christianity, which became a dominant religion in the Roman Empire, and overlook the true diversity that was inherent in the Jesus movement from its inception. Nor should one denigrate the contributions that Judaism made to Christianity. A popular introductory New Testament textbook by Bart Ehrman is written to emphasize the history behind the biblical narrative and successfully sidesteps any taint of triumphalism. Ehrman goes to great pains to describe a wide variety of early forms of Christianity, including what he describes as the "proto-orthodox" stand that would eventually become dominant.[17]

A close cousin to triumphalism is the problem known among historians as Whig history. The error takes its name from the Whig historians who are often described as a so-called school of researchers active in England during the Victorian era. They tended to write histories about their own country and possessed a common methodological outlook: "The Whig historians emphasized—their later critics say over-emphasized—history as a story, continuity, a development and, by implication, a progress towards a free liberal, enlightened present."[18] While there is nothing inherently wrong with this—after all, progress was a key component of many speculative histories in the period—unfortunately the Whig version had a significant flaw. Its interpretation of progress included a value judgment wherein the present was deemed to be superior to the past. One is said to be doing Whig history when one falls into the trap of assuming that people living in earlier time periods are primitive, or lacking in some way, and prior events are merely pale shadows of the glories of one's own era.[19] Taken to its most extreme form, the past may end up dismissed as completely irrelevant or "dead" to the present.

War," in *Cold War Triumphalism: The Misuse of History After the Fall of Communism* (ed. Ellen Schrecker; New York: New Press, 2004), 2.

17. Bart D. Ehrman, *The New Testament: A Historical Introduction to the Early Christian Writings* (4th ed.; Oxford: Oxford University Press, 2008), 3–7.

18. Roger Spalding and Christopher Parker, *Historiography: An Introduction* (Manchester: Manchester University Press, 2007), 13.

19. This is essentially a version of an *argumentum ad novitatem* fallacy, the notion that something is better simply because it is newer or more recent than something else.

Problems in studies related to perception-based difficulties are an outcome of the desire for history to be relevant and useful. This is a noble goal that can be achieved if history is done carefully and our biases don't lead us to abuse it. That being said, a mundane type of flaw that sneaks into studies is one that simply stems from how the project was conceived and structured at its outset.

4.4. Problems with Project Design

One result of holding a day job as the director of a theological library is that I often encounter patrons who are struggling with the basics of designing research projects. There are those who select topics that are so broad that it would take a lifetime, not a mere semester, to conduct the research needed to prove the intended thesis. Conversely, there are those who have signed up for a topic but now cannot find any resources. Although on rare occasions the subject is in fact one that is cutting edge or has never been tried and there are few published scholars with whom to engage in dialogue, in most cases the difficulty that the student has in finding material is one involving terminology, professional vocabularies, and definitions. The researcher is hunting for information about Y and coming up dry, when in fact an entire ocean of research on the topic is available by searching for Z instead.

If it is true that the key to any successful real estate transaction is "location, location, location," then in the field of history a crucial activity of research is making certain one is clear about the "definition, definition, definition." The whole purpose of academic writing is to have a conversation about a subject with others, and the recipe for success in that endeavor is making certain that all parties are on the same page. Defining terms carefully can also help authors to avoid two logical impediments to sound scholarship in history: equivocation and reification.

4.4.1. Equivocation and Reification

Equivocation is a logical fallacy that occurs when a word or phrase has multiple meanings and the researcher shifts between them. This involves making a widely accepted or "true" assertion using the word one way, but then formulating additional steps in the argument where the term has a different shade of meaning altogether. For instance, at first glance the following argument seems persuasive:

A. Zacchheus is a really cool cat.
B. Cats love to chase birds.
C. Therefore, Zacchaeus loves to chase birds.

Absurd though this example might be, premises A and B may both be correct by themselves. The argument is incorrect, though, because it turns on two very different meanings of *cat*—the first being a debonair, self-assured man and the second, a four-footed, furry pet.

Sometimes using terminology in a slippery way with inconsistent meanings is not the result of a formal logical argument but arises from ambiguities in sentence construction or lack of structural elements such as "transition markers" in writing. When ambiguity of various sorts is introduced into a work intentionally, it may be described as obfuscation. Haziness of argument in a work may arise from another quarter in addition to equivocation—reification.

Carl Trueman gives reification this weighty definition:

> Reification is the act by which an abstraction is given an existence it does not really possess and, from the historian's perspective, can therefore take on a life of its own. It ceases to be the endterm of a process of historical interpretation and becomes rather something that stands as an *a priori* category of analysis.[20]

Basically, when historians are trying to make sense of the past, they may make up terms and categories like the descriptive term *antiquity*. People who actually lived in that time period, however, did not know that they were living in antiquity, and it is very difficult to describe exactly when that age began, when it ended, how it differed from region to region, and what all of its characteristics might be. Still, it is popular to use this very vague and abstract category as if it is something that really exists. At some point, the problem of reification becomes so cumbersome that it makes sense to jettison a baggage-laden term entirely.

4.4.2. FORMULATING THE QUESTION

"A moment's reflection should suffice to establish the simple proposition that every historian, willy-nilly, must begin his research with a question."

---

20. Trueman, *Histories and Fallacies*, 142.

So begins the first chapter of David Hackett Fischer's text on fallacies.[21] It is fairly obvious that sometimes the simple way a question is asked determines the answer that is expected. A common example in comedy routines that demonstrates this is the query, "Do I look fat today?"—a question that immediately puts the person attempting to answer in a bind. The answer "no" implies that the person asking the question may look a bit hefty on other days, but not at the moment, while an affirmative answer would also carry an insult. A more open-ended "How do I look today?" would provide the interviewee with many more options for replying.

Historians, too, can fall into the snag of setting the stage for obtaining a desired outcome for their research by the way questions are posed. Take the thorny issue of Paul's view of women in ministry. One might ask, "What circumstances give rise to Paul's seemingly contradictory references about women and women's roles in ministry?" or conversely, "What do Paul's comments about women tell us about the oppression of women in Early Christianity?" Although the first query is fairly broad and permits various avenues of exploration, the latter starts steering the investigation along a set path.

Essentially, the second question includes a presupposition about women's roles in the early empire. Variations of this problem of framing questions involve structuring an inquiry so that multiple questions are asked but a single answer desired, or even advancing a truly complex investigation but demanding a simple solution.[22]

Both Fischer and Trueman are also concerned about creating questions that are based on false dichotomies. Later on in this book we will explain Marxist interpretations of history in detail. When it comes to that method of doing history, however, Trueman is disturbed that in the Marxist dialectic, the question, "Does this event reflect a class struggle?" is supplanted by the loaded question, "How does this event reflect the class struggle?"[23] It is a historian's insider joke that Trueman, or his editors, chose to feature a photograph of Karl Marx right in the center of the front cover of his book, directly under the word *fallacies* in his title.

Although there are other difficulties that relate to structuring the central points for a historical investigation, the final one to briefly toss out

---

21. Fischer, *Historians' Fallacies*, 3.

22. Ibid., 8.

23. Trueman, *Histories and Fallacies*, 161–62, See also Fischer, *Historians' Fallacies*, 9–12.

here is the fallacy of metaphysical questions. As Fischer puts it, "these are questions which will not be resolved before the oceans freeze over."[24] It is terribly easy for New Testament historians to find themselves in short order on one of the numerous picturesque trails that have no end.

4.4.3. Limits of Particular Methods

Before leaving the topic of some of the typical pitfalls that crop up related to project design, it is important to provide a reminder that a key task for historians in planning research is matching up the appropriate method with the available facts. Quantitative methods, for instance, require that the available data be suitable for statistical analysis. This means that if the evidence that is consulted resists quantification because it is unique, or is present only in a small sample size, there may be bumpy roads ahead. Readers should be alert to the fact that historians ought to be careful to determine whether this would be a fatal weakness or simply a difficulty that could be acknowledged up front when describing the method that informs the research.

4.5. Developing an Eye for Good History

Carl R. Trueman offers the sage advice that the best thing a historian or even an aspiring historian should do to hone his or her craft is read history. Further, when undertaking this onerous task (or pleasure, as the case may be), any given study should be read on two levels. The first is reading to see what the historian says. This entails learning about the subject matter. Histories are written to inform and educate about a particular event, phenomenon, or person in the past, and a reader should be able to increase his or her knowledge about the topic that is presented. Trueman, however, cautions that one must not linger at this type of reading alone. Instead, one should also dig into the text on a second level, the one that reveals what the historian does. In addition to the facts that are presented about the historical event being discussed, one can discover how the historian who is writing handles evidence, constructs arguments and narrative, and even comes to grips with biases related to his or her own culture, place, or period.

---

24. Fischer, *Historians' Fallacies*, 13.

The historian hones his or her craft throughout the course of a career. One is always acquiring knowledge about new subjects, branching out into new subjects, and giving new methodologies a whirl. Roger Spalding and Christopher Parker sum up the historian's challenge and, indeed, the occasional encounter with flaws and fallacies:

> Some historians are more conscientious researchers than others, more accurate, more learned and clear in their arguments. Many deliberately set out to participate in a continuing debate, perhaps to support an ally or a mentor, or to challenge an opponent. There are established rivalries, even hostilities. Some, one suspects, are being deliberately provocative, perhaps to establish a reputation. Others have career-defining projects. Some are methodologically explicit; others leave the readers to their own devices. It helps to know about these things. Very few disputes are settled by outright victory, though occasionally a fatal flaw is revealed in the methods, the concepts, or the research finding of an influential work.... The study of history has an apparently inexhaustible capacity for moving on.[25]

Thus we come to the end of this chapter on the stumbling blocks that historians must transcend. And, with its close, we have also finished the overview of the various theories, philosophical tenets, and tools that historians employ in their discipline. The next step is to explore how these fundamentals have been combined in various ways in the individual methods that Western historians have employed across the ages when writing histories.

---

25. Spalding and Parker, *Historiography*, 3–4.

PART 2
HISTORIOGRAPHY: THE HISTORY OF WRITING HISTORY

5
EMERGENCE OF A DISCIPLINE: METHODS FROM ANTIQUITY TO THE MODERN ERA

Toward the close of the last century, a group of scholars held a symposium on the city of Ephesus at Harvard Divinity School. The meeting was cosponsored by both the divinity school and the department of classics at Harvard, and archeologists, classicists, historians, and New Testament scholars all joined together to have an interdisciplinary conversation about this ancient city.[1] Despite the fact that this meeting took place almost two decades ago and both historians and New Testament scholars were exchanging ideas at the meeting, sometimes the nitty-gritty techniques that historians use when exploring the past are still not very familiar to many of those involved in New Testament studies. In the words of Mark Noll, understanding of historical practices, assumptions, and arguments "remains in short supply."[2] Certainly, some New Testament researchers do have training the area of the techniques of modern history, but Michael Licona, a New Testament scholar, recently wrote a book that was driven by his concern that a knowledge gap continues to exist between the two fields. In fact, he is so convinced that this disparity is widespread that he subtitled his book *A New Historiographical Approach*, even though the methods he employed in his project are well known to historians. At heart, Licona essentially ponders the question of what might happen in the field of New Testament studies if more students and scholars were

---

1. Helmut Koester, ed., *Ephesos: Metropolis of Asia: An Interdisciplinary Approach to Its Archaeology, Religion and Culture* (HTS 31; Valley Forge, Pa: Trinity Press International, 1995).

2. Mark A. Noll, "History," in *Dictionary for Theological Interpretation of the Bible* (ed. Kevin J. Vanhoozer; Grand Rapids: Baker Academic), 294.

better informed about historiography, the methods that historians use when plying their craft.[3]

In this chapter and the two that follow, a survey of the Western tradition of historiography is presented. Being familiar in a general way with how the work of historical writing in the West has been accomplished in the past and understanding the fundamentals of the business of doing history constitute an exercise that is of value on two fronts. From one perspective, knowing the techniques that characterize the works of past historians allows the present-day reader to determine where any given work fits on the continuum. Indeed, there is no "perfect" way to do history, and each tried and true approach has strengths and weaknesses. It is useful to know both the potentialities and limits of any work of history that is presented. From another vantage point, being familiar with the wider stream of contemporary historiography may even encourage a historian of the New Testament to take up the gauntlet thrown down by Licona and experiment with approaches that colleagues in the cognate field of history have used. Indeed, employing an untried, overlooked, or previously unexplored methodology that is in vogue in the field of history in general but has not gained mainstream currency in New Testament studies increases the possibility of yielding new results or different insights to questions that have been perennially sticky in our own subject.

The overview here will be painted in broad brushstrokes. No attempt is made to be comprehensive, and many significant figures will be left out. But the purpose is to provide a wide-ranging introduction to some of the major movements, schools, trends, and paradigm shifts that have marked the practice of writing history. The presentation also will be roughly chronological. When, however, a technique that gained currency in the past continues to have an influence in the present time, those themes will be highlighted and drawn out. It has been reported that Stephen D. Moore, a witty New Testament scholar who tends to push boundaries in scholarship, once wryly commented, "the rise of a new movement in biblical studies often coincides with its decline or even demise in its field of origin."[4] While likely a slight exaggeration made for dramatic impact, there is nevertheless some truth in the idea that the adoption of techniques and new

---

3. Michael R. Licona, *The Resurrection of Jesus: A New Historiographical Approach* (Downers Grove, Ill.: InterVarsity Press, 2010), 19.

4. As reported by Gina Hens-Piazza in *The New Historicism* (Minneapolis: Fortress, 2002), 69.

outlooks proceeds at various paces from discipline to discipline. So any chronological treatment of developments related to historiography in the field of history occasionally must be bent at points to account for shifts and trends in our own field.

5.1. History in Western Antiquity

5.1.1. Hebrew Historiography

In Ernst Breisach's introductory textbook on Western historiography,[5] he chooses to focus exclusively on early traditions of history writing that were located in the Greek world, thereby completely circumventing the troublesome problem of the place of ancient Jewish historiography, which, it may be granted, is more aptly categorized as ancient Near Eastern rather than Western.[6] Nevertheless, a few very brief comments about the nature of Jewish historiography[7] are apt, since it is one of the foundations of Christian conceptions of history as it is practiced in the Western tradition, as even Breisach himself concedes.[8]

Contrary to an understanding of the past characterized by prehistorical, agrarian-based cultures in which the cycles of seasons and days blended together in endless repetition and subsequently blurred concepts of chronology, Jewish history recognized that there was meaning, struc-

---

5. Breisach, *Historiography*.

6. Mario Liverani, "The Chronology of the Biblical Fairy-Tale," in *The Historian and the Bible: Essays in Honour of Lester L. Grabbe* (ed. Philip R. Davies and Diana V. Edelman; LHBOTS 530; New York: T&T Clark, 2010), 73.

7. Without a doubt, now and again scholars today have concerns about whether the Jewish Bible is actually history since the Tanak is a product of religious experience and faith, and may use fictive elements in the narrative. See Rainer Albertz, "Secondary Sources Also Deserve to be Historically Evaluated: The Case of the United Monarchy," in Davies and Edelman, *Historian and the Bible*, 31–45. This nervousness about the historical weight that Hebrew texts might bear is seen especially in regard to whether some of the more mythic stories, like the Abraham accounts, may actually relate to specific historical contexts in the Persian and Hellenistic periods. See, for instance, Thomas L. Thompson. "Reiterative Narratives of Exile and Return: Virtual Memories of Abraham in the Persian and Hellenistic Periods," in Davies and Edelman, *Historian and the Bible*, 47. See also the overview of the discussion in Mark W. Chavalas, "Recent Trends in the Study of Israelite Historiography," *JETS* 38 (1995), 161–69.

8. Breisach, *Historiography*, 77.

ture, and process in events.[9] This is exemplified by the Deuteronomistic Historian, who goes beyond the task of chronicling or merely listing happenings to point out the relevance of the events as they occur in the flow of time.[10] Ancient Hebrew historical writing also, at points, reveals some understanding of the ideal of professional detachment in the way characters are portrayed, a hallmark of good historiography. Very clearly, heroes in the biblical story are not whitewashed but may be depicted with their flaws or even criticized.[11]

Despite the convention of exercising professional detachment, however, the problem of the use of myth-like stories that would not meet modern standards for what constitutes history proves to be troublesome to those who write about historiography in the Hebrew Bible.[12] But one must be cautious both about anachronistically applying modern standards of history to historical writing of the past and about assuming that there are clear divisions between literary techniques and history. Just because a text makes use of literary devices does not mean it should automatically be classified as literature rather than history. After all, history is by nature narrative in format and must use the conventions of solid and lively prose composition to convey the past. So both Jewish historians and those of other cultures utilize speeches by prominent figures, as well as present history in terms of periods. These are, naturally, literary and structural elements, respectively.

Another aspect of Jewish historiography is the fact that the Deuteronomistic documents have a unifying thesis about how earlier time periods impacted the Israelite nation. As John Van Seters puts it, the historian of ancient Israel attempts "to communicate through this story of the people's past a sense of their identity—and that is the *sine qua non* of history writing."[13] For the Jews, as will be true for the Christians who enter this stream of history, this identity hinges on the special relationship between

---

9. Gilderhus, *History and Historians*, 13.

10. Van Seters, *In Search of History*, 358.

11. Gilderhus, *History and Historians*, 15–16.

12. John Collins goes so far as to use the modifier *history-like* when describing the Old Testament in his article "The 'Historical Character' of the Old Testament," in *Israel's Past in Present Research: Essays on Ancient Israelite Historiography* (ed. V. Philips Long; SBTS 7; Winona Lake, Ind.: Eisenbrauns, 1999), 150–69.

13. Van Seters, *In Search of History*, 359.

God and God's people. At its heart, Jewish writing about history might be described as "theological historiography."[14]

Unfortunately, Jewish interest in historiography declined throughout the Second Temple period. Despite works like 1 Maccabees and the texts of Flavius Josephus, there are no extant rabbinic writings from the period 60 C.E.–500 C.E. that are histories.[15] Instead, recording the past during that later timeframe "ceased to be a central feature of Jewish self-expression," and the activity of writing history is replaced by study of the Torah.[16] Thus, when looking for historical writings contemporary with the Christian era and associated with the Mediterranean region, biblical scholars will discover that the materials available for study are Greco-Roman in origin and part of the Western tradition rather than Near Eastern.

5.1.2. GREEK HISTORIOGRAPHY

Historical writing in the Greek world did not emerge fully formed but developed from a long tradition of other types of nonfiction writing. Stephen Usher, for instance, comments that historiography was a close cousin of geography, a type of writing where a drive to explain the structure of the physical world had its cognate in investigations into the origins of human societies.[17] History is also related to the activity of those who kept records and annals and are known as logographers. These logographers were writers of prose, including speeches, and as part of their tasks they recorded local events, preserved stories of neighborhood mythology, and kept chronological lists of Olympian winners, political dignitaries, and the like.

Where Ernst Breisach chooses to begin his treatment of ancient Western historiography, however, is not with a historical work at all, or even with the logographers, but surprisingly with the epics of Homer (ninth or eighth century B.C.E.). Aside from the fact that the bard's writings are lyric

---

14. Amram Tropper, "The Fate of Jewish Historiography after the Bible: A New Interpretation," *History and Theory* 43 (May 2004): 187.

15. Ibid.

16. Ibid. Tropper provides several reasons for this shift, including the failure of the Jewish revolts against Rome, which lessened the Jews' sphere of political influence, and the emergence of the Second Sophistic—a preference of which was the idealization of the past rather than contemporary history.

17. Stephen Usher, "Greek Historiography and Biography," in *Civilization of the Ancient Mediterranean: Greece and Rome* (ed. Michael Grant and Rachel Kitzinger; New York: Charles Scribner's Sons, 1988), 1525.

rather than prose, the epics are clearly different from Israelite historiography in another way. Specifically, the Greek gods behave quite differently in the stream of time than does the deity of the Hebrew people. Unlike the Deuteronomistic History, wherein divine purpose drives events, within the Greek epic the gods have a distinct lack of direction or plan when they act in human affairs. For instance, the *Iliad* takes up the story of the siege of Troy with the arbitrary interference of Apollo, who was miffed about an insult paid to one of his priests.[18] This sets the stage for the remainder of the story, in which the gods interact with humans at a whim, sometimes assisting, sometimes hindering, and often driven to intercede for particular humans by the prevailing emotional response of the given deity on the spur of the moment.

To be clear, Breisach does not want to make the case that Homer's works are in fact history; they are not. Actually, as E. V. Rieu emphatically expresses it, Homer is not providing a true account of the past "in even its most diluted form."[19] Rather, Breisach is making the more modest claim that embedded within the Bard's works are elements upon which subsequent authors will eventually draw and that will become characteristic of some early forms of Greek history.[20]

First of all, the epic poets created an appreciation for and an interest in the past, a prerequisite for the field of history to even develop in a culture.[21] Beyond that, though, they set the stage for the selection of subject matter that would be undertaken once history comes into its own. In particular, Breisach observes that the *Iliad* is concerned with aristocratic life, not the trials and tribulations of merchants, fishermen, tax collectors, or peasants. The characters that are the center of focus are instead heroes

---

18. Homer, *The Iliad* (trans. E. V. Rieu; London: Penguin, 1950), 23.

19. E. V. Rieu, introduction to ibid., xiv.

20. As an aside, it is important to note that Homer's poetic writings also became foundational in the basic educational system that was in place throughout the early years of the Empire. See Karl Olav Sandnes, *The Challenge of Homer: School, Pagan Poets and Early Christianity* (LNTS 400; London: T&T Clark, 2009), 22. As a consequence, Homer may have exerted some level of influence (even if it was reactionary) on New Testament writings, even if only select passages from him were learned. See William V. Harris, *Ancient Literacy* (Cambridge: Harvard University Press, 1989), 227. Sandnes is a bit clearer about the piecemeal nature of the Homeric materials available to students in his subsequent work, *The Gospel 'According to Homer and Virgil' Cento and Canon* (NovTSup 138; Leiden: Brill, 2010), 8, 23.

21. Breisach includes with Homer a treatment of Hesiod, another ancient poet.

guided by personal codes of honor. Israelite history understood the role of the people as a collective on the stage of human affairs, and that genre at least rudimentarily acknowledged cause and effect, as exemplified by the notion that faithfulness and apostasy alternately trigger periods of peace and domination by enemy nations, respectively. Homeric "heroic history" instead focused on timeless, virtuous deeds practiced by extraordinary individuals. The historical writings of the Hellenic people also lacked a clearly developed sense that past events might impact those in the present.[22] Instead, the Greek historians assumed the Homeric mantel and took as their "central themes human arrogance, self-indulgence, and brutality leading to disaster."[23] Homer, then, is significant for Greek historiography because he helped to color perceptions of which aspects of the past made worthy subject matter for historical writing. In other words, he influenced selectivity.

Herodotus (ca. 484 B.C.E.–430/420 B.C.E.) illustrates this point. His *Histories*—or, as the title of his work is sometimes translated, *Researches* or *Inquiries*—tend to focus on the activities of "great men." This gender-limited agenda is clearly laid out in his opening paragraph.[24] Women, while present in the body of his text, generally take minor roles. The historian does differ slightly from the bard, however, in his willingness to admit characters from a variety of social strata to the storyline. Although not shifting focus entirely from the aristocrats, he at least acknowledges the common people who made up the troops and for whom the war was part of general human experience.[25] Despite this small deviation, Herodotus still

---

22. Breisach, *Historiography*, 6–7. Also, Usher makes the comment that even Xenophon makes no attempt to establish causal connections. See Usher, *Greek Historiography*, 1530. There are some hints of, if not causality, at least a sense of mechanisms for change in Thucydides, who begins his tale of the origins of the Greek people with the observation that economic conditions related to the arable capacity of various regions of the land resulted in migratory movements and conflicts over wealth and resources among the Greek people (*Peloponnesian War* 1.2.3 [Smith, LCL]). All further direct quotes from Thucydides will be from the Smith translation.

23. Robert W. Wallace, "Historiography, Greek" in *Oxford Encyclopedia of Greece and Rome* (ed. Michael Gagarin and Elaine Fantham; Oxford: Oxford University Press, 2010), 4:7.

24. Herodotus, *Hist.* 1.1 (Godley, LCL). The title of the book ends up providing the name *history*, by which the genre as a whole eventually comes to be known. All further direct quotes will be from the Godley translation.

25. Breisach, *Historiography*, 13.

follows the bard's lead in remaining preoccupied with military endeavors. Even though the historian's concern in book 2 is largely an ethnographic treatment of Egypt, nonetheless, in the style of Homer, the work as a whole is an account of armies and their battles. Herodotus's main focus is largely limited in scope to the Persian-Greek conflicts between the years 550 and 480 B.C.E.[26] This is a dramatic contrast to the Hebrew accounts of their history, which seek to present the past on grand scale that stretches back over generations to the origins of the world.

Even given the debt to Homer, the *Histories* evidence the first glimmers of other techniques for "history" and historical methodology that would be foundational in Western traditions of historiography. Several deserve mention. First, rather than the convention of the muse who inspires and is the "source" of the story, as is the case in Homer's epics, Herodotus claims his own authorial authority. In the opening paragraph of the *Histories*, for example, the historian states his name and the fact that he is the publisher of his own work, a distinct break from Eastern historiography, including Hebrew history, where the material is either attributed to the deities or the author remains anonymous.[27] Granted, the so-called father of Western history[28] does give a nod to the muses by adding the name of each of the nine goddesses who inspire the arts to each of the nine books of his composition, but his work does not claim to be inspired or revealed. Furthermore, although the gods are mentioned during the course of the text, the relationship between the deities and human fate is more obscure in the work of the historian than was the case in Homer since humans tend to shape their own lives and their failures are due to human weaknesses.[29]

Hand in hand with the new approach—that the writer is the author of his own account—is Herodotus's clear attempt, as a reliable author, to gather his own material, and his role in the development of the use of sources was mentioned in the prior chapter. Herodotus personally col-

---

26. Frances Hartog, "The Invention of History: The Pre-History of a Concept from Homer to Herodotus," *History and Theory* 39 (2000): 394. The influence of Homer even extends to Herodutus's use of Homer as a source (*Hist.* 2.118–20).

27. Hartog, "The Invention of History," 393.

28. Hecataeus of Miletus was a historian who preceded Herodotus. Usher notes that he does have some claim to the title "Father of History" ("Greek Historiography," 1525), but his works only survived in small fragments, which make them difficult to assess.

29. Breisach, *Historiography*, 14.

lected many of the legends, anecdotes, and even geographical details in his work throughout his travels. Furthermore, he is careful to cite his sources, indicating where and from whom he heard particular details, such as one group of reports that he gathered "from the people of Delphi" (*Hist.* 1.20). Where he feels compelled, he does speculate as to the veracity of the stories, and he offers his own opinion. At other points, he lets the reader decide. Yet when sources disagree, he nonetheless reports them both, noting their tendency to contradict each other. An example that illustrates this attempt at objectivity in relation to his sources appears in book 1. After he recounts some of the Persian legends related to the abduction of three women named Io, Helen, and Europe as triggering events for the war, he comments,

> Such is the Persian account of the matter: in their opinion, it was the taking of Troy which began their feud with the Greeks. But the Phoenicians do not tell the same story about Io as the Persians. They say that they did not carry her off to Egypt by force: she had intercourse in Argos with the captain of the ship; then, perceiving herself to be with child she was ashamed that her parents should know it, and so, lest they should discover her condition, she sailed away with the Phoenicians of her own accord. These are the stories of the Persians and the Phoenicians. For my own part, I will not say that this or that story is true. (*Hist.* 1.5)

Herodotus's drive for objectivity has another facet as well. In particular, he attempts to present his subject matter, from the exclusive to the mundane yet fanciful, without rendering judgment about its value. This is apparent where he sets out the program for the ethnographic section of the text and stresses his intention to portray cities both humble and great:

> I will name him whom I myself know to have done unprovoked wrong to the Greeks, and so go forward with my history, and speak of small and great cities alike. For many states that were once great have now become small; and those that were great in my time were small formerly. Knowing therefore that human prosperity never continues in one stay, I will make mention alike of both kinds. (*Hist.* 1.5)

Herodotus's heir in historiography, Thucydides (ca. 460 B.C.E. or earlier–404 B.C.E. or earlier) continued the tradition of objectivity but was more particular about his sources. Generally, where Herodotus's sources were partisan and personally involved in the events they recounted, Thucydides "edited and impersonalized" his.[30] Further, since he was a commander in the Peloponnesian War between Athens and Sparta, which is the subject of the history he writes, Thucydides was able to draw upon eyewitness accounts and was critical of histories that rely on hearsay, observing:

> Now the state of affairs in early times I have found to have been such as I have described, although it is difficult in such matters to credit any and every piece of testimony. For men accept from one another hearsay reports of former events, neglecting to test them just the same, even though these events belong to the history of their own country. (*Peloponnesian War* 1.20.1)

Moreover, Thucydides was more circumspect about his use of Homer as an interlocutor than was his countryman from the prior generation, noting at points that one shouldn't give greater credence to the poets than to other sources. When forced to rely on the bard when other evidence was lacking, he expressed skepticism about the amount of weight one might lend to accounts designed to be performed and please the ear.[31]

One point, however, in which Thucydides, like Herodotus, was indebted to Homer was with the use of "live speech," a convention that appears in the epics, is continued by the father of history, and is used extensively by the military commander turned historian. It appears that both of the major Greek historians "regarded the inclusion of what was said as necessary in order to explain what was done."[32] Not knowing precisely what any individual figure uttered, of course, the authors were forced to be inventive. Thucydides, who employs speeches extensively and often presents pairs of orations when representing the pep talks given by generals from opposing sides in the conflict, confesses,

> As to the speeches that were made by different men, either when they were about to begin the war or when they were already engaged therein, it has been difficult to recall with strict accuracy the words actually spoken, both for me as regards that which I myself heard, and for those who from various other sources have brought me reports. Therefore the

---

30. Usher, "Greek Historiography," 1528.

31. Thucydides, *Peloponnesian War* 1.21.1. See also 1.9.3–4; 1.10.3–4. He does employ Homer as a primary rather than secondary source when he observes that the name *Hellene* was a later development and was not even used by Homer (1.3.2).

32. Usher, "Greek Historiography," 1527.

speeches are given in the language in which, as it seemed to me, the several speakers would express, on the subjects under consideration, the sentiments most befitting the occasion, though at the same time I have adhered as closely as possible to the general sense of what was actually said. (*Peloponnesian War* 1.22.1)

Certainly, the idea of "making up" addresses that only convey the gist of what might have been spoken in the past as opposed to presenting a record of the actual words uttered would be a practice anathema to the modern-day historian, who has access to technological innovations and mass media for preserving oral history. Nevertheless, the use of discourses, and particularly those that convey arguments from opposing viewpoints, in the ancient form of scholarship represented sound techniques of presenting information and drew on approaches from the field of rhetoric and even sophistic philosophy.[33] Ultimately, the difference between current-day practice and antiquity might be expressed thus: the ancient "historians regarded speeches as a method of analysis by which the motives of a character could be made explicit. A modern historian delivers analytical judgments in his own voice, but ancient historians preferred the dramatic and rhetorical mask of a speech."[34] Ernst Breisach observes that the practice of using speeches was such a useful narrative device that historians employed them intermittently in the later Middle Ages straight up to the dawn of modern historiography.[35]

In addition to the convention of using speeches, Greek historians are generally said to have one other pronounced methodological preference. Several of the extant writings reveal a fondness for a cyclical view of time. Polybius (ca. 200 B.C.E.–ca. 118 B.C.E.), for instance, made use of a cycle based on the human life span, with the key spokes on the wheel of time being birth, maturity, death and decay.[36] Even Thucydides had a cyclical concept of the passage of time since he conceived his history to be a guide to actions in the future:[37] what happened in the past was likely to come around again, so his readers should be prepared.

---

33. Ibid., 1527.

34. Ronald Mellor, "Roman Historiography and Biography," in *Civilization of the Ancient Mediterranean: Greece and Rome* (ed. Michael Grant and Rachel Kitzinger; New York: Charles Scribner's Sons, 1988), 3:1553.

35. Breisach, *Historiography*, 17.

36. Howell and Prevenier, *From Reliable Sources*, 4–5.

37. Gilderhus, *History and Historians*, 18.

5.1.3. ROMAN HISTORIOGRAPHY

Roman historiography was deeply indebted to that of the Greeks. Marcus Tullius Cicero (106–43 B.C.E.), who was writing in the last decades of the Republic, almost a century before the New Testament documents were penned, makes a joke concerning the inadequacy of Roman historians. He denigrates the Romans as "mere chroniclers" compared with their Greek counterparts, whom he praises for turning their rhetorical skills to the field of history. He jests, "What class of orator, and how great a master of language is qualified, in your opinion to write history?" The reply is a scathing assessment of Roman endeavors: "If he is to write as the Greeks have written," answers Catalus, "a man of supreme ability is required; if the standard is to be that of our fellow-countrymen, no orator at all is needed; it is enough that the man should not be a liar" (*De Oratore* 2.12.51).[38] Later in the discussion on history, Cicero has the character Antonius remark,

> No wonder … if this subject (history) has never yet been brilliantly treated in our language. For not one of our own folk seeks after eloquence, save with an eye towards its display at the Bar and in public speaking, whereas in Greece the most eloquent were strangers to forensic advocacy, and applied themselves chiefly to reputable studies in general, and particularly to writing history. (*De Oratore* 2.13.55)

Cicero then goes on to list a wide variety of Greek historians whom he believed were gifted with eloquence. Herodotus and Thucydides head the list (*De Oratore*, 2.13.55–58). While the Romans had not necessarily applied rhetoric to the field of history in the past, its absence is, according to Cicero, a defect that should be rectified in the future. Reportedly, Cicero's friends constantly hoped that this leading light in rhetoric would himself undertake to write a major work of history, a wish that remained unfulfilled.[39]

What is interesting in this discussion, however, is that according to Cicero historiography should not be merely the dry reporting of facts but, as was the case with oratory, ought to evidence attention to the narra-

---

38. Trans. Rackham, LCL. All further direct quotes from Cicero will be from the Rackham translation.

39. A. J. Woodman, *Rhetoric in Classical Historiography* (London: Croom Helm, 1988), 70. For the full discussion on Cicero's views of oratory and history, see 70–116.

tive art (*De Legibus* 1.2.5). The idea of a link between rhetoric and history in the ancient world is not far-fetched. The construction of the speeches that were used by historians for their heroes and generals no doubt bore a verisimilitude to the oratorical addresses with which their readers would have been familiar. Another connection between history and the art of spoken narrative is part of history's legacy from Homer because the epics were intended for oral performance. Or perhaps histories in the ancient world were themselves originally intended for presentation before crowds by their authors as part of the process of "publication." Certainly Lucian of Samosata (120–180 C.E.), the second-century satirist, hints that such is the case when he portrays Herodotus as shamelessly flogging his *Histories* by reading them aloud to audiences at Athens, Corinth, and Sparta, but not achieving the acclaim he craved until having the audacity to recite them at the Olympic games.[40]

In our current time period, it is sometimes fashionable to distinguish between "history" and "narrative artistry" or between "history" and "rhetoric." Clearly, firm distinctions such as these did not exist in the ancient world.

Despite Cicero's envy of the skill displayed by the Greek historians, there were other points at which Roman history differed from that of the Hellenes. First, where Thucydides had been a military man, authors in the Latin areas tended to be Roman senators.[41] As a consequence, subject matter was often political and narrowly focused on Roman interests. A travel log of countries and foreign sights such as the one that appears in the second book of Herodotus would find no place in Roman histories because it had little to do with Rome itself. Second, for the Romans, history was the forum through which to work out moral questions and make moral judgments. As such, the impartiality and objectivity that characterized Thucydides would be absent from Roman works.[42] The Romans were also never able to achieve as critical a view of their sources as had Thucydides. As Mellor summed it up, "As long as there was no blatant improbability and no obvious bias, a Roman historian would accept his

---

40. Lucian of Samosata, *Herodotus and Aëtion* in *The Works of Lucian* (ed. H. W. Fowler and F. G. Fowler; Oxford: Clarendon, 1905), 2:90–91.

41. Livy was an exception.

42. Ronald Mellor notes that the Greeks, in contrast to their Latin counterparts, used philosophy as the vehicle for exploring morality ("Roman History and Biography," 3:1541–42).

source at face value. That the source contained information that could not possibly be based on knowledge or verified is irrelevant."[43] Furthermore, despite the presence of an increasing amount of documentary evidence as the empire matured in the form of rescripts, annals, and laws, Roman historians did not tend to do archival work or original research. Instead, they relied on other historians or a limited number of favorite sources. Yet they did seek to present the "truth" rather than outright fiction.

5.1.4. Ancient Historiography and the "Truth"

Standards and expectations in any field change and develop. A Model T automobile, for example, would not be outfitted with GPS technology, electric windows, air conditioning or even a basic AM/FM radio. Still, car buffs trolling antique automotive shows would be able to recognize a primitive four-wheeled contraption that is devoid of these features for the car that it is and would not expect it to meet modern standards for comfort and functionality. History as a field includes historical methods that also keep developing with time. Therefore, applying modern standards for "truth" and accuracy to ancient documents in this genre is problematic.

When Herodotus reports, for instance, that the flooding of the Nile is due to the actions of the sun moving to Libya and pulling the water to itself (*Hist.* 2.24–27), is that to be taken as "truth"? Likewise, what is the modern reader to think about the father of Western history's assertion that in the final battle with the Persians the Greeks managed to amass 110,000 fighting men (*Hist.* 9.30), a number that is in all likelihood exceedingly inflated, given what is known about techniques of ancient warfare? Further, how is one to come to terms with Thucydides's use of speeches, which he himself concedes are to some extent fabricated? These elements, for their lack of accuracy by today's standards, do not make ancient writings any less "history." Nor do they imply that these works should be categorized as "historical fiction" because of the questionable reliability of the facts that they contain. They must be allowed to stand within their own time and place.

But that is not to say that the modern historian should emulate these early methods and techniques for writing history any more than today's Detroit automakers should commence turning out Model Ts on their assembly lines. It does mean, however, that when encountering histori-

---

43. Mellor, "Roman History and Biography," 3:1552.

cally oriented sources about the past that were written in eras other than our own, we should not conflate the concepts of precision and truth that characterize our own contemporary historical methods with ancient standards. Ancient historiography was correct to the extent that it was an attempt to convey underlying realities related to actual events in the past. It was not necessarily an endeavor preoccupied with exact details.

If present-day historians of the first century concede that this is logical, then it is reasonable to apply this same leniency about precision and accuracy to documents produced in early Christian communities that are historical in nature. But that raises the question about the "truth level" of any New Testament texts that are "histories."

Certainly many of the books in the canon are, at heart, historical. For instance, they present a viewpoint where the Old Testament was written in anticipation of Jesus, a fact that demonstrates that the early Christians had a healthy engagement with the past.[44] And even Luke-Acts takes on some of the attributes of a universal history through its efforts to show that Jesus' life and message had significance not only for their own community but also for pagans. Indeed, this cosmopolitan focus is markedly different from the self-centered approach to history practiced by the Romans.[45] One troubling aspect of early Christian history, however, is the fact that the status of some of the works as "sacred" tends to muddle the distinctions between truth, precision and "Absolute Truth."

For instance, knowing that historians in antiquity, like Herodotus, tended to estimate crowds and armies, is it necessary to assume that exactly 5,000 persons, not one more and not one less, were present at the meal Jesus shares with the throng (Mark 6:44)?[46] Likewise, if historians even of Livy's stamp were not able to correct conflicts in his sources, should we be surprised when New Testament texts include doublets? Along these same lines, should the individual speeches and sermons of Jesus as recounted in the Gospels, inspired though they may be for persons of the Christian faith, be taken as word-for-word accurate if, in fact, ancient historiography

---

44. Gilderhus, *History and Historians*, 20.

45. Ibid.

46. The other three Gospels seem to grant that the number 5,000 is an approximation (Matt 14:21; Luke 9:14; John 6:10). There is also some trouble in how to take the "feeding of the 4,000," which appears in Matthew (15:32–39) and Mark (8:1–10), a doublet not present in the other two Gospels. Were there two separate feedings?

itself did not expect speeches to represent transcript-like reporting?[47] In other words, is it misguided to construct "red-letter" versions of Jesus' sayings based on imputing to the Gospels standards for speeches, sayings and addresses from our own time period? These types of questions are important to ask even if the conundrums they pose will not be resolved here.

In any event, to automatically consign ancient documents, including the Gospels to one side or the other of a history–fiction polarity[48] based on modern perceptions of factual reliability is to impose modern sensibilities anachronistically on the text. The inevitable result is the generation of a false history–fiction dichotomy or a supercilious dismissal of ancient writings as too archaic to have contemporary relevance. Both of these positions do a disservice to the ancient authors and to the truth they were trying to convey using the conventions they had at their disposal.

5.1.5. The Role of Biography in the Classical World

Because the New Testament contains a few documents that have been considered to be "lives of Jesus" and may be compared to ancient writings such as Plutarch's (46–180 C.E.) portraits of philosophers or even Tacitus's (50–120 C.E.) biography of his father-in-law, a general named Agricola, saying a few words about the relationship between ancient historiography and biography is in order. Indeed, just as researchers must be careful about fiction–history dichotomies, there are also troublesome aspects about driving too wide a wedge between "history" and "biography."

Today members of the general public often recognize biography and history as part of the same discipline; a biography being an account of the past of an individual while works that are "histories" are accounts concerning the past of events, communities, or wider phenomena. Thomas Carlyle, writing at the end of the late nineteenth century, demonstrated how thin a dividing line there actually is between history and biography

---

47. With regard to speeches in the New Testament, see Osvaldo Padilla, *The Speeches of Outsiders in Acts: Poetics, Theology and Historiography* (SNTSMS 144; Cambridge: Cambridge University Press, 2008). For further discussion on the topic of Acts' speeches, see also Stanley E. Porter, "Thucydides 1.22.1 and Speeches in Acts: Is There a Thucydidean View?" *NovT* 32 (1990): 121–42.

48. Francis Watson, *Text and Truth: Redefining Biblical Theology* (Grand Rapids: Eerdmans, 1997), 33.

when he asserted, "History is the essence of innumerable biographies."[49] To some extent, one might say that the book of Acts adheres to this notion by presenting in-sequence details about Peter, Stephen, and Paul when describing the history of the early church.

Nevertheless, some ancient authors themselves tended to distinguish sharply between biography and history as different genres. Biography, though popular, was to some degree regarded as history's inferior cousin.[50] The division appears to be significant enough that even Plutarch insisted that he was a biographer rather than a historian.[51] Perhaps Plutarch's inclination to separate the two genres stems from their respective origins. We have already seen that history, although it had affinities with epic poetry, likely originated with the logographers and geographers. By contrast, the first known monograph covering an individual was written by Isocrates (436–338 B.C.E.), an orator, and took as its subject Euagoras, the fourth-century B.C.E. king of Salamis. Isocrates taught rhetoric, and thus the biography genre is essentially thought to be a derivative of one of the three types of rhetorical speeches—panegyric, or eulogy.[52] The funeral orations that are given today in funeral homes or at wakes are the offspring of this type of speechmaking about individuals.

During the end of the Roman Republic, the reputation of biography as a field also suffered by virtue of the use to which it was put. Politicians who sought to promote themselves commissioned biographies, and obliging historians like Theophanes of Mytilene (mid-first century, B.C.E.), whose patron was Pompey, were not above shading their accounts to portray their benefactors in favorable light.[53] Truth be told, though, this practice is not unique to antiquity. In the later Middle Ages, historians pandered to elite aristocrats, for whom they created glorious pasts and treated "evidence" in a cavalier manner in order to show their subject to best advantage.[54] Even in the Internet age, one may find historians for hire who are willing, if the price is right, to craft anyone's life story.[55]

---

49. Thomas Carlyle from the 1830 essay "On History," reproduced in Stern, *Varieties of History*, 93.

50. Mellor, "Roman Historiography," 3:1554.

51. Breisach, *Historiography*, 71.

52. The other two are forensic and deliberative.

53. Usher, "Greek Historiography," 1537.

54. Howell and Prevenier, *From Reliable Sources*, 7.

55. For instance, the "Remembering Site" will provide biographers who will com-

One must be careful, however, that the distinctions that some of the ancients themselves made not be overdrawn. The historian Tacitus (56–120 C.E.) wrote not only his biographical notes about Agricola but also two works of history, his *Annals* and *Histories*, demonstrating facility with both types of historical writing. The idea that biographies originated with those trained in rhetoric apparently was no barrier for Roman orators like Cicero who did not feel compelled to limit themselves to that genre, but, as we have already seen, thought that their artistic gifts and eloquence should be brought to bear on writing histories like those authored by Herodotus or Thucydides. Finally, the dividing line between biography and history appears to have been blurred by cross-over works such as Varro's (116–27 B.C.E.) *De Vita Populi Romani* and, on the Greek side, Dicaearchus's (ca. 320 B.C.E.) *Life of Greece* (βίος Ἑλλάδος), neither of which are biographies in the strict sense, despite the use of the word *life*, frequently associated with works about individuals, in the titles.

Given this ambiguity between what is and isn't a history and what constitutes a biography, scholars like Hubert Cancik are justified in describing Luke not as a biography of Jesus as an individual but as an institutional history that continues in Acts.[56] By the same token, one can understand the origin of Darryl Palmer's reticence to classify the Gospels, including that of Luke, as examples of the genre of history, which he defines narrowly to exclude biographical works.[57]

Perhaps a way forward is the technique modeled by Rosamund McKitterick in her work on the early Middle Ages,[58] the next time period upon which we will focus. Rather than getting bogged down with categorizing works by specific genres too closely, McKitterick regards an author's fascination with the past as the key in identifying a writing as historical.

---

plete the task for $15,000–$30,000. These appear to be based on a "formulaic" format that is focused on a set stable of questions asked in an interview of the subject. See http://www.therememberingsite.org/resources.php.

56. Hubert Cancik, "The History of Culture, Religion and Institutions in Ancient Historiography: Philological Observations concerning Luke's History," *JBL* 116 (1997): 673, 679.

57. Palmer, "Historiographical Literature," 163.

58. Rosamund McKitterick, *Perceptions of the Past in the Early Middle Ages* (Notre Dame, Ind.: University of Notre Dame Press, 2006).

5.2. The Middle Ages: Speculative History Triumphs

An important source for the patristic period is Eusebius of Caesarea (260–340 c.e.), an early fourth-century bishop and advisor to Emperor Constantine. This so-called father of ecclesiastical history provides material that fills the gap between the events recorded in the New Testament and the triumph of Christianity under the patronage of the emperor. Nevertheless, by modern standards his skills as a historian are dubious at best, largely due to his thoroughgoing apologetic agenda on behalf of the faith and reliance on sweeping generalizations. For instance, his chronological work lists events from the pagan world, events of the state, and a plentitude of miscellaneous information, but when he turns to history events are subordinated to Christian agendas and moral lessons.

In any event, the paradigm for historical writing in western Christendom during the middle ages was set by Augustine (354–430 c.e.) rather than Eusebius. His famed work *The City of God* contained both an apology in reaction to the notion that the Christian faith was to some degree culpable for the fall of Rome and an extensive historical theology. He echoes Eusebius by conflating world history with Christian history but diverges by disentangling Christianity from too close an identification with the fallen Roman Empire. This bishop of Hippo sets out his objective for the historical section of the treatise, stating,

> Now, recognizing what is expected of me, and not unmindful of my promise, and relying, too, on the same succor, I will endeavour to treat of the origin, and progress, and deserved destinies of the two cities (the earthly and the heavenly, to wit), which, as we said are in this present world commingled, and as it were entangled together. And, first, I will explain how the foundations of these two cities were originally laid, in the difference that arose among the angels. (*Civ.* 1.11)[59]

He then begins his account by referring to creation, roughly following the outline of Genesis. Because his interest is theological as well as historical, he intersperses his description of the beginning of the world with conjecture concerning when angels might have been created and a theological digression about the role of the nature of the trinity which takes its cues

---

59. Trans. Marcus Dods, LCL. All further direct quotes from Augustine will be from the Dods translation.

from the opening chapter of John's Gospel (*Civ.* 11.10, 11.24). Along the way, however, Augustine both describes his sources and details his understanding of time.

Naturally, when it comes to sources the churchman holds the canonical scriptures to be the primary storehouse from which to retrieve historical information—a position that he confirms when he writes, "This mediator, having spoken what He judged sufficient, first by the prophets, then by His own lips, and afterwards by the apostles, has besides produced the Scripture which is called canonical, which has paramount authority, and to which we yield assent in all matters of which we ought not to be ignorant" (*Civ.* 11.3). His reliance on scripture notwithstanding, when seeking to make philosophical or theological points relative to the history he sets out, Augustine stoops to summarize arguments made by pagan authors or from other sources, such as Porphyry (234–305 c.e.) or Plato (428/427–347 b.c.e.).[60] However, when he does so, the profane always is distinguished from the sacred.[61]

With regard to time, Augustine's perception is very linear and thus represents a complete departure from Greek cyclical conceptions.[62] For the church father, time commenced with the creation of the world (*Civ.* 11.5), before which only a timeless eternity existed. And although this primordial eternity is immutable, time itself can accommodate change and thus has a past, present, and future.[63] As a consequence, events may be understood to occur prior to or after one another in sequence. This very well-thought-out conception of time allows Augustine to present an exposition of history that is divided into periods such as that from Noah to the Kings of Israel and the span from the era of the prophets to Christ since events may occur in series.[64] All in all, Augustine identifies six ages within

---

60. Augustine, *Civ.* 22.26–27. He references Sallust (2.17) and even quotes Cicero (2.14). In his role as bishop, he also learned of miracles and both interviewed those healed and relied on the testimony of others who witnessed the miracles. See especially the story about Curubis, *Civ.* 22.8.

61. Gilderhus, *History and Historians*, 22.

62. Ibid., 23.

63. As Augustine puts it, "For that which is made in its time is made both after and before some time—after that which is past, before that which is future.... But simultaneously with time the world was made, if in the world's creation change and motion were created, as seems evident from the order of the first six or seven days" (*Civ.* 11.6).

64. Augustine, *Civ.*, books 16 and 17.

time.[65] Yet time also has an ending. Following last judgment, time ceases and an eternal seventh age will flourish. In that final period, a state of eternal blessedness or punishment as foretold in Revelation will be experienced by each individual according to his or her due.[66] Since humans will be outside of time and no longer able to change during the seventh age, at that point everyone will be immortal and God "shall be the end of all our desires who shall be seen without end, loved without cloy, praised without weariness" (*Civ.* 22.30). To the extent that judgment and this blessed state where humanity basks in the beatific vision are still to come and affect all of creation, Augustine's history is both universal in scope and speculative in its underlying philosophy.

During the entire medieval period, Augustine's influence held sway, and, as a result, focus centered on sacred rather than secular history. This is evidenced by a wide array of genres that all reflect an interest in religious matters, including ecclesiastical histories, church and monastic

> ### Elements of
> ### Medieval Historiography
>
> - *Orientation and Bias:* History is Christian history.
> - *Objectivity:* Not an issue. Goal is simply to "write the truth."
> - *Sources:* Histories are largely derived from other earlier histories. No primary research using resources from the past.
> - *Time:* Linear and progressive.
> - *Philosophical Stance:* Histories are speculative. Focused on the beatific vision after time ends.
> - *Scope:* Universal. History fits into the Judean-Christian tradition beginning with Genesis or the birth of Christ, which is seen as relevant for all humankind.

---

65. Augustine, *Civ.* 22.30: age 1: Adam to the flood; age 2: the flood to Abraham; age 3: Abraham to David; age 4: David to the exile; age 5: the exile to Christ; age 6: the current period; age 7: the eternal Sabbath. Eventually, in the Middle Ages, other schemes of periodization were adopted. Ernst Breisach includes helpful charts for the tripartite divisions (analogous to the three parts of the Trinity) developed by Rupert von Deutz and Hugh of St. Victor along with the radical millenarian concept put forth by Joachim of Fiore in his own tripartite version of history. (See especially Breisach, *Historiography*, 140–42.) For more on the strand of speculative history in the Middle Ages that had an apocalyptic flavor like that found in Fiore, see Marjorie Reeves, *The Prophetic Sense of History in Medieval and Renaissance Europe* (Variorum Collected Studies Series; Aldershot: Ashgate, 1999).

66. Augustine, *Civ.* 20.16; cf. Rev 15:2; 21:1.

annals (taking the form of registers or lists), church chronicles (which included some narrative), the acts of church leaders, martyrologies, collections of canon law, and the like.[67] Moreover, modern historians would classify historical writing from the period as derivative. This is because—just as Augustine relied primarily on his key source, scripture, rather than looking for other primary resources—so too did the heirs to his tradition of historiography eschew primary research to depend to a great extent on the work of the historians who preceded them.

Mark Gilderhus provides a nice overview of the main elements that characterized medieval histories in Western Christendom in his introductory text on historiography. These include a summary of universal history from the time of creation, an affirmation of God's purpose and will, statements about occurrences in recent times, and a demonstration of divine immanence in events.[68]

That is not to say, however, that historical writing from the Middle Ages might be dismissed as uninventive. Rather, there are subtle developments. For instance, Rosamund McKitterick notices that gradually the city of Rome emerged in accounts as a key political and religious center.[69] And, while new primary written sources about the past were not consulted, many works did take into consideration the relics of the saints. In fact, McKitterick goes so far as to claim that, at least as far as the martyrs are concerned, the medieval historian's perception of time and geography were innovative as well. When it came to detailing where the martyr originally died (the past), where the relics now rested when they were relocated from Rome and other locations (the present), and the individual martyrs' places in heaven (the future kingdom), time coalesced. In essence, a saint represented the coming together of past, present and future since, although dead, the saint was still alive in the memory of the church.[70] The

---

67. By the thirteenth century, chronicles had become encyclopedic storehouses of new as well as old information. An example would be Salembene's *Chronicle*. See Breisach, *Historiography*, 147.

68. Gilderhus, *History and Historians*, 24. McKitterick notes that some histories, particularly Carolingian and Frankish, start not with Genesis but with Abraham. *Perceptions*, 9. By the early fourteenth century, Angelo Clareno begins his chronicle of the Franciscan order with the birth of Christ (*A Chronicle of History of the Seven Tribulations of the Order of Brothers Minor* [trans. David Burr and E. Randolph Daniel; Saint Bonaventure, N.Y.: Franciscan Institute, 2005], 2).

69. McKitterick, *Perceptions*, 55.

70. Ibid., 54.

slight warping of time with regard to the martyrs combined with historians' attempts to detail the exact locations with which individual saints were associated created a sort of "hagiogeohistorigraphy," to use McKitterick's neologism.[71]

In addition to this particular strain of originality, historical writing in the Middle Ages also took many formats. While traditional narratives were present, works like the *Chronicon* of Eusebius of Caesarea pairs a narrative in the first part of his work with a chart or table in the second. For his part, Angelo Clareno (1247–1337 B.C.E.) makes use of techniques that harken back to Thucydides and the Greco-Roman tradition. The monk starts his chronicle of the Franciscan order with two speeches that Christ purportedly delivered directly to Saint Francis (1181/82–1226 C.E.) in the way that the Messiah had previously spoken to Saint Paul at Damascus. Even speeches given by St. Francis appear in Clareno's text. In a way, Calreno's reliance on speeches in his work, which was written in 1320, foreshadows the enthusiasm for the use of speeches in the Greek and Roman style that was evidenced in the late fourteenth and early fifteenth centuries by the humanist Leonardo Bruni (ca. 1370–1444 C.E.)[72] By then a revival of all things Greco-Roman was in full swing.

5.3. The Early Modern Period: The Advent of Philological History

If the Middle Ages were dominated by an interest in universal, speculative histories in which the Old and New Testaments were accepted unquestionably as sources that testified to God's interaction with and plans for humanity throughout the course of time, then Renaissance historiography represents a shift away from this paradigm.

Leonardo Bruni, for instance, wrote a *History of the Florentine People*, which owed much to classical rather than medieval models. In addition to the recovery of live speech that was already mentioned as a deviation from medieval treatments, ecclesiological concerns were no longer the primary driving force and subject of history. Bruni himself emphasized politics. He also was interested in accuracy to an extent that the precritical chroniclers in prior centuries were not. As a result he compared his sources to one

---

71. Ibid., 55.

72. David Burr and E. Randolph Daniel, introduction to Clareno, *A Chronicle of History*, xii.

another rather than imitating the earlier practice of reproducing the content of each individual source like separate beads on a string.

The humanists were a bit more careful than their predecessors about sources in other ways too. In general they eschewed unsubstantiated anecdotes and even began to worry about cultural context and anachronism in relation to ancient witnesses. This was the advent of philological history, yet only in its most rudimentary form. As Gilderhus observes, historians were actually still more interested in imitating the style of the authors of antiquity than they were in actually interpreting them.[73]

Another innovation was a modification to the scope or span of the past considered in humanist works in comparison with those of their predecessors. Instead of beginning with creation and focusing on a broad history of the world, as did Augustine and his historiographical heirs, the histories of the humanists reflected the rise of secular interests on a more limited plane. Specifically, concentration shifted from universal history to Western history. This included, for instance, attention to writing biographies of individual rulers. Even regional histories became increasingly dominant. Along with this trend was an accompanying weight assigned to human activity in history rather than preoccupations with the actions of the divine. This is best exemplified by the fact that, rather than periodization of history taking the form of eras marked by specific actions anchored to the Bible like "the period of Noah" or the "period of the Patriarchs," the humanist historians developed a novel threefold division that included ancient history, the dark ages, and their own age. As Breisach is quick to point out in his summary of this phenomenon, however, the new understanding on the part of the humanists did not mean that the Renaissance historians were any less Christian in their personal beliefs, nor that they disagreed in principal with the religiously themed universal histories of the prior ages. Instead, they merely chose new subject matter and a new style for their projects.[74]

During the Reformation, history took on still another role. It became a tool used to discredit opponents in political and religious wrangling. Martin Luther (1483–1546 C.E.), models this. He employed principles

---

73. Gilderhus, *History and Historians*, 32.

74. Breisach, *Historiography*, 160. In any event, Joseph Levine asserts that it was during the Renaissance that seeds were sewn that would allow history to "declare its independence from every other form of knowledge" and become its own discipline. *The Autonomy of History* (Chicago: University of Chicago Press, 1999), viii.

analogous to those about the value of sources in his effort to understand the history of the church and critique Catholicism. To be specific, one of the objectives of the Protestant Reformers involved stripping away human inventions related to the practices of the Catholic Church that had accumulated in prior centuries, much as philologists sought the original form of a document. The purpose of this exercise was to return to the earliest understanding of the Bible and religious practices of the apostolic era. The *Magdeburg Centuries*, edited by a team of Lutheran scholars, was a thirteen-volume history in this vein. It sought to identify the corrupting influences and accreted traditions that had dulled Christianity and accomplished this task by using primary, or original and authentic, sources as opposed to those it deemed secondary or inferior ones.

In any event, Luther himself did not escape criticism and even mudslinging from his opponents when they penned their own polemically charged and biased histories. In fact, in one history of Malta that was translated by Antonfranceso Cirni Corso, Luther was described as the "filthiest of evildoers and great fore-runner of the Antichrist."[75] The fact that early modern historians took no pains to hide their biases was also evident in biographies of monarchs and rulers. Tudor historians, for example, employed ancient myths to validate the claims that dynasty had to the throne. Meanwhile, John Rastell (ca. 1475–1535) in his *Pastyme of People* used his own volume of history as a means of protest against the ruling party, subtly making the point that in England the law, not the monarch, should reign supreme.[76] The idea that impartiality should be a hallmark of historiography, however, would become an issue with which scholars in subsequent centuries would wrestle.

5.4. The Industrial Age and Objective History

Concurrent with the pinnacle of the industrial age in the nineteenth and early twentieth centuries, historical approaches in the modern era became wholeheartedly positivistic. Taking its cue from the achievements in the

---

75. Helen Vella Bonavita, "Key to Christendom: The 1565 Siege of Malta, Its Histories, and Their Use in Reformation Polemic," *Sixteenth Century Journal* 33 (2002): 1031.

76. Peter C. Herman, "Rastell's *Pastyme of People*: Early Monarchy and the Law in Early Modern Historiography," *Journal of Medieval and Early Modern Studies* 30 (2000): 285.

hard sciences, history was hailed a professional discipline and established its own journals such as *Historical Zeitschrift* (1859), the *American Historical Review* (1895), *Review Historique* (1876), and the *English Historical Review* (1886). In addition, during this time period, history achieved its own departmental presence in university systems and developed a methodology that was likened to the scientific method. With these tools and this sparkling new method of analysis, the actions, motivations, values, and intentions of the persons and institutions that were active in the past could become knowable to historians. In other words, earlier events and periods were "objective" realities that could be perceived and known by investigators who were able to look at historical occurrences impartially. Three terms—*objectivism, positivism,* and *realism*—are variously marshaled to denote the historiographical approach of this time period. Perhaps it would be helpful to break each of these down in turn.

5.4.1. The Elements of Historicism

Realism presupposes that veracity and facts exist independent of an individual's mind. Reality is immutable and knowable when it is observed. *Objectivism* is essentially an alternate label for realism. It is not redundant to observe that objectivism (or realism) maintains that objects (a shorthand term for truth and facts) have an ontological reality apart from an individual's perception. There is a "sharp separation between knower and known, between fact and value, and, above all, between history and fiction."[77] Positivism, which was defined a previous chapter, is the application of a scientific method–styled approach to study those phenomena that are available for inspection by the intellect and involves repetition and verification to confirm the truth or knowability of a fact. It assumes that events, rather than being one-off occurrences, have some degree of universality that allows the reduplication required for authenticating the event. Although positivism cannot be linked exclusively to objectivistic interpretations of history and has indeed been used with other methodologies, the historiography popular at the turn of the last century relied on the scientific method so heavily that *positivism* became a designation for it. In some literature, *positivism* is even used as if it were a synonym for *objectivism*.

---

77. Peter Novick, *That Noble Dream: The "Objectivity Question" and the American Historical Profession* (Cambridge: Cambridge University Press, 1998), 1–2.

In addition to being referred to as positivism, historical realism, or even objectivism, sometimes the historical methodology of the eighteenth-nineteenth centuries is also known as historicism. *Historicism* as a term came into vogue after being associated with the German historian Leopold von Ranke, whom we met earlier in chapter 2. In his 1824 history, *Die Geschichte der romanischen und germanischen Völker von 1494 bis 1514* (*History of the Latin and Teutonic Peoples from 1494 to 1514*), von Ranke, who is sometimes recognized as one of the founders of modern history, laid out the objectivist agenda. For instance, history was to follow the rule that "the strict presentation of the facts, contingent and unattractive though they may be is undoubtedly the supreme law,"[78] an assertion that affirms the impartiality with which the historian was to approach his or her subject.

The ability of a historian not only to treat subject matter in a balanced manner but also to wall off his or her own biases from the material was the ideal of objective history. This latter point is exemplified by Lord Acton, who edited a twelve-volume work entitled *The Cambridge Modern History* but did not include personal details about the contributors, as is customary, on the grounds that, "Our scheme requires that nothing shall reveal the country, the religion, or the party to which the writers belong. It is essential not only on the ground that impartiality is the character of legitimate history, but because the work is carried on by men acting together for no other object than the increase of accurate knowledge."[79]

Another characteristic of von Ranke's method, to review from the earlier chapter, was that primary sources, rather than derivative works, were to be preferred in historical investigation. All of this, so far, does not sound too different from the approach of Thucydides, who also was concerned about an impartial approach to the subject and use of reliable sources![80] Yet, Ranke does clearly go beyond the ancient historian to declare the positivist agenda when he states, "the discipline of history—at its highest—is itself called upon, and is able, to lift itself in its own fashion from the investigation and observation of particulars to a universal view of events, to a

---

78. From the introduction reproduced in Stern, *Varieties of History*, 57.

79. Quote taken from the introduction to *The Cambridge Modern History*, reproduced in Stern, *Varieties of History*, 248.

80. This point is also made by Georg Iggers, *Historiography in the Twentieth Century: From Scientific Objectivity to the Postmodern Challenge* (Middletown, Conn.: Wesleyan University Press, 2005), 2.

knowledge of the objectively existing relatedness."[81] History is about real actors and events that actually did take place. And these things are comprehensible. As a result, "Truth is one, not perspectival. Whatever patterns exist in history are 'found' not 'made.'"[82] In other words, history isn't what is perceived. History is what *is*.

In addition to being based in realism and boasting a positivistic underpinning, objectivism had additional elements. First, influenced by the great progress of the Industrial Revolution, which was undergoing great leaps forward with manufacturing, productivity, and efficiency, there was a sense among many nineteenth-century historians not only that time was linear or ever forward moving but that it was progressive. Essentially, for industrial-age historians, civilization as a whole was moving toward an ever better and prosperous future.[83] Of course, this was a significant departure from the ancient historians, who assigned a role to destiny in turning the wheel or history or even the speculative histories of the medieval era were humans always yielded center stage to divine providence.

That is not to say, however, that this trend did not have detractors. A few historians preferred cyclical schemes and held to the idea that periods of deterioration followed periods of improvement.[84] Nonetheless, there was a sense of optimism that colored not only the perception of time but also viewpoints

---

Elements of Historicism

- *Objectivism*: Facts are real and exist outside of the mind of the one perceiving them.
- *Researcher Bias*: Researchers are able to approach a subject with neutrality.
- *Balance*: If an event is both good and evil, or has worthy and unworthy elements, both sides are to be taken into account.
- *Positivism*: The scientific method may be applied in analyzing historical phenomena.
- *Sources*: Primary, accurate sources are to be preferred.
- *Polarities*: There are stark differences between fact and fiction, history and literature.
- *Scope*: Focus on "great men" and political history.

---

81. Von Ranke, in Stern, *Varieties of History*, 59.
82. Novick, *That Noble Dream*, 2.
83. Breisach, *Historiography*, 205–6.
84. Ibid., 213–14.

on the accuracy and certainty that historians could claim about their portraits of the past. Perhaps it was due to this sanguine view of history that historians of this period focused their efforts on recording the histories of remarkable individuals—those illustrious talents (usually male) who helped to propel nations toward their grand destinies—and the political arena in which they worked.

A second important point is that, by identifying so thoroughly with the hard sciences, historicism implied "a sharp division between scientific and literary discourse."[85] Literature was not history. And that was that. Contrary to the position laid out a few pages above which concerns the fuzzy borders exhibited by texts in the classical era in various arenas, like the use of "live speech," the boundaries between the two in the eyes of historicists were inviolable. A text was classified as either history or fiction by virtue of its adherence to reporting brute facts. A made-up speech such as Thucydides's would no doubt be dismissed as fantasy. By the first decades of the twentieth century, although many of the precepts of objective history would continue to influence historiography, criticisms were being raised about some of the more traditional aspects as formulated by von Ranke. As it turns out, the world, and history, would end up being rather more gray than black and white.

Pointing out flaws or weaknesses in historical objectivity as a method is not a task to be undertaken lightly since, within the discipline of history itself, objectivity has shifted from being a mere philosophical question to one that is ideological. As Peter Novick observes,

> It is an enormously charged emotional issue; one in which the stakes are very high, much higher than in any disputes over substantive interpretations. For many, what has been at issue is nothing less than the meaning of the venture to which they have devoted their lives, and thus, to a very considerable extent, the meaning of their own lives. "Objectivity" has been one of the central sacred terms of professional historians like "health"; for physicians or "valor for the profession of arms."[86]

How doubly complicated, then, is a discussion of history, truth, and objectivity within the context of biblical studies! In our discipline it is easy for historicism as a method to become conflated with issues of faith on a

---

85. Iggers, *Historiography*, 2.
86. Novick, *That Noble Dream*, 11.

number of levels, perhaps not least of which is the unspoken assumption that known facts and an objective basis for faith would resolve conflicts of interpretation and result in a unified history, a unitary understanding of the Christ event, and, ultimately, a single faith tradition that would transcend denominationalism. Yet, no matter how tenaciously historians hold to objectivism as a historical presupposition, impartiality, which is a central tenet of objectivism, calls for honest and evenhanded presentation of the critiques of the method of historicism.

From as early as the nineteenth century, the question of research bias and the level of subjectivity in historical research was as much a challenge for historicism as were problems with the concept of realism. Johann Gustav Droysen, for instance, writing nationalistic history that focused on "great men" and the political situation of Germany and thereby conforming to the wider trend of historicism with regard to content and subject matter, nevertheless did remain somewhat skeptical about the knowability of events in a realist model, stating, "This critical view that past events be before us no longer directly, but only in a mediate manner, that we cannot restore them 'objectively,' but can only form out of the 'sources' a more or less subjective apprehension...this, so it seems, must be our point of departure."[87]

By contrast, Frederick Jackson Turner, an American historian, retained the tenets of realism but did understand the whisper of bias that permeates the relativistic needs that the researcher brings to the historical project, stating, "Each age writes history anew with reference to the conditions uppermost in its own time."[88]

Likewise, even the sharp distinction between history and literature was challenged. Thomas Babington Macaulay, to illustrate, reminded those in the profession that history is expressed in narrative form and thus, while not abandoning or embroidering the facts, must be written with attention to stylistic elements and ornamentation. As he picturesquely remarks,

> The effect of historical reading is analogous, in many respects, to foreign travel. The student, like the tourist, is transported into a new state of society. He sees new fashions. He hears new modes of expression.

---

87. As recorded in Stern, *Varieties of History*, 140.
88. "The Significance of History," reproduced in Stern, *Varieties of History*, 200.

His mind is enlarged by contemplating the wide diversities of laws, of morals, and of manners.[89]

Following this literary bent in history, George Macaulay Trevelyan goes so far as to assert that history cannot merely be a science for surely the first duty of the historian is to "tell the story."[90] And, in telling the story, historians eventually became aware that there was not just a tale to be spun about political institutions and "great men," but there was a vast storehouse of subject matter upon which to draw.

Ultimately, by the early part of the twentieth century, historicism found itself increasingly besieged. By the time the older versions of historicism reached the United States, the social and political conditions it presupposed in Europe in a post-Napoleonic era had already been fundamentally transformed.[91] As a consequence, there was a greater need to expand the scope of historical inquiry to take into account social and even economic realities that contravened theories of perpetual progress such as World War I and the Great Depression. In the discipline of history today, historicism in its traditional form has been largely abandoned, though certain aspects, such as an objectivistic view of facts, linger in some quarters, such as in our own field of biblical studies. Even these are under increasing pressure from a variety of competing philosophies that began to have strong influence on historical methodology in the latter part of the twentieth century.

New Testament studies' relationship with historicism is a stormy one, with some factions embracing it while others lambast its weaknesses. The susceptibility to researcher bias, despite historicism's ideal of neutrality, was one point with which historians of first- and second-century Christianity always struggled. This was aptly demonstrated in 1906 by Albert Schweitzer, an Austrian musician, theologian, and physician who published a work that was translated into English as *The Quest of the Historical Jesus*. In that book Schweitzer traced the fruits of critical historical conceptions of Jesus' life during the period in which historicism was flourishing—from Reimarus in the eighteenth century to the close of the nineteenth century. Instead of finding *the* historical Jesus, however, Schweitzer was forced to conclude that

---

89. Reproduced in Stern, *Varieties of History*, 85.
90. From "Clio, A Muse," reproduced in Stern, *Varieties of History*; see 230, 233.
91. Iggers, *Historiography*, 5.

each successive epoch of theology found its own thoughts in Jesus; that was, indeed, the only way in which it could make Him live. But it was not only each epoch that found its reflection in Jesus; each individual created Him in accordance with his own character. There is no historical task which so reveals a man's true self as the writing of a Life of Jesus.[92]

Objective history had failed to produce a unified portrait of Jesus and to eliminate the personal bias of the individual historian who was working within the spirit of his or her own time period. Schweitzer's work essentially preempted any studies seeking the historical Jesus for almost fifty years on the grounds that it was impossible to "recover" the Jesus of history and "theologically unnecessary to base one's faith on the uncertain results of historical research."[93]

Although conscious of the limits of the method of historicism, in the 1950s New Testament historians again took up the search for the teachings of the historical Jesus. Yet this quest, too, was still influenced by the classic realist slant inherent in historicism. As Günther Bornkamm, a leading light of the "New Quest" asserted, "bare facts" existed beyond the mind of the historian.[94] Bornkamm revealed an almost textbook understanding of historical realism when he stated,

> the Gospels justify neither resignation nor skepticism…. Quite clearly what the Gospels report concerning the message, the deeds and the history of Jesus is still distinguished by an authenticity, a freshness, and a distinctiveness not in any way effaced by the Church's Easter faith. These features point us directly to the earthly Jesus.[95]

But, as in the first quest, researchers in this new search for Jesus undertaken in the middle of the twentieth century also were not able to rise above their own place in time and the predispositions of their own contexts but

---

92. Albert Schweitzer, *The Quest of the Historical Jesus* (trans. W. Montgomery; New York: Collier/Macmillan, 1968), 4. See the similar conclusions of Martin Kähler, *The So-Called Historical Jesus and the Historic Biblical Christ* (Philadelphia: Fortress, 1988).

93. David B. Gowler, *What Are They Saying about The Historical Jesus?* (Mahwah, N.J.: Paulist, 2007), 15.

94. Günther Bornkamm, *Jesus of Nazareth* (trans. Irene McLuskey et al.; San Francisco: Harper & Row, 1960), 14.

95. Ibid., 24.

ended up producing a Jesus who "came off sounding like an existentialist philosopher."[96] They too had fallen into the trap of reflecting their own various ideologies, cultures, and places in history in their research.[97] As a result, this second quest was largely abandoned by the late 1960s.

Research focused on the historical Jesus was begun anew in the 1980s, and one strand in particular, the Jesus Seminar, exemplified not progress away from historicism, but rather entrenchment within that paradigm. Designed to determine an accurate list of what Jesus said and did, which implies the actions and words were perceived to be objective realities that participants might know, the seminar was devoted to separating fact from fiction. In a nutshell, its members wanted to point to solid evidence where they could declare "That's Jesus!" as opposed to what was attributed to him by later tradition.[98] And why was this process necessary? Because the seminar members believed that there was a weakness with the sources about Jesus. The Gospels were not the primary sources that practitioners of historicism preferred but "hearsay evidence" that scholars had to be cautious about taking at face value.[99]

But making a hard distinction between fact and fiction and being concerned about the reliability of sources were not the only points at which the Jesus Seminar held fast to the precepts of historicism. The participants also sought to limit the problems with bias that had been inherent in earlier quests to discover the Jesus of history. To achieve this goal, the seminar structured the investigation as an effort of a scholarly collective rather than the undertaking of individuals, thinking this would mute the bias of any single individual. Further, the group would use democratic vote in order to arrive at consensus, thereby, in theory, avoiding partiality. These proceedings also employed a scientific-style method. Each pericope was submitted to rigorous analysis comprised of a common set of "rules of evidence" that had been formulated by members of the seminar. These included such criteria as "Jesus sayings and parables are often characterized by exaggeration, humor, and paradox"[100] and the idea that

---

96. Ben Witherington III, *The Jesus Quest: The Third Search for the Jew of Nazareth* (Downers Grove, Ill.: InterVarsity Press, 1995), 11.

97. Gowler, *What Are They Saying*, 24.

98. Robert M. Funk and the Jesus Seminar, *The Gospel of Mark: Red Letter Edition* (Sonoma, Calif.: Polebridge, 1991), xx.

99. Ibid., 29.

100. Ibid., 33.

"hard sayings are frequently softened in the process of transmission to adapt them to the conditions of daily living."[101] Furthermore, the scientific aspect was inherent in the uniform application of these criteria. No passage would receive preferential treatment. All passages would be examined equally—or at least that was the original ideal.

In actuality, despite clinging to the precepts of historicism rigorously, the Jesus Seminar was ensnared by the same pitfalls that earlier quests experienced. First, while bias of an individual may be subverted by a democratic process, it would be fallacious thinking to insist that a collective is impartial. If groups were free of preconceived notions, by analogy politicians would have no need to tailor campaign speeches to specific voting demographics and lobby groups! As it turned out, the Jesus Seminar participants, as a group, were not as theologically diverse as might be hoped, and their ideology shaped their results.[102] Second, some of the individual "rules of evidence" were questionable in their own right. To be sure, any scientific experiment is valid only to the degree that the method is accepted as compelling to others in the field. Third, the assumptions with which the Jesus Seminar operated were a reflection of its own time period. To illustrate, while it was true that there seemed to be an emerging consensus that the Gospels were not eyewitness accounts at points in the twentieth century, that assumption is no longer viewed with as much accord as it has been, particularly in the case of the Fourth Gospel, which claims to contain firsthand evidence.[103]

Lest this exposition about the prevalence of historicism in research concerning the life of Jesus leave the impression that this method, which has long fallen out of favor in the wider field of history, is limited to topics related to the Gospels, it is important to note that historicism is pervasive in many historical investigations of New Testament texts. One must concede, however, that scholars who employ newer and different methods have been gaining attention and stronger followings during

---

101. Ibid., 37. The full list of criteria may be found on pp. 29–52.

102. An extensive overview of the criticism that has been launched against the Jesus Seminar may be found in Gowler, *What Are They Saying*, 43–56.

103. Richard Bauckham, *Jesus and the Eyewitnesses: The Gospels as Eyewitness Testimony* (Grand Rapids: Eerdmans, 2006), 6. See also Arthur J. Dewey "The Eyewitness of History: Visionary Consciousness in the Fourth Gospel," in *Jesus in Johannine Tradition* (ed. Robert T. Fortna and Tom Thatcher; Louisville: Westminster John Knox, 2001).

the past quarter century. The late Pauline scholar J. Christiaan Beker, for instance, signaled that he had made a shift away from historicism in 1984 when he wrote:

> Present hermeneutical debate teaches us that there is no exegesis without eisegesis: interpretation does not take place within a vacuum, but includes necessarily the particular perspective of the interpreter, without thereby licensing a distortion of the text. Although my book focuses on a historical investigation of Paul's thought, my stance as a Christian theologian should have penetrated this work.[104]

This quote shows two aspects of Beker's break with historicism. On the one hand the assumption that neutrality on the part of the historian is possible has been abandoned. On the other, Beker is linking history with interpretation. History is not merely the recitation of bare objective facts but is mediated through interpreters.

Nonetheless, two years after Beker published these comments and almost fifty decades after historicism had given way to other methods and a focus on social history in professional history, Howard M. Teeple was still busy codifying historicism in his introductory New Testament textbook on the method of historical criticism. In this primer for students he outlined an approach that was, in his words, "consistent with scientific methodology" while at the same time stressing that students and researchers must be willing to put away bias in favor of what the evidence revealed. They could, he believed, achieve objectivity.[105]

In all of this, Teeple seemed unaware that decades earlier in the run-up to World War II the tide was already turning against historicism in academic departments of history. Certainly in the 1930s speakers at the American Historical Society recognized that "one generation's truth was not another's" while at the same time acknowledging that the selection and ordering of materials was always influenced by "biases, prejudices, beliefs, affections, general upbringing, and experience, particularly social and economic."[106] Granted, there was a revival of a more modest form of

---

104. J. Christiaan Beker, preface to *Paul the Apostle: The Triumph of God in Life and Thought* (repr.; Philadelphia: Fortress, 1984), xiii.

105. Howard M. Teeple, *The Historical Approach to the Bible* (Evanston, Ill: Religion and Ethics Institute, 1982), excerpted from 145–53.

106. Novick, *That Noble Dream*, 254.

historicism following World War II, yet even then historians were a bit more hesitant about the extent to which "scholarship was value-free and objective."[107] Nonetheless, by 1982, when Teeple's work was fresh off the press, even the premises of objectivity and the reliability of the scientific method had become increasingly sidelined in the historical guild. The field of history moved on while, isolated in his own discipline, Teeple was still practicing the method of historicism.

The idea that biblical scholarship might lag behind another discipline by a decade or two should not be unduly surprising. After all, it takes time to research currents in other cognate disciplines, write textbooks reflecting new viewpoints, and subsequently train a new generation of students who will employ the new methods. In the information age, multidisciplinary databases and electronic books and articles help speed up the processes of intellectual exchange between academic fields. This is reflected by the fact that, during the waning of the twentieth century, New Testament scholars would increasingly experiment with a wider assortment of historical approaches. But communication between disciplines still isn't infallible.

5.4.2. New History/New Historicism

Each field has its own specialty vocabulary, professional journals, and methodological paradigms that, at times, make communication between disciplines difficult. Back in the age of the dinosaurs, when I was a student and indexes were in paper format, I remember an afternoon of research agony in which I searched the paper journal holdings for hours trying to track down an article on the *Fiscus Judaicus* that had been mentioned in a footnote. I was convinced that I should be able to find it in the *Journal of Religious Studies*, but it simply wasn't there. I went back to the footnote to confirm the citation. Yes, I should be looking in *JRS*. So I returned again to the stacks and the *Journal of Religious Studies*, thinking that I must have overlooked it. But I failed again. Finally, I humbly approached a reference librarian, who pulled out a trusty list of journal abbreviations and directed me to the *Journal of Roman Studies*. Apparently, I had been locked into my "disciplinary country" and needed to cross the border into classical studies.[108]

---

107. Ibid., 321.

108. In my discipline centrism and naiveté, I had conflated the abbreviations *JRS* and *JRelS*.

In the midst of a discussion on historicism, it is important to acknowledge that there are a number of terms that seem at first glance to be similar to *historicism* but, much as the designation *JRS* created confusion for me many years ago, are not easy to unravel. Thus, even though it requires stepping a bit out of our chronological treatment of historiography, it is important to address and define New History[109] and New Historicism.

One definition of New History is that it is an alternate name for Progressive History, a pre–World War II American reactionary movement against histories that were European in focus. Taking the name *New History* from a 1912 publication by James Harvey Robinson, progressive historians otherwise known as New Historians called for history to be more relevant to the contemporary American situation, which at the time was marked by frontier expansion. Thus, the focus of traditional historicism on "great men," military history, and politics that was popular in many history departments at the turn of the last century was superseded in New History by economic interests and concerns for the social ills that were side effects of the uncontrolled momentum of industrialization. It even began to draw ever more broadly from the social sciences including sociology, psychology, and anthropology in terms of method.[110]

But even though the term *New History* was used to describe a turn in history that was preoccupied with recording the triumphs and failures of American democratic society of the early twentieth century,[111] it is also used in a completely different way in the contemporary era—as a synonym for *New Historicism*.

The present-day term *New History* or *New Historicism*, among other designations,[112] is nomenclature for a method employed primarily by literary critics, not historians. Now, at this point, it would make sense to

---

109. The use of *New History* is a problem of reification. *New history* has been used for a century to describe various movements. Even Peter Burke, who employs the term to describe various practices that developed in the 1970s and 1980s, is troubled by it. He traces the various iterations of *New History* back to 1867, when Rankean history itself was described as "the New Historiography." See "The New History: Its Past and Its Future" in *New Perspectives on Historical Writing* (ed. Peter Burke; University Park: Pennsylvania State University Press, 2004), 7.

110. For more detail on the progressive historians, consult Richard Hofstadter, *The Progressive Historians: Turner, Beard, Parrington* (New York: Knopf, 1969). See also Breisach, *Historiography*, 417.

111. Iggers, *Historiography*, 34.

112. New Historicism also goes by names other than *New History*, including his-

offer up a definition of New Historicism and say, "New Historicism is x and it does y and z," but that would do a disservice to one of the central tenets of New Historicism—that the method should be open ended and defy attempts to describe or classify it. Ultimately, in this section we will go against this premise in the method itself and use terminology and categories that are associated with the philosophy of history to define New Historicism fairly precisely. We will even list its characteristics in a neat sidebar, but when we do so, it is important to remember that we will be imposing structure on a method that conceives of itself as having no structure. So hang tight: we will gradually tease out the description. But to get there and be as true as possible to the heart of New Historicism we will use an inductive method that first describes the general background of the movement and hopefully helps convey the very unique freewheeling aspect of this method, which in and of itself is an important contribution to a survey of techniques for interpreting texts.

Those who label themselves literary critics who make use of New Historicism deliberately choose "their various practices in contradistinction to those of their forerunners, the hordes of traditional literary historians whose naive historicism the new historicists were allegedly trying to overcome."[113] The New Historicism movement originally took off in the literature department at the University of California in the 1980s. Eventually, though, the trend came to the attention of biblical scholars, who, after being preceded by a consultation unit at the Society of Biblical Literature in 1999, began a six-year group on New Historicism and the Hebrew Bible in 2002.[114]

New Historicism in the style of the last thirty years considers itself cross-disciplinary. Historians such as Georg Iggers and Peter Jürgen, however, do not yet seem ready to embrace these new "new historians" as fellow practitioners of the discipline of history but describe them instead as postmodernist literary critics.[115]

That being said, because the new New Historicism has—despite being a literary endeavor—borrowed heavily from many disciplines, it is pos-

---

torical-materialist criticism, cultural materialism, and critical historicism. See Hens-Piazza, *New Historicism*, 5.

113. Jürgen Pieters, "New Historicism: Postmodern Historiography between Narrativism and Heterology," *History and Theory* 39 (2000): 21.

114. Hens-Piazza, *New Historicism*.

115. Iggers, *Historiography*, 10–11.

sible to draw some broad comparisons between it and familiar turn-of-the-last-century historicism. The first characteristic of literature's New Historicism relates to conventions of style. This type of interpretation by the literary critic is often peppered with anecdotes, which help to illustrate that there is a personal encounter between the reader or researcher and the subject matter.

Anecdotes also serve another purpose. For those who favor this rhetorical device when writing about literature, an anecdote is separate from a time continuum and "just lets history happen."[116] To put it another way, rather than a cause-and-effect or linear sense of time, for postmodern New Historians time is chaotic. Imagine a herd of cows grazing in a field. While one may occasionally bump into another, there often does not appear to be any planned trajectory on the part of one cow to intercept a peer in the pasture. Two of the placid beasts may simply go for the same clump of grass at the same time and knock noses. For the postmodernist new historian, each point of interaction may be expressed as an anecdote.

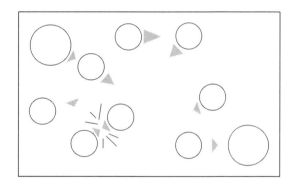

If the cows were people encountering a text, or a variety of texts, each bump represents a change in the reader's personal history and hence in one's impression of the text. And, the text may be perceived variously by different people (or even disparate communities) at other points in time.

Consequently, this element in New Historicism explains my own choice to start a survey of this literary method the incident about my confusion between *JRelS* and *JRS*. It was an attempt to illustrate how the story as expressed in a text is freed from its original sequence to allow for a serendipitous encounter with other communities and readers. In essence, in such a scheme there is no reason not to juxtapose my own introductions and interactions with a classical periodical that occurred many years ago

---

116. Hens-Piazza, *New Historicism*, 4.

in the United Kingdom with my first encounter with the phenomenon of literature's version of New Historicism while writing this book.

Because the phenomenon of New Historicism, postmodern style, is a reaction by literary critics against the traditional historicism that had seeped into their discipline, there are other elements besides the philosophical understanding of time that may be compared and contrasted between the two approaches. First, as opposed to an interpreter approaching his or her subject as a neutral agent, as is assumed in simplistic formulations of the scientific method in the mode of old fashioned historicism, the act of analyzing a piece of literature inevitably involves subjectivity. Again, my choice of using a personal anecdote and writing in first person is intended to highlight this subjective element of scholarship. My own experience of modern-day New Historicism itself and, to be certain, how I would approach interpreting a text from a new historical perspective, differs from how another individual might experience it and proceed. This subjectivist underpinning of New Historicism explains why postmodern New Historians themselves are reluctant to define or lay out "a method" of interpretation, preferring instead to present New Historicism as an ethos or sensibility expressed variously by individual literary critics.[117]

Elements of Current Day New Historicism

- *Objectivism replaced by skepticism*: Past may not be known; language is inadequate to the task of true communication.
- *Researcher Bias*: Researchers are products of their time, places, and experiences and bring these backgrounds to the table when interpreting texts. Interpretation is subjective.
- *Method*: Declines identifying a single method or theory. A typical technique, though, is the use of anecdotes.
- *Time*: Chaotic.
- *Polarities disappear*: There are no essential differences between history and literature. Literature shapes communities, and communities shape literature.
- *Sources*: How the source was produced, not what it indicates about the past, is of primary interest.
- *Scope*: Focus is on literature, specifically the communities in which it is produced and the communities that consume it. Also a tendency to look for the "marginalized" in texts.

---

117. Ibid., 5. Pieters maintains that Greenblatt's approach itself is a combination of psychoanalytical and discursive. See Pieters, "New Historicism," 22.

In addition to rejecting traditional historicism's claim of impartiality on the part of the researcher, New Historians also question the realism or objectivism inherent in historicism. Not only are there concerns about the use of language and signifiers as one aspect of this tension between reality and the expressions that attempt to represent it, but also some postmodernists approach antirealism—the idea that there is no world outside of an individual's mind. At the very least, there is a skepticism that is broad enough to allow for alternate theories and interpretations of the past to exist side by side. To put it simply, there are "pasts" rather than "the past."

Perhaps this viewpoint about the dubious knowability of the past has affected the use of sources by New Historians. The professional historian uses the source to point to something external to itself; the New Historian is focused on what gave rise to the source or how it came to be produced.[118] To illustrate, given a pottery shard Z, the New Historian would treat the shard no differently than a text and might ask what social, political, and other forces gave rise to the production of a pot like pottery shard Z. By contrast, a historian wants to look beyond the text to explore other questions: What does pottery shard Z tell us about the family who dwelled here and used this pot? What does finding this shard in this place tell us about trade routes in this part of the world at the time this type of pottery would have been in use? Why is it here, and how did it get here? Between the two disciplines of history and literature, the questions and starting places related to sources are different.

To some extent, however, the concerns that New Historians have about production reveal that they are heavily influenced by the thought of Karl Marx. Marx was one of the most influential thinkers in the twentieth century and had a significant impact not only in the discipline of literature but also on history. But the way Marx helped to shape the field of history is a story for the next chapter, where we will jump back into our place in the chronological treatment of the methods of writing history.

---

118. Hens-Piazza, *New Historicism*, 28–29.

6

HISTORY BLOSSOMS: THE MODERN ERA TO THE MID-TWENTIETH CENTURY

In any discipline, some methods may have bursts of popularity and then wane. Others may be transformed by subsequent generations of researchers and endure in their new forms for decades, or else they may have basic tenets that are adopted by the practitioners of yet other methods. In any event, the approaches that historians take for their investigations tend to reflect the larger interests and intellectual streams of the societies that give rise to them. Historicism, for instance, was forged in the crucible of the Enlightenment and Industrial Revolution, where optimism that science could unravel the mysteries of the world and make it knowable was echoed in historians' realism and positivism; the seemingly never-ending forward momentum and innovation of the Industrial Revolution justified confidence in speculative histories and linear or progressive concepts of time; and the educational systems and values of the culture at large kept the content of history largely focused on political matters and the contributions made by great men, as opposed to women or the marginalized.

Even though the twentieth and early twenty-first centuries have been distinguished by a proliferation of historiographical methods that gradually moved away from historicism, they too are a reflection of larger intellectual currents that affected how historians viewed time, used sources, and even selected their materials and subjects for study. Martha Howell and Walter Prevenier identify two primary influences that impacted the way that historians chose to do their work throughout this period: interdisciplinarity and "a self-consciousness about the assumptions that propel their inquiry."[1] At the risk of being overly simplistic, it is possible to assert that these two factors are changes that may be traced to the

---

1. Howell and Prevenier, *From Reliable Sources*, 109.

shift from the industrial age to the information age. Interdisciplinarity is facilitated when specialists from disparate fields have the opportunity to dialogue and exchange ideas with ease. Innovations such as the automobile, the telephone, air travel, television, mass-market publications, copy machines, personal computers, the Internet, and a host of other inventions made this increasingly possible throughout the twentieth century. Likewise, self-consciousness about methods is driven by the same innovations because communication and travel technology provide outlets for those who have had no power or who reside in far-flung corners of the globe to communicate their own viewpoints. When these voices are heard, they consequently make it obvious that there are more ways to approach subjects than those in the particular intellectual stream in which a given researcher is fishing.

In this chapter we will explore the methods that reveal the interdisciplinary nature of historiography in the first half of the twentieth century. In the one that follows, attention will shift to the methods that incorporate new lenses or vantage points that have become prevalent in the last few decades. Between the two chapters there are nine brief sketches of some of the major trends in the craft of writing history in the Western tradition. They are presented roughly in chronological order based on either when the thought was first conceived or, alternately, when it became practiced on a wide scale within history writing. There is, though, a caveat about the chronological presentation. While it is true that to some extent some later developments depend on, react against, or rework select earlier methods, the reader is cautioned not to assume that later methods supersede earlier ones. Many of these methods still have their adherents and the various techniques are practiced simultaneously in the academy just as, in our own field, literary criticism, poststructuralism, and redaction criticism each stepped onto the stage of biblical interpretation at different times yet all still inform research in various quarters of our subject.

Also, historians well versed in historiography may recognize that several methods or trends are missing from the treatment in these chapters. For instance, there is no separate section on oral history. Similarly, the changes wrought on national histories in the period between the two world wars are not addressed. National histories and oral histories are, in a way, remote from the interests of New Testament scholars, whose primary focus is on antiquity. In addition, professionals in the field of history will notice that the examples selected to illustrate each method will not be drawn from the usual canon of notable historians. E. P. Thompson, Fernand Braudel and others will be conspicuously absent. Instead, because this is an interdisciplinary work, the writings of New Testament scholars will be referenced as models that make use of a particular historiographical approach whenever possible.

Selecting a place at which to begin the sketches of the various methods is fairly obvious. Karl Marx is the thinker who comes to mind. Although chronologically Marx's publications first appeared in the mid-1800s, he is still the "single most influential theorist for twentieth-century historical writing."[2] Not only would his thought have lasting influence on what came to be known as Marxist history but the theoretical underpinnings of his approach would be adopted by some revisionist historians and even post-colonial interpreters of the later twentieth century. Both of these movements will receive their own treatments later in chapter 7.

6.1. MARXIST HISTORY

6.1.1. AN OVERVIEW OF MATERIALISM

The most comprehensive statement of Marx's theory of history is found in *The German Ideology*, a work that he coauthored with Friedrich Engels in 1846.[3] Broadly speaking, Marx's understanding of history is interdisciplinary to the extent that it draws inspiration from or resonates with three distinct fields in the academy, the first of which is philosophy.

In their writings, Marx and Engels thoroughly engage the philosophical system of Hegel. The German philosopher is well known for promoting a dialectic in which simple ideas are subject to underlying conflicts. This friction is resolved by the formation of more complex ideas wherein each previous conflict is sublated, or incorporated into a newer principle that is broad enough to handle it. Sometimes this is simplistically expressed as a cycle of thesis, antithesis, and synthesis. The gritty aspect upon which Marx chose to ground his version of Hegel's dialectic was class struggle, a feature of society that Marx believed characterized all of human experi-

---

2. Ana Green and Kathleen Troup, *The Houses of History: A Critical Reader in Twentieth-Century History and Theory* (New York: New York University Press, 1999), 33.

3. Karl Marx with Friedrich Engels, *The German Ideology* (Great Books on Philosophy; Amherst, N.Y.: Prometheus, 1998).

ence. Ultimately this focus on class dynamics in Marx's thought foreshadowed trends that would develop in the field of sociology.

Sociology and philosophy, however, were just two legs of Marx's system. The third was economics. He asserted that class struggle was precipitated by unequal distribution of the means of production—both raw materials and the labor that transformed them. This particular aspect of the theory is why Marxism sometimes goes by the name *materialism*. In this worldview, the privileged elites, or ruling class, exploit and oppress the masses by obtaining power through control of the political, legal, and other societal structures in order to safeguard their economic interests.

In spite of how grim such a system sounds, Marx's use of dialectic comes into play at this point to inspire hope. The tensions caused by severe inequality coupled with occasional breakthroughs in technology result in instability that permits dramatic upheavals or even revolutions. As a result of this conflict, existing social systems and class structures are re-engineered. The goal of these changes is to better value the contribution of all individuals, whose separate identities had previously been subsumed under the laborer role. These modifications to the social structure in turn set the stage for a new era of exploitation and oppression when the newly emerged dominant class gains control over economic resources and, in its own time, will eventually be overthrown by a group with less power.

Even though at first glance this view of history is cyclical and has an inherent determinism, there is a twist. With each turn of the dialec-

---

Elements of Marxist Histories

- *Philosophy*: Speculative. The future is envisioned as a classless utopian society.
- *Method*: The system is propelled by dialectic that turns on the concepts of class struggle, unequal distribution of material resources and labor, control of power and wealth by the elites, and ultimately revolution.
- *Scope or Type of History*: Focus is on economic history, particularly the history of labor or the underclass. Political history also plays a large role because political structures are tools by which the powerful retain control of resources.
- *Time*: Although there is a looping aspect inherent in the dialectical method, there is an overarching forward progress in the pattern.

tic wheel, modest progress is made toward a utopian, classless society in which leaders are no longer necessary.[4] To put it another way, time is more like a spring that curls ever forward toward a positive end, enabling this method of history to be classified as speculative rather than analytical.

6.1.2. KNOTTY ISSUES FOR MARXISM AND BIBLICAL INTERPRETATION

In the past few decades, Marxism has had a significant influence on New Testament studies, despite a reluctance by some biblical interpreters to identify their work as Marxist.[5] The use of Marxism in our discipline has taken two tracks. First, it has been paired with liberation theology and then focused on texts that contain apocalypses, as has been pointed out by Randall Reed.[6] Reed is concerned that this three-way connection between Marxism, liberation theology, and apocalypticism is untenable. Basically, Reed finds it perplexing that biblical interpreters such as Ched Meyers and José Porofino Miranda have taken several precepts of Marxism to heart in their interpretive strategies without wrestling with the very real issue that Marx himself viewed religion as the "opium of the people."[7] To be sure, Reed is right to emphasize that Christianity, with its view of the apocalyptic end time brought about through God's intervention, and Marxism, which is characterized by a vision of a socialist utopia that is achieved without divine influence, are fundamentally different systems with different ends.[8]

The second sphere in which a few scholars, such as Richard Horsley, have adopted Marxism involves the dynamics and tension between a peasant class and wealthy elite in Judea. Horsley sets out the basics of class conflict in a work that he wrote with John S. Hanson in 1985 entitled *Bandits, Prophets, and Messiahs: Popular Movements at the Time of Jesus.*[9] In more

---

4. Howell and Prevenier, *From Reliable Sources*, 142.

5. Neil Elliott, "Marxism and the Postcolonial Study of Paul," in *The Colonized Apostle: Paul through Postcolonial Eyes* (ed. Christopher D. Stanley; Paul in Critical Contexts; Minneapolis: Augsburg Fortress, 2011), 34.

6. Randall W. Reed, *A Clash of Ideologies: Marxism, Liberation Theology, and Apocalypticism in New Testament Studies* (PTMS 136; Eugene, Ore.: Pickwick, 2010), ix.

7. Ibid., 3.

8. Nonetheless, Mark T. Gilderhus comments that most historians prefer to avoid the predictive elements inherent in philosophies of history such as Marx's *History and Historians*, 49.

9. Richard A. Horsley with John S. Hanson, *Bandits, Prophets, and Messiahs: Pop-*

recent decades he has applied the same sensitivity about social conflict to the complex relationship between the Roman Empire and early Christianity, a religion whose adherents were from far-flung regions yet still subjugated to Roman rule.[10]

While Horsley has not been the only one to write on this topic in recent years, some works that focus on issues related to empire and what impact Roman rule had on societal dynamics are akin to postcolonial historiography, which studies the reactions of a given group has in coping with the cultural legacy of imperial hegemony.[11] That being said, books on the New Testament and empire at the present time are concerned with issues of power and authority, the unequal distribution of resources between those who rule and their subjects, and struggle or opposition between the two groups, all of which are classic ingredients in Marxism. These elements are all clearly articulated by Richard A. Horsley in his 2004 edited volume, *Paul and the Roman Imperial Order*. In his introduction to that book he identifies the "Roman imperial order as the context of Paul's mission" and asserts, "instead of being opposed to Judaism, Paul's gospel of Christ was opposed to the Roman Empire."[12] A few sentences later, Horsley even talks about first-century "class struggles," "power," and "wealth" in true Marxist fashion, saying, "Paul set his gospel of Christ ... in opposition to the Roman imperial order: the whole system of hierarchical values, power relations, and ideology of peace and security generated by the wealthy, powerful, and nobly born and dominated by the rulers of this age."[13] The use of these key Marxist catchphrases, particularly "opposition" indicates a very clear grasp of the Marxist dialectic. Despite the helpful insights that arise from utilizing a Marxist methodology, there are a few difficulties in such a strict dialectical theory that must be acknowledged.

---

ular Movements at the Time of Jesus (New Voices in Biblical Studies; San Francisco: Harper & Row, 1985).

10. Richard A. Horsley, ed., *Paul and Empire: Religion and Power in Roman Imperial Society* (Valley Forge, Pa.: Trinity Press International, 1997).

11. See the treatment by Neil Elliott, "Marxism and the Postcolonial Study of Paul," in Stanley, *Colonized Apostle*, 34–50. Stephen Moore worries about the anachronism inherent in projecting "postcolonialism," a post-WWII concept, onto Rome's relationship with its provinces: "Paul after Empire" in Stanley, *Colonized Apostle*, 21–22.

12. Richard A. Horsley, *Paul and the Roman Imperial Order* (Harrisburg, Pa.: Trinity Press International, 2004), 3.

13. Ibid.

Setting up binary opposites between oppressed and oppressor, or ruled and ruler, can automatically cause one to overlook the fact that each of the two groups may not be as homogenous as appears at first glance. The oppressed, rather than merely being unified, may include a variety of different subgroups with different interests, cultures, and ideologies of their own. All of these may be subaltern, or without a voice, because they have been silenced by the dominant ideology.[14]

Another difficulty with some, though not all, Marxist histories is the danger of slipping into an oversimplified economic determinism. It is not necessarily the case that every incident, reaction, or accomplishment in the past stems from economic causes. As Carl R. Trueman observers, one must be wary of reducing "history to a sound bite.... Class struggle is helpful for understanding some events, but clearly inappropriate in addressing others."[15]

Lest one think that this exposition is overly critical of Marxist history writing, it must be pointed out that there isn't a single extant theory about how to investigate the past that is without points of vulnerability. However, it is worth noting that, at the same time Marxism was becoming more prevalent in New Testament studies, in the 1980s and 1990s,[16] other historiographical methods in the field of professional history deliberately distanced themselves from Marxism. Social history is one of them.

6.2. SOCIAL HISTORY

Even though he served in the prior section as the poster child of Marxist history, Richard Horsley has been accused of keeping his methodological cards close to his vest[17] and using alternate terminology when describing his approach to the past. It is true that in *Bandits, Prophets, and Messiahs* he never uses the word *Marxism*, even though he and his coauthor, John S. Hanson, are preoccupied with concerns related to the "Jewish peasantry,"[18]

14. In theories that have been developed by Marxist historians, it is possible that at least one or more of these factions has "false consciousness" and identifies with interests that are the same as those of the oppressor.

15. Carl R. Trueman, *Histories and Fallacies* (Wheaton, Ill.: Crossway, 2010), 107.

16. See Elliott, "Marxism," 45–50.

17. Ibid., 34.

18. Horsley and Hanson, *Bandits*, xviii.

are worried about Josephus, who is "hostile" to the common people,[19] and seek to understand the "social conflicts" and "turmoil and revolt" in the era of Jesus.[20] Instead, Horsley and Hanson profess to be exploring the "social history of selected groups"[21] and using "social scientific methods."[22]

Although it is the case that Marxism does have a sociological element, as has been pointed out in the previous description of the method, Anna Green and Kathleen Troup are quick to note that "to conflate the broad body of social history with the work of Marxist historians may be to miss the very clear distinction between them."[23] To be certain, while Marxism takes capitalism as its starting point and is concerned with the economic and political structures that impact wider culture, social history more widely construed tends to investigate social phenomena apart from politics and is skeptical of Marxism's economic determinism.[24]

At this point, it is probably good to take a step back and define terms a little more carefully. The phrase *social-science approaches*, which appears in Horsley and Hanson, if we recall from chapter 1, in which we were defining how historical criticism related to history, is an umbrella designation employed by biblical scholars and not necessarily historians. It designates methods influenced by many disciplines outside of the natural sciences like psychology, economics, and, of course, sociology, just to name a few. Within that descriptor, the

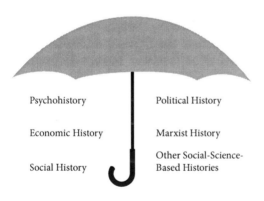

Psychohistory   Political History

Economic History   Marxist History

Social History   Other Social-Science-Based Histories

term *social history* refers to the approach that stemmed from sociology itself, even though, as we shall see, social history has an amoeba-like tendency to try to engulf other branches of social science history for itself.

---

19. Ibid., xix, xxi.
20. Ibid., xx.
21. Ibid., xvii.
22. Ibid., xx.
23. Green and Troup, *Houses of History*, 33.
24. Ibid., 34.

Social history is the subject that will occupy our attention for the next few paragraphs.

Social history, which claims to have no single methodological predisposition despite the tendency of many practitioners to try to explain human behaviors in terms of socially determined patterns and categories, comes in various flavors depending on the nationality and specific context of the researcher. Thus there are few common denominators.[25] This is, of course, only natural since each nationality tends to have its own social conventions and social institutions, the building blocks of social theory. To be sure, researchers living in far-flung places have the advantage over outsiders when it comes to "knowing their own cultures, social conventions and local geographies well."[26]

The most well documented strand of social history is associated with France. That country has given birth to at least three and perhaps four waves of social history.[27] In fact the third, which blossomed in the 1970s, is sometimes known in France as *nouvelle histoire*, or "new history."[28] Of course, this adds one more layer of confusing taxonomy to a list of labels that favor the word *new*, including *New Historians*, *new progressives*, and *New Historicism*, which were all discussed at the end of the previous chapter.

In any event, the first version of the French social-history approach got its start under the influence of those thinkers who published in the journal *Annales: Économies, Sociétés, Civilizations*, which was begun by Lucien Febvre and Marc Bloch in the late 1920s. Taking a cue from title of this journal, these French social historians came to be known as the *Annales* School or, simply, the *Annales*.

In its earliest formulation, rather than giving priority to political history, as Marxist historians often do, or to biographies, which were popular in traditional historicism, social historians explored how various elements of sociology and the other social sciences play contributing roles

---

25. Iggers, *Historiography*, 42.

26. Peter N. Stearns, "Social History Present and Future," *JSH* 37 (2003): 15.

27. Green and Troup, *Houses of History*, 93.

28. Peter Burke, "The New History: Its Past and Its Future," in *New Perspectives on Historical Writing* (2nd ed.; ed. Peter Burke; University Park: Pennsylvania State University Press, 2001), 2. Theodore Zeldin resists the term *new history* when applied to social history, given his conception that social history has "always represented dissatisfaction with existing explanations" and had, since its very earliest time, demanded "new clues to understanding the past" ("Social History and Total History," *JSH* 10 [1976]: 238).

in developing pictures of the past. The advantage of this was twofold. By sidestepping biographies, which tended to focus on "kings, politicians, and parliaments," history was democratized history; other groups of people, not just those individuals who garnered the most attention, also had pasts. [29] The second benefit from this stance was that it permitted an interest in economics that didn't depend on Marxian economic determinism. It is worth noting that the de-emphasis on politics was held so stringently by social historians that well into the 1970s the editorial board of *Annales* refused to print articles dealing with political problems or social hierarchies.[30]

Although claiming neutrality in regard to the wide variety of methods with which it experimented, one phase of social history evidenced a love affair with quantitative analyses where all available records, such as parish registers, were broken down statistically to garner insights into moral behavior, sexuality, and a host of other topics. Although still boasting a substantial following, this trend has subsequently faded from its domination of mainstream social history.

Another characteristic associated with social history was "rebellion against the specialisation of history into a distinct discipline."[31] Instead, members of the *Annales* School advocated boldly breaking out of the ruts of traditional history by exploring the other social sciences more broadly. In essence, apart from political science, social history envisioned a grand "total history" that encompassed vast regions of subject matter and even subsumed within its amorphous borders disciplines that previously had not previously fallen within the purview of historiography. As social historian Peter Stearns himself quips, "I once argued that no aspect of human behavior should be denied to social history, not even sleep. And now we have some really promising efforts even on sleep."[32] Social history, however, is not without limitations. It has a tendency to ignore individuals in favor of "group categories and social structural explanations,"[33] and it is possible to question its prejudicial stance against political history

---

29. Zeldin, "Social History," 238.

30. Michael Harsgar, "Total History: The 'Annales' School," *JCH* 13 (1978): 8.

31. Zeldin, "Social History," 239.

32. Stearns, "Social History," 12.

33. Paula S. Fass, "Cultural History/Social History: Some Reflections on a Continuing Dialogue," *JSH* 37 (2003): 39.

since political history may offer viable explanations for social and cultural phenomena.

Despite its weaknesses, social history is a vibrant strand of historiography and has much to offer New Testament interpreters, particularly in regard to its call for scholars to constantly explore new ideas and new topics as part of historical investigations. Indeed, a fair number of biblical scholars have taken this challenge to heart when studying the early Christian epoch. There is no shortage of examples of social-history approaches, but one of the classic texts is Gerd Theissen's *The Social Setting of Pauline Christianity: Essays on Corinth*. The final chapter of his work concerns methodological considerations and includes his helpful working definition of the sociological project. He writes,

> A sociological statement seeks to describe and explain interpersonal behavior with reference to those characteristics which transcend the personal. First of all, then, a sociological question is less concerned with what is individual than with what is typical, recurrent, general. Second, it is less concerned with the singular conditions of a specific situation than with structural relationships which apply to several situations. There fore, a sociology of primitive Christianity has the task of describing and analyzing the interpersonal behavior of members of primitive Christian groups.[34]

Sociology, however, represents only one arena in which historiography in the twentieth century demonstrated its interdisciplinary interests.

6.3. PSYCHOHISTORY

Martha Howell and Walter Prevenier observe that "not all of historians' encounters with the social sciences have been successful."[35] Most certainly, the intersection between psychology and history has had an extraordinarily rocky reception in the academy. Anna Green and Kathleen Troup, for instance, describe psychohistory as "one of the most controversial areas of twentieth-century historiography"[36] and mention that it

---

34. Gerd Theissen, *The Social Setting of Pauline Christianity: Essays on Corinth* (trans. John H. Schütz; Philadelphia: Fortress, 1982), 176–77.

35. Howell and Prevenier, *From Reliable Sources*, 95.

36. Troup and Green, *The Houses of History*, 59.

is an approach that the historical community regards with suspicion.[37] Its troubled reception is largely due to problems in "obtaining the appropriate evidence on which to base a psychoanalytic interpretation," since the psychological norms of bygone eras are not necessarily known.[38] There are two other barriers to the widespread acceptance of this mode of historical interpretation. The first is that the empathy that the researcher employs as an integral part of the analytic process results in the conundrum that "no two researchers will interpret the data in an identical way."[39] To put it bluntly, the ability to verify the claims made by psychohistory is frequently in question. Truth be told, though, in more recent years there is growing recognition that all interpretations are subjective and objectivity in history is ever more elusive. Thus this argument no longer has the force that it did when psychohistory was first taking off in the 1960s.

A second difficulty in the execution of the method involves the level of technical knowledge that is required for this interdisciplinary approach. Mark Gilderhus notes that, for studies in this arena to be done well, practitioners need formal training in both history and psychoanalytical theory, a feat that few can master. Clearly this onerous knowledge base is a significant weakness that prevents widespread adoption of this methodology.[40]

Before looking at the intersection of New Testament studies and psychohistorical methods today, it is important to note that psychohistory has been fascinated with religious subject matter since the method's inception. Perhaps the most well known psychohistory of a religious figure is Erik Erickson's text on Martin Luther, the German religious Reformer.[41] Erikson's analysis situated Luther's rebellion against the church within the context of the regular, personal emotional crises that individuals experience in late adolescence and early adulthood when they are forced to redefine their prior youthful ideologies.

---

37. Ibid., 62.

38. Ibid., 65.

39. Ibid.

40. Gilderhus, *History and Historians*, 106. Most of the contributors to *Jesus and Psychology* (ed. Fraser Watts; Philadelphia: Templeton Foundation, 2007) possess formal training in psychology.

41. Erik Erickson, *Young Man Luther: A Study in Psychoanalysis and History* (1962; Austen Riggs Monograph 4; New York: W. W. Norton, 1993). Green and Troup credit Erickson and this work with spurring interest in psychohistory in the latter half of the twentieth century (*Houses of History*, 59).

How this plays out in *Young Man Luther*, however, is that, even though faith convictions were the wheel upon which the Reformation at large turned, religion is incidental to Erickson's psychological portrait of the sixteenth-century reformer. Since religion was just the particular ideology that triggered the identity crisis in the monk, Erickson was not interested in Luther's theological thoughts or the "validity of the dogmas which laid claim to him."[42]

When one turns from the era of the Reformation to the earlier centuries in which the New Testament documents were first written and read, one finds that producing a psychoanalysis of New Testament figures is a precarious task, given the extant source material. To some extent, when one engages in psychoanalysis, one must know who exactly is the subject of the study. In a field where the authorship of many texts is unknown, where the thoughts and feelings of the characters that are portrayed in the some of the texts are often supplied by omniscient narrators rather than the subjects themselves, and where the primary preoccupation of biblical scholars is with the truth or meaningfulness of religious ideology itself rather than the psychological predispositions of biblical figures, psycho-historical methodologies have not always found fruitful ground.[43]

Nevertheless, there have been some forays into this inhospitable academic terrain. Given that there is consensus that Paul authored several of the letters attributed to him, attempts have been made from time to time to offer psychohistorical assessments of the apostle. Predating Erikson by just over a half century, Nietzsche, for instance, presents what may be described as a protopsychological treatment or case history of the pre-conversion Paul, who he believed was "more important to the development of Christianity than the misunderstood soul for whom (the) religion was named."[44] Nietzsche concludes that the key to unlocking the Pauline psyche is the law, which he believes Saul subconsciously realized he was

---

42. Ibid., 22.

43. Victor Paul Furnish adroitly skirts the problematic issues by examining Pauline portraits that are theological character sketches, *Paulusbild*, rather than full-fledged psychological profiles. See "On Putting Paul in His Place," *JBL* 113 (1994): 3–17.

44. Morgan H. Rempel. "Daybreak 68: Nietzsche's Psychohistory of the pre-Damascus Paul," *Journal of Nietzsche Studies* 15 (Spring 1998): 50. Another early study is Sigmund Freud's *Moses and Monotheism* (New York: Vintage, 1967).

unable to fulfill.[45] This frustration was essentially projected upon the early Christians, whom he persecuted in a misplaced "psychic expulsion" of his own self-loathing.[46]

Psychology has come a long way since the days of Nietzsche, and the 1990s biblical interpreters began exploring the potential of psychohistory in earnest, as evidenced by the publication of *Jesus at Thirty: A Psycho-historical Inquiry*[47] and by the recognition of the Psychology and Biblical Studies Section as group that received the go-ahead to meet regularly at annual meetings of the Society of Biblical Literature beginning in 1998.

It is likely that, in the hands of those who are trained in both the fields of New Testament studies and psychology, interesting and valuable interpretative insights might be brought to light. But scholars who tread this path must be able to acknowledge the respective limits of both fields and the controversial status of psychohistory in the academy.

6.4. Economic History and the Numbers

At roughly the same time when professional historians were exploring links between psychology and history, another branch of the social sciences caught their attention: economics. In the 1950s and 1960s "new economic history" blossomed. It was heavily inspired, on the one hand, by Marx's economic emphasis on the means of production and, on the other, by progressive historians[48] who suspected that economic motives where the true dominant forces in history.[49] While Marxist historians and the progressive historians spawned studies that were qualitative, however, their "new economic history" successors in the early Cold War era gave history a novel twist. They capitalized on subjecting economic data to quantitative analysis. History, to them, was all about crunching numbers. Known sometimes as econometrics or cliometrics, this particular strain of economic history sought to define variables, build models, produce data

---

45. Rempel, "Daybreak," 54.

46. Ibid., 56.

47. J. W. Miller, *Jesus at Thirty: A Psychohistorical Inquiry* (Minneapolis: Fortress, 1997); see also Michael P. Carroll, "Moses and Monotheism and the Psychoanalytic Study of Early Christian Mythology," *JPsychohist* 15 (1988): 295–310.

48. The progressive or "New Historians" were mentioned in chapter 5, §5.4.

49. Breisach, *Historiography*, 302.

or evidence for the model, and then test the model. By the 1970s, economic patterning was even being generated by computer.

A key ingredient in the cliometric method was the use of counterfactuals—imagining alternate scenarios that each have one single element that differs from the original happening and then rerunning the numbers on the new models. The similarity or dissimilarity of the results in the modified scheme relative to the original historical event assisted the historian in assessing how integral that one variable really was. The new economic historian then used the results of this modeling to provide explanations about why something in the past happened the way that it did.

But new economic historians were not necessarily content with explaining the past. Many were speculative historians at heart. Therefore, they studied the trends of the past in order to attempt to predict how the economy might behave in the future. Pondering the absence or addition of certain variables to any given model functioned like the turn of a tarot card in a fortune-telling booth. The predictive abilities of the new economic historians, despite the use of complex models, ended up being of dubious value at best.

Unfortunately, their capacity to forecast the future relied on the twin assumptions that humans behave in an economically rational way and that there are never extreme variables for which one cannot account.[50] These assumptions proved to be terribly naive. In hindsight it is fairly clear, for instance, that after natural disasters and other unpredictable events, there is much economic wreckage with which to wrestle. Likewise, if human beings were truly rational, investors would never panic without cause and send stock markets into tailspins. Other additional assumptions held by the new economists related to the ideas that capitalist economies always grow and that economic modernization leads to political modernization,[51] but these have also been proven faulty in light of the worldwide "great recession."

Despite the weakness of econometrics as one expression of economic history, individual elements within the method are of value. For instance, on their own, quantitative methodologies, counterfactuals, and a focus on economic history in general all continue to play a strong role in today's historiography. Further, today's economic historians now engage in quali-

---

50. Green and Troup, *Houses of History*, 143.
51. Iggers, *Historiography*, 146.

tative as well as quantitative approaches and generate many worthwhile studies. The subjects of demography and content analysis, for instance, provide significant resources for New Testament historians. To illustrate, since the 1980s demographic data gathered from tomb inscriptions across the empire have been mined and subjected to rigorous statistical analysis in order to allow evaluation of factors such as population size, mortality, fertility, marriage, and even gender. The inscriptions also provide clues to family structures and how slaves and others related to households.[52] These data are invaluable in our field.

Content analysis, by comparison, is a quantitative research arena of a slightly different cast. Essentially, texts and inscriptions can be rendered in digital format, from which they are coded and subjected to numerical scrutiny. This procedure highlights features related to their content that may be overlooked due to subjective elements in structured readings.[53]

Shifting gears slightly, an exposition of economic history would not be complete without mentioning several solid works using the method and published by biblical scholars. First up are Bruce W. Longenecker and Kelly D. Liebengood, who edited a work entitled *Engaging Economics: New Testament Scenarios and Early Christian Reception* (2009).[54] A contributor to that volume, Stephen C. Barton emphasizes that knowledge of first-century economics is vital for understanding the context of the New Testament. After all, he remarks, "the title 'Paul the accountant' is not often heard. Yet, in Paul's remarkable autobiographic statement in Phil 3, the language of accounting, of gains and losses, is pronounced."[55]

---

52. Walter Scheidel, "Epigraphy and Demography: Birth, Marriage, Family and Death" [cited 23 June 2011]; online: http://www.princeton.edu/~pswpc/pdfs/scheidel/060701.pdf. See also W. Scheidel *Measuring Sex, Age and Death in the Roman Empire: Explorations in Roman Demography* (JRASup 21; Ann Arbor: Journal of Roman Archaeology, 1996); R. P. Saller, *Patriarchy, Property and Death in the Roman Family* (Cambridge: Cambridge University Press, 1994).

53. Green and Troup, 147. For more detail on this method, see Klaus Krippendorf, *Content Analysis: An Introduction to Its Methodology* (2nd ed.; Thousand Oaks, Calif.: Sage, 2004).

54. Bruce W. Longenecker and Kelly D. Liebengood, eds., *Engaging Economics: New Testament Scenarios and Early Christian Reception* (Grand Rapids: Eerdmans, 2009).

55. Stephen C. Barton, "Money Matters: Economic Relations and the Transformation of Value in Early Christianity," in Longenecker and Liebengood, *Engaging Economics*, 37.

While Barton's study is qualitative, two of the other authors with the *Engaging Economics* project are not afraid to swim in math-infested waters and have proven their methodological versatility in other publications. In particular, Bruce Longenecker explores his interest in the socioeconomic status of Greco-Roman city dwellers in *Remembering the Poor* (2010).[56] Longenecker devises a model poverty scale that posits the percentages of the ancient Roman population that would have been at various economic levels at the time of Jesus—from the elite to those below subsistence level.[57]

Douglas E. Oakman, for his part, shifts gears away from economics and into demographics in one chapter of his book, *Jesus and the Peasants* (2008).[58] Demonstrating both an extraordinary facility with mathematics and a high level of technical savvy, Oakman executes a computer-generated model based on archeological data about the size of towns. His objective? To shed light on the magnitude of the crowd of five thousand mentioned in Mark 6:34, given regional population densities. He concludes that five thousand persons would represent half of the residents of a fair-sized city or, alternatively, all of the residents of one to five towns combined.[59]

So, while the new economic historians produced studies that were based on problematic assumptions, subsequent generations of scholars were able to unsnarl the kinks in the methodology. Fortunately, as Longenecker and Oakman demonstrate, in the last decade both economic history and quantitative methods have really begun to prosper in New Testament studies. There is ample room, though, for many more.

For those for whom economics or quantitative methods are not the most flavorful of teas, however, historians in the latter half of the twentieth century developed a panoply of historiographical methods from which the New Testament scholar may choose. Some of these will be surveyed in the next chapter.

---

56. Bruce W. Longenecker, *Remember the Poor: Paul, Poverty and the Greco-Roman World* (Grand Rapids: Eerdmans, 2010).

57. Ibid., 53. Longenecker takes a study by Steven J. Friesen as his starting point: "Poverty in Pauline Studies: Beyond the So-called New Consensus," *JSNT* 26 (2004): 232–61.

58. Douglas E. Oakman, *Jesus and the Peasants* (Matrix: The Bible in Mediterranean Context 4; Eugene, Ore.: Cascade, 2008).

59. Ibid., 52.

7
New Lenses for History: The Late Twentieth Century to the Present

In a small, isolated, rural Kansas community with only five hundred residents, many citizens own passports because they serve as volunteers in agricultural exchange programs. Their cosmopolitanism does not stop there. The town provides free wireless Internet access to everyone in its borders so they can communicate with the world. Sure, the inhabitants still earn very modest livings by growing wheat, but that doesn't mean the remote location translates to this tiny populace having tunnel vision or close-minded perspectives about what is taking place in the wider United States or even abroad.

The previous chapter focused on one peculiar consequence of the early information age, the elimination of silos between academic disciplines. The result was the rise of cross-disciplinary methods such as social history, psychohistory, and economic history. But the information revolution and the resultant globalization had another side effect that manifested in the latter half of the twentieth century. Just as the residents of the tiny Kansas town now are exposed to different vantage points, and their perceptions about the world are subsequently altered or broadened, so too does history now have new methods that promote exploring the past through fresh lenses. One is known as revisionist history.

7.1. Revisionist History

There is an African proverb that states, "Until lions have historians, tales of the hunt shall always glorify the hunters." This saying encapsulates the central premise of those who practice revisionist history—that the interpretations provided by historians are colored by the historian's context and that, more often than not, history is told from the perspective of those who represent the majority or the mainstream interests within a culture. As a result, revisionist historians want to examine the received view of past events to see what those accounts might have missed, marginalized, or downplayed. And, where huge gaps are found, their objective is to revise the accounts so that the perspectives, facts, and contributions of suppressed voices or sidelined groups might be heard. In the United States, for instance, the voices of women and ethnic minorities are typically absent from accounts that record the nation's past accomplishments. This is troublesome because what is at stake is not only the accuracy of accounts of the past but issues related to power and control. Joyce Appleby, Lynn Hunt, and Margaret Jacob pull no punches about this fact when they write,

> Having a history enables groups to get power, whether they use a past reality to affirm their rights or wrest recognition from those powerful groups that monopolize public debate. History doesn't just reflect; it provides a forum for readjudicating power and interests.[1]

In the United States, the 1960s and 1970s were decades of social unrest during which established societal structures were challenged across the board. This tumultuous period provided the backdrop for the birth of revisionist history in America. In those decades one particular cadre of historians, who were known as the New Left, set out to practice a "revolutionary historiography on behalf of all disadvantaged groups…and destroy harmful institutional remnants in the present."[2] When it came to distinctive elements of their method, the New Left members on the West Coast were reluctant to incorporate Marxist theory because of the economic determinism inherent in that system,[3] though this stance would change with time and was not ubiquitous throughout the United States[4] or other parts of the world because early British feminism always had a Marxist flavor.[5] For another distinguishing feature, New Left members in the movement's earliest days were also extraordinarily critical of prior generations of historians and condemned most existing histories. These radicals, though, were

---

1. Joyce Appleby, Lynn Hunt, and Margaret Jacob, *Telling the Truth about History* (New York: Norton, 1994), 289.

2. Breisach, *Historiography*, 364–65.

3. Ibid., 366.

4. The *Radical History Review* at Duke clearly linked Marxism and revisionism. See Michael Merrill, "Introduction," *RHR* 9/10 (1975): 1.

5. See Iggers, *Historiography*, 89–92; Green and Troup, *Houses of History*, 254–55.

not organized as a whole. Thus, while they envisioned revisionist works that would retell history from new perspectives, they themselves didn't actually produce them.

This task was left to their intellectual progeny, the well-organized advocates within marginalized groups. These were the bona fide revisionist historians who were able truly to make a difference in how mainstream history was reported. On example of the influence revisionist historians could wield occurred in the late 1980s and early 1990s, when there were calls for reforms related to the history curriculum that was taught in the public schools in the United States. At that time, participants in the National Women's History Project (NWHP) stepped up and conducted a literature survey of the resources that were being used to teach children. They were able to demonstrate that no more than 3 percent of the content in U.S. history textbooks mentioned women's contributions to the past.[6] As a result of this work by the NWHP as well as various projects by activists for other interest groups such as the National Association for the Advancement of Colored People (NAACP),[7] what were considered to be self-congratulatory histories of earlier decades began to change. Despite resistance, the older, biased histories were gradually replaced by accounts that better demonstrated the gender, ethnic, race, and class diversity of the country.[8]

In biblical studies, gender-based interpretations of the history of the biblical era followed the trajectory of the cultural milieu in which the women who were working with the texts were formed. Reflecting an approach that echoed the thoroughly critical stance of the more extreme New Left was Mary Daly. She was actively publishing in the 1970s and came to "judge the Hebrew and Christian texts, and the entire Judeo-Christian tradition, to be hopelessly sexist and patriarchal."[9]

By contrast, much of the work by feminist New Testament scholars that has been published in the last decade represents a more moderate position. These scholars embrace the canon and Christianity as a faith

---

6. National Women's History Project, "About the NWHP: Our Past" [cited 21 June 2011]; online: http://www.nwhp.org/aboutnwhp/history.php.

7. The NAACP was successful in having the month of February designated Black History Month.

8. Appleby, Hunt, and Jacob, *Telling the Truth*, 293–94.

9. Cherith Fee Nordling, "Feminist Biblical Interpretation," in Vanhoozer, *Dictionary for Theological Interpretation of the Bible*, 229.

system as opposed to rejecting them, and they offer interpretations that seek to fill the gaps about our knowledge of New Testament women. To put it plainly, they are more revisionist than radical. Two recent publications have been chosen to represent the sort of work that is being done.

The first is a book on the reception history of the New Testament edited by Christine E. Joynes and Christopher C. Rowland and entitled *From the Margins 2: Women of the New Testament and Their Afterlives.*[10] The use of the word *margins* in the title provides an immediate hint that the subject of the book is history that has been overlooked by the mainstream and reflects the revisionist agenda of the contributors. Specifically, Joynes and Rowland focus on how obscure female New Testament characters are portrayed in art, music, and poetry in order to "put women back on the agenda of ancient texts" despite the fact that the biblical documents themselves have "been focused on the lives and actions of men."[11]

The second work that provides an example of gender-focused revisionist history, yet one that has a touch of socialist sympathy, too, is Reta Halteman Finger's *Of Widows and Meals: Communal Meals in the Book of Acts.*[12] The socialist overtones creep in when she draws out the stark disparity between the elite who own land, the key means of production in an agrarian society, and the impoverished peasants who make up the majority of the populace. All of this plays out like Marxist ideology sans the element of violent revolution—not surprising, since Finger is from a Peace Church tradition. The revisionist agenda of desiring to clarify and flesh out the history of a sidelined group is, of course, Finger's primary objective, given that the role of widows in Acts is often "overlooked by most scholars."[13]

To sum up this discussion on revisionist history, Dick Gregory, the civil rights advocate, serves as an excellent spokesperson. About the weaknesses of history texts, he once wryly observed, "we used to root for the Indians against the cavalry, because we didn't think it was fair in the history books that when the cavalry won it was a great victory, and when the

---

10. Christine E. Joynes and Christopher C. Rowland, *From the Margins 2: Women of the New Testament and Their Afterlives* (BMW 27; Sheffield: Sheffield Phoenix, 2009). Volume 1 deals with women from the Hebrew Bible.

11. Ibid., 1.

12. Reta Halteman Finger, *Of Widows and Meals: Communal Meals in the Book of Acts* (Grand Rapids: Eerdmans, 2007).

13. Ibid., ix.

Indians won it was a massacre."[14] The revisionist historians, both in our own discipline and in the wider field of history at large, have an important function to play in historiography. They seek to make certain that the histories that we write and those from which we learn reflect all of us.

7.2 Cultural History and Approaches Influenced by Anthropology or Ethnology

Essentially, revisionist history and cultural history are two sides of the same coin. Both are efforts to sweep corners of the past for information and subject matter that traditional forms of history writing had missed. They are using new lenses for their research. In the case of revisionist history, we have seen this manifested in a desire to tell the stories of marginalized groups that historians of prior generations had overlooked. In the case of cultural history, the focus shifts from looking for forgotten stories to unpacking sources that mainstream historians had either disdained or merely failed to notice. For the cultural historian, no piece of evidence about the past is too lowly, too mundane, or too ubiquitous to ignore or take for granted. To the extent that there is a drive to be comprehensive or to explore what is new, the cultural historian is in sympathy with the social historian. The practice of using previously disregarded sources in history, however, distinguishes them in some regards.

The scorn to which cultural historians may sometimes be treated as a result of using common or lowbrow materials is reflected by a bit of striking dialogue from a Dean Koontz novel. In the scene, Arkadian, a gas-station owner, is talking with two police officers:

"Do you know," he (Arkadian) said incredulously, "there are professors who have written books on the value of graffiti? The *value* of graffiti? The *value?*"
"They call it street art," said Luther Bryson, Jack's partner.
Arkadian gazed up disbelievingly at the towering black cop. "You think what these punks do is art?"
"Hey, no, not me," Luther said.[15]

---

14. Dick Gregory with Robert Lipsyte, *Nigger: An Autobiography* (New York: Simon & Schuster, 1964), 39.

15. Dean Koontz, *Winter Moon* (mass market ed., 2011; New York: Bantam, 1993), 5.

For the cultural historian, graffiti provides as many important clues to the past as do inscriptions painstakingly chiseled on marble monuments or the official political documents that are housed in presidential libraries, zydeco is as worthwhile as the purest chorale, and the Sears Roebuck catalog is as indispensible a source about American history as is the Declaration of Independence. Boldly put, a cultural historian would not balk at the idea of using a piece of popular fiction such as Koontz's *Winter Moon* as a legitimate resource in a piece of formal academic writing.

Although cultural history and ethnohistory blossomed post-1950 and are being treated along with other methods that emphasize new perspectives on the past, like the earlier social-science histories, they also were heavily influenced by other cognate disciplines in the social sciences, such as anthropology, sociology, ethnology, and archeology. In particular, cultural history is heavily weighted toward anthropology because it tends to focus on popular history. And popular history is often expressed in customs, the arts, and rituals—hence, the value of graffiti, typically an art form of inner-city youth.

Ethnohistory, by contrast, draws a little more strongly on archeology and ethnology. This branch of history is not limited to popular or contemporary society, which tends to be the primary interest of cultural historians, but explores the past of ethnic groups in general, whether a particular group is still a force in present society or just an echo from the distant past. With regard to resources, therefore, the ethnohistorian is free to collect folktales, oral histories, or recorded music from more recent eras but when dealing with obsolete groups or those from past centuries will rely more strongly on the paintings, architectural details, and other remains, both objects and narratives, turned up by archeologists.[16]

The fascination that culturally and ethnologically influenced historians have with using the stuff of everyday life as resources for their studies has an interesting effect on the scope of their projects. Since everything related to a given segment of the past is deemed relevant, rather than producing broad sweeping histories that cover great swaths of prior eras, the cultural historians sometimes tend to deliver extremely detailed studies that target a tiny sliver of the past, or a small group, or a very specifically defined location, or even a very narrow type of history—like medical history or the

---

16. Green and Troup do an excellent job of demonstrating the subtle differences between British and American expressions of ethnohistory and cultural history (*Houses of History*, 172–82).

history of education. In essence, cultural historians and ethnohistorians are experts at producing microhistory. As an alternative to microhistory, historians in this mode may also write histories of private life. Such studies focus on the ordinary daily tasks, rituals, and family structures of the run-of-the-mill citizen of a particular culture, time period, or geographic location. No topic is too commonplace. Anything is fair game for analysis—from dating to cooking to clothing to gardening to the traditions by which individuals mark birthdays to vacations to the rhythm of a typical workday.

Microhistories and histories of private lives, as they continued to develop in the later decades of the last century, intentionally challenged the presuppositions of other modes of early twentieth-century historiography. For instance, while traditional social history–oriented historians tended to subscribe to the philosophy that modernization was positive and that society was gradually progressing in constructive ways, the cultural historians and ethnohistorians were "a good deal less sanguine" about the outcome of social development.[17] In short, although earlier social historians might maintain a speculative view of history, the historians that drew more broadly from anthropology and ethnography were more sympathetic to the analytical philosophy of history.

There are two other ways in which the cultural historians differ from many of their earlier social science–inspired siblings. First, tracing the impact of political forces is no longer a dominant preoccupation, even if not subject to scorn, as it was in the *Annales*. We have already mentioned that in cultural history itself medical history, agricultural history, educational history, and a host of other "types of history" can take center stage. Political history just isn't often in evidence. Second, Marxist and some social-history undercurrents are set aside. In effect, the obsession with power structures, particularly as expressed in politics, was removed from the equation to allow the historian to focus not on macrohistorical concerns but on the disharmony and diversity that is actually part of everyday life. And in the process the social-science emphasis on groups also faded. As Iggers puts it, what is more important now is "the individual lives of the many" rather than abstract generalizations.[18]

---

17. Iggers, *Historiography,* 101.

18. Ibid., 103. In actuality, Marxism in its pure form is extraordinarily concerned with the individual. While in oppressive societies labor and productivity are valued

To risk a bit of glibness in the interest of clarity, Marxist historians would be concerned about whether or not the masses have bread and what forces keep them from getting this basic foodstuff. The cultural or ethnohistorian, by contrast, would be interested in how regional recipes for baking bread differ and what particular subgroups use a specific recipe to produce loaves that are used to mark specific occasions or within particular rituals.

**Elements of
Cultural and Ethno-histories**

- *Philosophy:* Analytical rather than speculative in outlook. Does not rely on Marxism as do some traditional social histories.
- *Method*: Interdisciplinary. Draws on techniques from the other social sciences, in particular anthropology, ethnology, and archeology, but not obsessively concerned with political history.
- *Sources*: Material and literary remains from everyday life. Will look at common, everyday materials that other types of historians might overlook.
- *Scope*: A narrow slice of ordinary life (focused on a short time period, specific location, or narrowly restricted topic) is treated thoroughly. Typically associated with microhistories or histories of private lives. Interested in the everyday, normal citizen, not heroes.

In biblical studies, a monumental work that owes much to anthropological and archeological influences in the mode of ethnohistory is E. P. Sanders's *Judaism: Practice and Belief 63 BCE–66 CE*.[19] In this book, which runs to a daunting 553 pages of text, Sanders's scope is very narrow. He examines the practice of Judaism in Palestine during one single century. In short, following along with the tradition of microhistory, he has set out a tiny subject for study: a single religious system during one century in a particular geographic area. Yet the fact that a study of this small slice of the past gives rise to more than five hundred pages of text provides a clue as to the wealth of detail that it contains. Sanders's work is a true microhistory to the extent that that covers everything and the kitchen sink. Well, this is a bit of an exaggeration. There is no kitchen sink, but there are *mikva'ot*, immersion

---

over the individual, one of the functions of revolution is to restore balance and focus back upon the individual.

19. E. P. Sanders, *Judaism: Practice and Belief 63 BCE–66 CE* (Philadelphia: Trinity Press International, 1992).

pools, and even a Roman-style *frigidarium*, all of which are used in clean-
liness rituals. How much detail is there? Sanders provides specifics on
temple plumbing when discussing temple sacrifices. To wit, he points out
that during sacrifice the blood of the slaughtered animals was flushed into
channels and a cistern provided water for the temple court.[20]

Although Sanders himself never uses the terms *microhistory, ethnohistory*, or even *anthropology* in his preface or in the first chapter, where
he sets out his methodology, it is clear that an interdisciplinary social-
sciences approach informs his writing. For instance, in concert with cultural history and ethnohistory's concentration on run-of-the-mill people,
Sanders states in the second sentence that in his book "the accent is on
the common people and their observances."[21] He even quips, "Mostly I
like the ordinary people."[22] In the mode of cultural historians and ethnohistorians, he also makes a conscious effort to engage all of the available
sources for the period to their fullest extent, to the point where he is able
to wring out information that others missed or to give greater emphasis to
underutilized resources.[23]

To illustrate, what is apparent in his book at large is that he not only
depends on literary evidence but also draws upon the findings of archeologists, a move well within the spirit of ethnohistory. This dependence on
archeology is readily obvious to the casual reader who flips through the
text. Bound into the center of the book is a smattering of plates that feature photographs of the synagogue at Gamla and even wall paintings from
Dura Europos that are meant to assist the reader in visualizing worshipers'
style of dress. There are also nine drawings of the architectural layout of
the temple that are scattered throughout the work.

Two final points may be made about Sanders's focus as it reflects a
cultural-history program. First, he has no interest in political history, as he
states clearly near the beginning of his text.[24] Second, unlike the Marxist
historians and even pure social historians, he is not particularly concerned
with groups, classes or social conflicts within Judaism per se. Rather, his
sketches of the main parties within Judaism are designed to serve as basic
background for understanding the practice of the religion in ordinary

---

20. Sanders, *Judaism*, 117–18.
21. Ibid., ix.
22. Ibid., 494.
23. Ibid., ix–x.
24. Ibid., 4.

households where the majority of the population was content to work within existing governing structures.[25] All five of these main features of Sanders's work, then—(1) the attention to the religious beliefs of everyday, ordinary people rather than aristocrats; (2) the insistence on leaving no source unexamined, both written and archeological, no matter how obscure they might be; (3) the desire to be comprehensive to the nth degree in providing detail about the subject being treated in the history; (4) a desire to avoid getting bogged down in political history; and (5) criticism of class-conflict models such as characterize Marxist approaches—are coincidentally hallmarks of cultural history and ethnohistory. As a consequence, Sanders serves as a solid model for this type of historiography.

7.3. THE POSTMODERN CRITIQUE OF HISTORY

At roughly the same time that cultural history was gaining momentum and popularity, professional history was also undergoing a discipline-wide and very dramatic period of self-reflection that was spurred by the flowering of postmodernism and poststructuralism. The postmodern movement was closely tied to linguistics and rooted in the philosophy of Martin Heidegger. This was a marked change from the period of the Industrial Revolution, when Hegel's thought held sway and provided the basic premises for understanding how reality worked. Because what was at stake was no less than the basic philosophical premises about certainty and truth that had formed the bedrock of the Western worldview, it is a bit imprecise to describe postmodernism as a historical method or to limit its effect solely to the writing of history. Rather, the shift in philosophical grounding affected society much more broadly and shook the fundamental presuppositions of many other fields too including architecture, music, sociology, and literature. That being said, what was its impact on historical writing in the 1980s and 1990s?

The transition from one underlying philosophical system to another was neither smooth nor comfortable and put historians on edge. This is evident in the language that is employed by historiographers when referring to these decades. Some talk about the "challenge" that poststructualism and postmodernism presented to the discipline of history.[26] Others

---

25. Ibid., 12, See also 36–43, 492.
26. Green and Troup, *Houses of History,* 297.

spoke of "the relativist attack" and the "fluid skepticism" that covered the intellectual landscape, "encroaching upon one body of thought after another."[27] Georg Iggers, the most alarmist of them all, inquires whether postmodernism marked the end of history as a scholarly discipline.[28] For his part, Iggers summarized the work of postmodernist historian Hayden White and wondered whether there is any difference between history or works of pure fiction—and, if not, why history was even needed.[29]

So what was postmodernism that it evoked such a negative reaction? At the risk of oversimplifying, within the field of history the collective influence of the works of Derrida, Foucault, Lacan, Saussaure, and others rang the final death knell for Ranke-style historicism and positivism. The critique was twofold. On the one hand, postmodernism questioned the knowability or, in its more extreme forms, the existence of objective truth. Now, this wasn't merely a case of pointing out that researchers had bias and could not, as a result, apprehend the truth. Rather, "truth" itself was relative. In the postmodernist worldview, either individuals define truth for themselves (subjectivism) or truth is a social construct created by culture (conventionalism). In short, realism was replaced by idealism at the same time positivism was giving way to pluralism, or the understanding that there are multiple cultural and historical realities.[30] But that is not all. On the other hand, the assertion that faith in progress was illusory was equally problematic for historians who were accustomed to viewing events on a continuum where there was progress and advancement. In postmodernism, time was neither linear nor progressive. Instead, continuity was considered to be a temporary human construct;[31] the sole temporal reality was change.[32] The understanding that time was chaotic and the world in

---

27. Appleby, Hunt, and Jacob, *Telling the Truth*, 243.

28. Iggers, *Historiography*, 118.

29. Ibid.

30. See the extended explanation in Pieter F. Craffert, "Multiple Realities and Historiography: Rethinking Historical Jesus Research," in *The New Testament Interpreted: Essays in Honour of Bernard C. Lategan* (ed. Cilliers Breytenbach, Johan C. Thom, and Jeremy Punt; NovTSup 124; Leiden: Brill, 2009), 90.

31. Breisach, *Historiography*, 422. It is important to note that postmodernism itself was not monolithic. The aspect of time mentioned here represents the later manifestation of postmodernism. An earlier strand, rather than focusing on flux, concentrated on the bland sameness of the postindustrial lifestyle for which time was essentially static (420).

32. Ibid.

constant flux dovetailed with the postmodernist assertion that truth could no longer be declared absolute. Neither time nor truth was static. The philosophy was consistent. But for once, historians were faced with a true chaos theory of time.

One might wonder how history as a discipline responded to this critique. Was it really necessary to throw out the entire discipline of history, as Iggers feared, because the past was unknowable and truth nothing more than an individual or collective illusion? Richard J. Evans, when interviewed in 2003, declared that the crises of the 1990s had passed. He remarked,

> there is a tendency for new methodological and theoretical approaches to begin by proclaiming their universal validity and their power to revolutionize the whole of historical study. Then within a short space of time, they tend to become subspecialties, with their own journals and societies where their adherents talk mainly to one another. And that is exactly what has happened to the extreme relativists among the postmodernists. Their critique has not left the practice of history unchanged, though the extreme skepticism that they voiced about historical knowledge has now subsided into a rather marginal phenomenon. After all, the only possible reaction from historians who actually did accept these notions was to stop writing history, and more history is being written today than ever before.[33]

The postmodern critique of history, however, was not without value. When queried further about the contributions that the postmodern challenge had provided for the field of history, Evans remarked that it helped to facilitate the shift in interest from socioeconomic models to cultural history. In addition, historians became more self-reflective about the presuppositions that informed their practice of history.

In any case, by bringing to light the idea that all historical interpretation involves a dose of not merely bias but also subjectivity, postmodernism paved the way for methods that had been explored earlier in the century but that were sidelined due to difficulties related to verifying their findings

---

33. Donald A. Yerxa, "On the Current State of History: An Interview with Richard J. Evans" in *Recent Themes in Historical Thinking: Historians in Conversation* (ed. Donald A. Yerxa; Columbia: University of South Carolina Press, 2008), 24. For an extended critique of postmodernism, see Steven B. Cowan and James S. Spiegel, *The Love of Wisdom: A Christian Introduction to Philosophy* (Nashville: B&H Academic, 2009), 34–35.

to make a comeback. It is likely no chance coincidence, for instance, that New Testament studies experienced a surge of interest in psychohistorical approaches in the same decades when historians were grappling with postmodernism.

In biblical studies the postmodern challenge to historiography as it applies to interpreting the New Testament has garnered two other responses in addition to the renewed interest in psychohistorical approaches. Both are related to historical-Jesus research and deserve mention.

For a start, Pieter Craffert attempts to outline a method that accepts multiple realities in the true spirit of postmodernism while preventing extremist, subjective interpretations from slipping into a dark swamp where "everything goes."[34] He advocates, if one may be so bold as to categorize it as such, a "moderate postmodernism" that includes three basic elements:

(1) Although naïve realism no longer holds water because the past is too alien to the interpreter who is separated from it by time, distance and culture, nonetheless an approximation of the past reality may still be reconstructed.[35]

(2) The focus on great men has been widened to include cultural history because realties are "expressions of the human spirit in its wide variety of forms" and "texts and artefacts are contextually and culturally bedded."[36]

(3) Cross-cultural interpretive strategies are necessary so we avoid projecting anachronistic categories and understandings from our own time period back onto the text.

Craffert's primary concern in his article, though, is not to define postmodernism. Instead, his key contention is that historiography outside of biblical studies has been undergoing a paradigm shift: "the most astounding feature about most current historical Jesus research is that it is still trying to answer the same old question and follow the same interpretive route" that was "first formulated in the time of positivistic, traditional historiography."[37] His article, then, is a call for scholars to undertake the

---

34. Craffert, "Multiple Realities," 89.
35. Ibid., 98.
36. Ibid., 100.
37. Ibid., 107.

challenge of "asking cultural(ly) sensitive questions about Jesus as historical personage and the sources as cultural artefacts."[38]

Michael R. Licona is the second New Testament scholar who attempts
to formulate a response to postmodernism for historical-Jesus research,
yet he does so in a way quite different from that of Craffert. Licona agrees
with Craffert to the extent that he too holds that naive realism is no
longer viable and extreme postmodernism is equally untenable. Instead
of attempting to make postmodernism palatable to moderates, as does
Craffert, however, he advocates a stance that is similar to that of Richard J. Evans. He asserts that there "are occasions when our knowledge is
adequate and when we may have reasonable certainty that our hypotheses
present an accurate, though imperfect and incomplete, description of the
past."[39] He proceeds to list several criteria used by professional historians,
either openly or implicitly, in weighing hypotheses to determine their level
of reliability.[40] These include:

(1) Explanatory scope: The most relevant data should be considered.
(2) Explanatory power: This is the principle of Ockham's Razor or
lex parsimonie—the idea that the simplest hypothesis is better
than one that is too convoluted.
(3) Plausibility: The more plausible hypothesis is supported by a
greater variety of background knowledge.
(4) Less ad hoc: A stronger theory is one where there are fewer
assumptions that are presented without evidence.
(5) Illumination: Does the explanation provide a solution to other
problems or have an effect on other areas of research?

In sum, while Craffert advances a "moderate postmodernism" and advocates proceeding along lines that resonate with cultural history, Licona
basically holds to what might be termed a "modified realism." He takes
into account his own personal bias and is aware that there is no absolute certainty that will result from his investigation, yet he does assert that

---

38. Ibid., 113.
39. Licona, *Resurrection of Jesus*, 89, 107.
40. Ibid., 109–11. As he confesses, "My desire is for the historicity of the resurrection of Jesus to be confirmed, since it would provide further confirmation of my
Christian beliefs" (130).

objective reality does exist apart from one's perceptions and that the scientific method of advancing a hypothesis and examining facts or data in its support may provide reasonable, if not absolute, explanations for events from the past.

Both Licona's and Craffert's approaches are viable ways to escape the paralysis of extreme forms of relativism and subjectivism that accompanied the postmodern paradigm shift. Yet postmodernism's concerns that truth is a social construct created by a group became an extremely important concept in post–World War II global politics as many nations began to achieve independence from the imperial forms of domination to which they had been subjected. Had the imperial powers created stories that shaped and colored the worldviews of the peoples over whom they held power?

7.4. POSTCOLONIALISM

In the twentieth century, the colonial relationships established by Britain, France, and other Western powers in Asia, Africa, the Caribbean, the Americas, and even Eastern Europe largely came to an end. Postcolonial theory is concerned with the power and continued influence of the worldviews of imperial nations on indigenous populations, even after colonial relationships have been severed. A key concept, which has been promulgated by Asian historians like Gayatri Chakravorty Spivak, is "subaltern." Essentially, a group is subaltern if it has no voice in or access to the prevailing culture.[41]

Belarus provides a good case study. Following the collapse of the Soviet Union in the early 1990s, Belarus, one of the former Soviet satellite countries, was faced with a new set of challenges about its identity as a standalone country. Those writing its history are still confronted with complex issues regarding the approach that should be taken in that enterprise. One involves the simple question of which language to employ when writing history texts. Russian, the tongue of the imperial overlords, had been the lingua franca for a handful of generations and taught in the public schools. Thus, many citizens are comfortable with it. But it presents a dilemma. If language helps to shape reality, then shouldn't historians

---

41. Leon de Kock, "Interview with Gayatri Chakravorty Spivak: New Nation Writers Conference in South Africa," *ARIEL: A Review of International English Literature* 23.3 (1992): 29–47.

write in their native dialect, Belarusian? While Belarusian might seem like the logical choice, it too presents difficulties. Which version should be preferred? Indeed, there are two distinct regional variations, complete with two slightly different Cyrillic alphabets. Which should be reflected in history books, and does the choice imply domination of one region by the other?

At bottom, if revisionist history is about giving the right to be heard to the marginalized, and postmodernism is concerned with how language shapes perceptions of reality, then postcolonial history is about how an entire country that has been decolonized deals with its new status by uniting the factions within it and learning to work together to find its historical voice and tell its own story.[42] This is not an easy task when the imperial powers have previously done it for them. There are many countries currently struggling with identity issues stemming from the decolonization of empires that began following World War II.

Before turning to the application of postcolonial history in biblical studies, however, a word should be said about the role of Marxism in this method. Stephen D. Moore comments that there are various traditions of postcolonial theory. One of them "has deep roots in Marxist theory and tends to frame (modern) colonialism squarely as an übercapitalist enterprise and to analyze it accordingly, with due attention to economic, military, political, and administrative matters."[43] In the case of Belarus, which was part of a socialist rather than capitalist empire, this Marxist flavor might be off-putting to those who wish to distance themselves from Soviet ideologies in emerging Belarusian historiography. Nonetheless, postcolonial methodology is one arena in which the Marxist legacy has been helpful to some indigenous peoples for expressing their experience under colonial domination.[44]

When it comes to biblical studies, Judea was not in a postcolonial context during the Christian era. It nonetheless was a country overshadowed

---

42. Green and Troup describe postcolonial historical writing as revisionist to the extent that "The colonized peoples may be placed at the centre of the historical process" (*Houses of History*, 278).

43. Moore, "Paul after Empire," 11.

44. Neil Elliott does note, however, that "the postcolonial criticism of the last few decades has so largely ignored Marx and Marxism as to give some observers the impression that its proponents wish to 'dump' Marx and 'forget Marxism'" ("Marxism," 40).

by Rome, an imperial power. This fact, in its very essence, raises question about the nature of the New Testament documents and hints at concerns that early Christians may have had that are to some extent analogous to those of persons who have experienced colonization. As Moore observes about New Testament texts, there is a tension between the point at which they are to be read as historical documents that represent a stand complicit with the Roman oppressors or, conversely, as resistance literature that is anti-imperial.[45] Perhaps Moore sums up the situation for a balanced approach to New Testament postcolonial biblical interpretation best when he writes, "Postcolonial criticism is not a method of interpretation (any more than is feminist criticism, say) so much as a critical sensibility acutely attuned to a specific range of interrelated historical and textual phenomena."[46] Moore himself provides examples of how this reading lens can illuminate particular aspects of the books of Mark, John, and Revelation. Efraín Agosto adds a bit more detail about one variation of the process when he talks about the hermeneutical moves made by those who have been colonized (or their descendants) when analyzing and reading first century texts.[47]

If anything, postcolonial history when done straight up as history, or when used as the foundation for exegesis, is grounded in a dour reality that human beings, even Christians, have not lived in harmony with one another. The past is marked on one side by colonialism and greed and on the obverse by struggle and oppression. By contrast, the next and final historiographical method to be covered in this chapter represents a complete change of pace. Its focus is not on the grim aspect of treatment of one another, but on the imaginative flights of fancy in which historians may indulge to stimulate insights about historical events. If postcolonialism is historiography at its most sober, then imaginative histories are the discipline at its most playful.

---

45. Stephen D. Moore, *Empire and Apocalypse: Postcolonialism and the New Testament* (BMW 12; Sheffield: Sheffield Phoenix, 2006), 13–14.

46. Ibid., 7.

47. Efraín Agosto, "Foreword," in Stanley, *Colonized Apostle*, xv. See also Hans de Wit and Gerald O. West, *African and European Readers of the Bible in Dialogue: In Quest of Shared Meaning* (Studies of Religion in Africa 32; Leiden: Brill, 2008).

7.5. Imaginative Histories

In the epilogue of his *Judaism: Practice and Belief 63 BCE–66 CE*, E. P. Sanders lays out an agenda for a technique for approaching the past of Judea entirely different from what he himself used in his book. He muses about what a historian might discover if she or he imagined the Romans taking an alternate approach to how they executed their control and influence over Judea than they actually did. Would the alternate actions have triggered the Jewish revolt or averted it? He notes that "speculation can help us see things in better perspective. 'What might have been', if considered in light of the basic realities of the eastern Mediterranean world, allows us to evaluate a little better what actually was."[48]

Although Sanders himself doesn't leap into a full-fledged imaginative history at this juncture—he is, after all, at the end of his cultural history book—he is nonetheless pointing to a legitimate historical methodology that New Testament studies has not really explored to its full potential. Since the turn of the millennium, however, professional historians have found a receptive audience for imaginative works in this vein among armchair history buffs.[49]

Imaginative history goes by many names, including *counterfactual history, speculative history, virtual history,*[50] and *alternate history*. But at base it is concerned with the use of hypothetical scenarios to provide insights into the past. It is represented by titles like *What if? The World's Foremost Military Historians Imagine What Might Have Been*, which became a *New York Times* bestseller,[51] and an essay by Geoffrey Parker,

---

48. E. P. Sanders, *Judaism*, 491.

49. Yet counterfactuals are not new. Philip E. Tetlock and Aaron Belkin (*Counterfactual Thought Experiments in World Politics: Logical, Methodological, and Psychological Perspectives* [Princeton: Princeton University Press, 1996], 3) reference the use of a counterfactual by Tacitus and the value that social scientists like Max Weber and Robert Fogel ascribed to counterfactuals.

50. In the interest of simplicity in this general introduction, I treat these as synonyms. There are actually subtle differences between these types of imaginative histories. See Allan Megill, "The New Counterfactuals," in Yerxa, *Recent Themes in Historical Thinking*, 103. Tetlock and Belkin provide an extremely helpful overview of five basic styles of counterfactual argumentation in *Counterfactual Thought Experiments*, 7–13.

51. Robert Cowley, ed., *What If? The World's Foremost Military Historians Imagine What Might Have Been* (New York: Berkley Books, 1999).

"Martin Luther Burns at the Stake: 'O God, is Luther Dead?'" (Luther actually died from what was likely a stroke or heart attack and was in poor health in his final years).[52]

Let's turn to some of the characteristics of this method. Perhaps the most obvious place to start is with the concept of time. The very act of creating an "alternative history" calls to mind "parallel universes" and presupposes a greater elasticity of time than found in some of the other methods that have been covered so far in this study. Allan Megill sums up the way in which imaginative historians treat time brilliantly: "The virtual historian cuts into the real past at some particular moment—normally just before one of the historical actors involved made a weighty decision." Then he or she "conceptualizes this moment as one of contingency" where the decision might have been different, and then the historian "exploits the supposed contingency at the beginning in order to launch his or her counterfactual history."[53]

In addition to time being contingent, the alternate scenarios are tethered to actual events in the past, and the virtual historian sacrifices any the idea that time is progressing forward or that there is a predetermined pattern that is leading to some grand future.[54] What remains is an emphasis on the arbitrariness of human existence.[55]

> **Elements of Counterfactual History**
>
> - *Philosophy:* Analytical rather than speculative in outlook. Does not rely on Marxism.
> - *Method:* Has established criteria for evaluating the plausibility, insightfulness, and viability of a construction. Most involve an element of consistency.
> - *Scope:* Any type of history and any event from the past. A given event, though, must be suitable for this sort of analysis.
> - *Time:* Contingent. What "happened" involves an element of arbitrariness.
> - *Sources:* Assumes historian has working knowledge of the facts and sources about the event. But the counterfactual exercise itself requires nothing more than the historian's imagination.

---

52. Ibid., 105–19.

53. Megill, "New Counterfactuals," 105.

54. This would be the case with the speculative philosophies of history as described in chapter 2.

55. Richard J. Evans, "Telling It Like It Wasn't," in Yerxa, *Recent Themes in Historical Thinking*, 78.

While this may seem unusually depressing in comparison with our particular discipline of New Testament studies due to the fact that many of us are related to the Judeo-Christian faith tradition and draw hope from the idea that God is active in history, there are, nonetheless, some points where imaginative history does recommend itself as a method in our field. For instance, it is not tethered to any particular "type" of history. While some of the other methods that have been covered were reactions against prior ways of doing history and thus deliberately steered toward or away from specific areas of study, that is not the case with imaginative history. It is a tool that may be applied easily to political history, religious history, economic history, social history, and any other. In addition, in an era where there is a decline in the use of Marxism as an ideological anchor in methodologies,[56] imaginative history has never had a close association with that ideology.

Another positive feature, methodologically, is that the use of imaginative historical exercises allows one to circumvent the extreme relativism associated with postmodernism. Although virtual history is a creative endeavor, nonetheless there are checks to help to assist in evaluating the legitimacy, plausibility, and insightfulness of specific counterfactuals. As Tetlock and Belkin put it, "anything-goes subjectivism"[57] is rejected. One place where extreme relativism is mitigated relates to sources. Even though a counterfactual scenario, when written down, may not include a single footnote or have a bibliography, imaginative historians must have a deep working knowledge of the primary and secondary evidence that relates to the event about which they were developing the alternate scenarios. So, while in one sense no sources are needed to write a virtual history but one's imagination, in another sense the exercise of executing a plausible counterfactual history requires a substantial pre-existing knowledge base. Thus the work of a counterfactual historian differs to some degree from that of a dilettante or the author who produces regency romances or other types of historical fiction.

In addition to the historian's command of the subject matter serving as a brake on more ridiculous scenarios, Tetlock and Belkin provide yet another check on rampant subjectivity: they developed a rubric. The duo came up with a list of six attributes that characterize ideal counterfactual exercises. These include clarity with regard to variables, logical

---

56. Ibid.
57. Tetlock and Belkin, *Counterfactual Thought Experiments*, 17.

consistency, historical consistency, theoretical consistency, statistical consistency, and projectability.[58] In essence, not only are researchers held to
standards of logic in the moves that are made but not every event from
the past is a good candidate for this type of methodological treatment.
Some happenings from the past, for instance, may be so complex that it
would be difficult to isolate sufficient variables to render undertaking the
investigation viable. So, while on the surface the subject matter available
for treatment seems limitless, in actuality each topic is circumscribed by
its inherent suitability to this type of analysis.

Now, before we go further, there are two caveats to be made. The first
concerns the words *speculative history*. While Sanders himself uses the
words *speculative* and *speculation* to describe imagining an alternative scenario for Roman governing tactics in Judea in the first century, imaginative histories as they are being discussed in this chapter are not to be confused with the philosophical stance known as speculative history that was
introduced in chapter 3. As laid out earlier, speculative histories, like those
of Augustine or even Marx, have an element that is predictive of the future.
By contrast, when historians engage in alternate history or counterfactual
history, their sights are firmly set on analyzing an event from the past and
they take an analytical approach. Their goal is to imagine a different twist
or scenario than what actually happened in order to either assess the relative importance of individual elements of the original event or to gain new
perspective that stimulates a new line of thought or investigation related
to the original happening. This should sound very similar to the way that
counterfactuals are used by economic historians.

A second caveat relates to the Geoffrey Parker title mentioned above,
"Martin Luther Burns at the Stake, O God, Is Luther Dead?" It is tongue
in cheek. But if it tempts some readers to think that virtual histories are
nothing more than childish pastimes or pieces of sheer fiction writing,
they would not be alone. Even Richard Evans, a professional historian, is
skeptical about the practice of indulging in writing counterfactual histories and caustically observes, "Historians have generally thought of such
mind games as entertainments rather than serious intellectual endeavors."[59]
Along these same lines, Philip Tetlock and Aaron Belkin readily admit
that, in publishing their book on counterfactuals, they might be convicted

---

58. Ibid., 18. The six are unpacked on pp. 19–31.
59. Evans, "Telling It Like It Wasn't," 77.

of luring "colleagues 'down the methodological rathole' in pursuit of unanswerable metaphysical questions."[60]

Yet many historians who delve into the activity are convinced of its value. Robert Cowley describes some important contributions that counterfactual histories have to make. First, regardless of historical method, researchers may lose sight of the fact that actors on the stage of the past made decisions. Outcomes were not always inevitable or obvious. Using a counterfactual approach, however, can highlight what occasions in the past were true turning points and "make a confrontation or a decision stand out in relief."[61] A second contribution that imaginative histories can offer is to eliminate "hindsight bias."[62] Loosely defined, this phenomenon is one in which the historian, because he or she knows the outcome of the event, is predisposed to examine only the factors that led to that event, giving short shrift to other causes or historical elements that were also present.[63]

Another role that imaginative history plays is it allows a historian to test hypotheses. In this regard, Richard Ledbow goes so far as to assert that "counterfactuals are essential to good history."[64] If a historian makes the case that episode X was the climax of an event or that factor Y was the root cause of an occurrence, than constructing an imaginative scenario with that element or factor removed will help confirm whether the degree of importance a historian is ascribing to it is actually warranted.

Finally, counterfactuals serve an important function when assisting us both to evaluate the merit of past events and to assess what policies and decisions we should be making in our current time given how those events turned out. Ledbow frames this beautifully by asking the question, "Was the development of nuclear weapons a blessing or curse for humankind?"[65] Only by imagining possible scenarios can we decide whether the ethical dilemma related to creating a weapon of such mass destruction was

---

60. Tetlock and Belkin, *Counterfactual Thought Experiments*, 3.

61. Cowley, "When Do Counterfactuals Work?" in Yerxa, *Recent Themes in Historical Thinking*, 116.

62. Ibid., 117.

63. Ibid. Cowley cites an example where counterfactuals corrected assumptions that had been made about one of Hitler's actions.

64. Richard Ned Ledbow, "Good History Needs Counterfactuals," in Yerxa, *Recent Themes in Historical Thinking*, 92.

65. Ibid., 93.

worth it. And, now that nuclear weapons are a reality, those scenarios help inform how we wish to proceed with their deployment or disarmament in the future.

Before leaving a discussion about the value of imaginative history, there is one important point to be made. Cowley emphasizes that within the practice of historiography the imaginative exercise is merely a tool that a historian uses in analyzing the original event.[66] Should the exercise become an end in and of itself, it is likely that even Cowley would concede that the author is producing a tall tale.

Examples of full-length counterfactual treatments of New Testament topics are relatively rare. One set of authors who do demonstrate interest in this particular method is D. James Kennedy and Jerry Newcome, who cowrote a work entitled *What If Jesus Had Never Been Born?* Their goal was to trace the impact that Jesus, and the church had on various institutions. One of these was the practice of exposing infants in the ancient world. After referencing passages like Matt 19:14a, in which Jesus remarks, "Let the little children come to me," the authors assert, "Through His Church, ultimately Jesus brought an end to infanticide. The influence of Christ brought value to human life, and infanticide was outlawed.... Christian influence in the Roman Empire helped to enshrine in law Christian principles of the sacredness of human life."[67]

While it is true that exposure was finally identified as a capital crime in 374 c.e.,[68] it is not clear that the birth of Christ and the growth of the Christian church were sole reason the practice was abolished. Kennedy and Newcome do not explore whether there were other causal factors at play in the decision, such as demographic pressures that required population growth; the influence of Judaism, which also looked unfavorably on exposure (Philo, *De Specialibus Legibus* 3.110–119), wars or threats of conflicts that inspired lawmakers to regard the survival and nurturing of infants as a necessary strategy in imperial maneuvers. Nor do they consider whether alternate institutions arose for the care of unwanted infants. In any event,

---

66. Cowley, as cited by Richard J. Evans in "Response," in Yerxa, *Recent Themes in Historical Thinking*, 130.

67. D. James Kennedy and Jerry Newcombe, *What If Jesus Had Never Been Born?* (rev. ed.; Nashville: Thomas Nelson, 2001), 12.

68. Josef (Kiel) Wiesehöfer, "Child Exposure," Brill's New Pauly [cited 1 April 2012]; online: http://referenceworks.brillonline.com/entries/brill-s-new-pauly/child-exposure-e613990.

legal prescriptions do not necessarily indicate compliance. For instance, infanticide in the form of smothering infants at night and exposure in the guise of abandoning infants at foundling homes continued in Europe well into the nineteenth century.[69] These issues do, however, point out the fact that not every subject readily lends itself to counterfactual treatments because institutions and events from the past are amazingly complex. Furthermore, they illustrate that the counterfactual exercise has two parts, the first is imagining "what if…" but the second is to return to the episode from the past that is being examined to weigh all the evidence and determine exactly how influential the single variable actually was.

Nonetheless, counterfactual exercises are an intriguing tool; one can only imagine the profitable use to which they might be put in New Testament studies.

7.6. SUMMARY

Even though it may be tempting to lump the various methodologies of twentieth-century historiography under the title *social-science history* or biblical studies' favorite umbrella term, *historical criticism*, and be done with it, these broad descriptors fail to do justice to the sometimes subtle, and at times rather dramatic, differences between the individual approaches to writing history that were developed in that time period. While the presentation in this chapter and the previous one are not exhaustive, and many methods were left out in the interest of brevity, hopefully fledgling New Testament historians will be tempted to drill down beneath the broad categories we biblical scholars sometimes use to the rich and spicy core of each one of these very varied methods and others besides.

Michael Licona asks two very intriguing questions in the introduction to his book on historiographical approaches to the resurrection of Jesus.[70] (1) "Are biblical scholars conducting their historical investigations differently than professional historians?" (2) "If professional historians who work outside of the community of biblical scholars were to embark on an investigation of the historicity of" any particular aspect of the New Testament era, "what would such an investigation look like?" Even though these two chapters on twentieth-century methods were not intended to provide

---

69. "Population," *Encyclopædia Britannica* [cited 1 April 2012]; online: http://www.britannica.com/EBchecked/topic/470303/population.
70. Licona, *Resurrection of Jesus*, 19.

an answer to Licona's musings, hopefully they have demonstrated that for each way of "doing history" there are at least some New Testament scholars who are well versed in it. In any event, knowledge of the fundamental characteristics of individual modes of history writing will promote clearer dialogue with colleagues in our sister field.

Let us now turn our attention to three essays that demonstrate how various historical methods might be adapted for application in New Testament exegesis.

PART 3
APPLICATION

8

COUNTING SHEEP: CLOTHING AND TEXTILES
IN LUKE'S GOSPEL

It is time to shift gears and actually apply what we have learned so far about methods and tools to an analysis of some sample New Testament texts. This particular study, in which references to clothing in Luke's Gospel are examined in order to shed light on the economic status of Luke's audience, straddles the fence between two historical methods. It is inspired by both economic history and cultural history. After all, clothing is the stuff of "ordinary life," common goods of the type that interest cultural historians and generally don't attract a lot of attention in biblical scholarship. Further, as is typical of cultural histories, these ordinary elements will be examined with careful attention to detail. So, for instance, several paragraphs will focus on minutiae such as how exactly ancient residents wore their clothes, down to the toggles or fasteners. This sort of narrow scope reflects the microhistorical element of cultural history.

At the same time, clothing is a commodity, and its presence or lack in relation to characters and storyline reveals something about its owner's economic condition. You will likely recall that economic history tends to incorporate mathematical models, charts, and graphs and is quantitative. Since this particular work blends cultural and economic elements, however, it will be by and large qualitative. That being said, there is one small section in which a model is created to determine approximate agricultural productivity related to sheep. Those paragraphs, as you will see, involve just a touch of math. Despite the interest in economics, however, the method employed here does not reflect a Marxist understanding of how economics work. Thus, there will be no presupposition that class conflict exists. The essay will also remain on the side of analytical history rather than speculative. In other words, it is focused on how simple items in everyday life worked in their own time period without hinting at how those elements might contribute to an end time.

Now, that is not to say that a historian would view the contents of this chapter as pure history. After all, it is exegesis and as such theological tendrils and redaction criticism creep into it. Nonetheless, the study must begin where all solid historical studies do: with defining terms and examining presuppositions. In this instance it is a matter of unpacking baggage associated with the words *wealth* and *poverty*.

The terms *wealth* and *poverty* are relative. Voting U.S. citizens, for instance, learned in the 2008 presidential election that a business with revenue that grossed over $250,000 per year was "wealthy" and should be subject to higher taxes than those at lower incomes. Meanwhile, on the opposite side of the spectrum, the U.S. poverty threshold for a family of four in 2009 was $21,954 per year.[1] Presumably, those living between those two extremes are the middle class. Yet it is hard to imagine that a family earning a dollar above the poverty threshold feels particularly middle class. Nor do those earning just above $250,000 likely consider themselves to be in the same echelon with the billionaires on Forbes's list of the four hundred wealthiest Americans.[2] So, if terms such as *wealth* and *poverty* are loaded (and somewhat subjective) today, how is one to judge the relative merit of labels like *elite*, *poor*, and *peasant* when they are used to describe the economy of the early Roman Empire? For those readers who remember our chapter on fallacies, this question is important because we are trying to avoid the danger of reification, a difficulty that is resolved by digging beneath terms to get at some actual data. So here goes.

In a preindustrial agrarian society such as the Roman Empire, where the urban population was never more than one twentieth of the rural[3] and where the land-owning "elite" composed only one percent of the total inhabitants of the empire overall,[4] it is tempting to take a primitivist

---

1. "The Census Bureau's Poverty Thresholds for 2009" [cited 10 November 2010]; online: http://www.irp.wisc.edu/faqs/faq1.htm#year2000.

2. "The Richest People in America" [cited 10 November 2010]; online: http://www.forbes.com/wealth/forbes-400.

3. Ian Morris, introduction to *The Ancient Economy*, by M. I. Finley (Berkeley: University of California Press, 1999), xxi.

4. William Scheidel, "Stratification, Deprivation, and Quality of Life," in *Poverty in the Roman World* (ed. Margaret Atkins and Robin Osborne; Cambridge: Cambridge University Press, 2006), 42.

stance in which it is assumed that the vast majority of residents would be rural peasants who lived barely above subsistence level.[5] Florence Dupont expresses this eloquently when she writes, "For either a Roman was very rich indeed, rich enough to lavish wine, food and entertainment on thousands of guests at a single feast … or his fortune was of no use to him whatsoever and he might just as well be poor." And what sort of life did the poor live? "A life of rustic poverty meant that one had few needs … one slept on straw, ate vegetables, bread and bacon, went barefoot, and wore a simple tunic."[6] Neville Morely, in taking up the thorny issues related to the concept of "the poor" in the Roman Empire, however, cautions that literary sources from the late Republic and early Empire that disparage the poor as needing the pacification of bread and circuses as portrayed in Juvenal were written by the elite,[7] and inherent biases due to this fact mean that the sources must be weighed carefully by historians before they are used.

In truth, there is no consensus concerning how the Roman poor should be identified, and historians must be careful not to fall into the snare of oversimplification. After all, Morely reminds his readers, there is a difference between poverty and destitution as well as between structural poverty (into which one is born and remains until death) and conjunctural poverty (which is the result of a misfortune). In sum, presuppositions of homogeneity among the masses must be abandoned.[8] This position is echoed by Walter Scheidel, who criticizes "overly dichotomized images of Roman imperial society"[9] and demonstrates that twenty to twenty-five percent of the population in Roman North Africa were neither rich nor poor but middling property owners secure from "chronic want."[10] Recently Bruce W. Longenecker, a biblical scholar, demonstrated that he is in tune with Morely and Scheidel when he adopted a scale for urban economies that avoids dualisms and instead provides graded classes for

----

5. This position is summarized by Neville Morely, *Trade in Classical Antiquity* (Cambridge: Cambridge University Press, 2007), 4.

6. Francis Dupont, *Daily Life in Ancient Rome* (trans. Christopher Woodall; Oxford: Blackwell, 1989), 31, 32.

7. Neville Morely, "The Poor in the City of Rome," in *Poverty in the Roman World* (ed. Margaret Atkins and Robin Osborne; Cambridge: Cambridge University Press, 2009), 26–27. See also Morely, *Trade*, 44, on his assertion that there are actually gradations of wealth and surplus production.

8. See Morely, *Trade*, 44.

9. Scheidel, "Stratification," 45.

10. Ibid., 49. See also 51, 53–54.

stable artisans, tradesmen, and merchants.[11] All of these studies, at core, are avoiding some of the pitfalls associated with older Marxist approaches to economic history that were discussed in chapter 6.

The question that provides the impetus for this particular exploration of Luke's Gospel is whether or not urban or village-dwelling Christians as portrayed in the text lived like Dupont assumes the rural population did—in a barefoot, tunic-wearing, straw-for-a-bed simplicity—or whether their standard of living was at least generous enough to offer some excess goods that might be used for trade or exchange, thereby offering a margin of security against the threat of destitution. It is framed as an open question of the sort presented in the last chapter warning about stumbling blocks in history projects; the answer is not presumed.

Since I am not a trained economist, the only accessible approach to me is a qualitative one that involves a close reading of the biblical text to search for evidence of the use and production of commodities in the daily lives of those portrayed in the narrative. In this case, the focus is on clothing and textiles, which constitute a stock element used by economists when calculating standards of living.[12]

That clothing was ubiquitous is asserted by Dupont, who observes that Romans "felt duty bound never to be completely naked," even if she portrays them as barely clothed in a single tunic.[13] In contrast to Dupont, Willem Jongman presents a portrait in which ancient workers rarely found themselves reduced to near nakedness and "modest but not impoverished citizens seem to have owned new garments of some quality."[14] If indeed clothing manufacture is the most important nonagrarian activity after building or construction and a leading indicator for standards of living above basic human survival, as Jongman contends, where on the con-

---

11. Bruce W. Longenecker, *Remember the Poor: Paul, Poverty, and the Greco-Roman World* (Grand Rapids: Eerdmans, 2010), 53.

12. On agrarian and fishing industries in Palestine, see K. C. Hanson and Douglas Oakman, *Palestine in the Time of Jesus: Social Structures and Social Conflict* (Minneapolis: Fortress, 1998), 99–129. In this particular volume, Hanson and Oakman appear to be heavily influence by the work of Moses Finley, a primitivist. See, e.g., pp. 116, 125.

13. Dupont, *Daily Life*, 258.

14. Willem M. Jongman, "The Early Roman Empire: Consumption," in *The Cambridge Economic History of the Greco-Roman World* (ed. Walter Scheidel, Ian Morris, and Richard Saller; Cambridge: Cambridge University Press, 2007), 609–10.

tinuum do Luke's characters fall? Just at the poverty level, or at a slightly better "modest but not impoverished "level?

8.1. Methodological Caveats

There are three caveats to offer at this point. First, focusing on a single commodity will not adequately answer the question of whether or not any individual is truly beyond subsistence. Although wool production and textile manufacturing could be found in every region of the empire,[15] other factors such as housing or food also impact economic status and security. Nonetheless, studying this one commodity at least provides a single, small step toward finding the answer to the question about the standard of living of the early Christians in the Lukan community. Clearly the text will also need to be excavated by subsequent studies for evidence of other basic goods beyond clothing before a full picture could be drawn and the answer reached with any degree of certainty.

In addition to limiting this study to one commodity, textiles, a second methodological peculiarity of this piece requires clarification. Much work by biblical historians, including those of the history of economics, appears to come out of a historiographical tradition that traces its roots back to Marxist theories of history. These center on conflict and class struggle. Oakman even calls this a "conflict" approach and describes it as one that "will tend to focus on the discontent of the subjugated and expose the harmful effects of the 'system,' as well as indicate its chief beneficiaries."[16] Granted, there are plenty of passages that do hint at conflict in the New Testament. In Luke's Gospel alone, Jesus is accused of stirring up people by his teaching (23:5), and his life is exchanged for that of Barabbas, who had been imprisoned for "insurrection" (23:25).

Yet, at core, agrarian economies are extraordinarily nuanced, so it is hard to impute feelings of subjugation and an inclination toward conflict to the masses due only to extreme poverty. As with other rural economies, families in Palestine likely supplemented their larders by hunting, engaged in cottage industries when weather prevented fieldwork outdoors, created redistribution chains where core goods were sold to others who in turn sold them further afield, and finally participated in a type of trade known

---

15. Morely, *Trade*, 20–21, 23. See also Jongman, "Early Roman Empire," 609.
16. Oakman, *Jesus and the Peasants*, 135.

by economists as reciprocity.[17] Reciprocity occurs when farmers borrow equipment from each other or neighbors pitch in to help with livestock care in the event of illness. So the economics of any given agrarian system are actually fairly complex. Scholarship that assumes that peasants are always unhappy with their lot and prone to rebellion, therefore, work on a troublesome premise. Instead, I am more inclined toward what Oakman labels a "functionalist" approach, one that looks at society as an "organic" whole.[18] In terms of historiography, this tendency to sidestep the use of Marxist elements is in keeping with studies that are aligned with cultural history approaches to the past, as was mentioned in the second section of chapter 7 above.

A final methodological consideration involves setting base levels of consumption for textiles in the Mediterranean region, against which the evidence from the Lukan account may be compared. In short, it must be determined how much cloth was necessary for a comfortable standard of living. This is where a quantitative element colors this study. To this end, Robert Allen is likely not far from the mark when he hypothesizes that five meters of textiles (roughly 5.4 yards, or 16.4 feet) of finished cloth represents an amount that would maintain a Mediterranean adult male at a consumption level equivalent with that of a "respectable working-class" European early modern male,[19] while three meters (roughly 3.5 yards, or 10.5 feet) is identified for subsistence level.[20] One can make a guess that this amount would be analogous to an agrarian-based economy in the classical world, but there is no absolute certainty—a fact which must be kept in mind in this exposition, lest we dance too terribly close to the fallacy of anachronism.

Aside from the limits inherent in attempting an analogy across centuries, another difficulty with Allen's formulation is that, while lengths of fabric might be easily measurable, widths vary based on the size of the loom used. Generally, on either an upright two-beam loom or a warp-weighted loom, which require passing thread from side to side with a

---

17. Morley, *Trade*, 10.

18. Ibid.

19. Robert C. Allen, "How Prosperous Were the Romans? Evidence from Diocletian's Price Edict (AD 301)," in *Quantifying the Roman Economy: Methods and Problems* (ed. Alan Bowman and Andrew Wilson; Oxford: Oxford University Press, 2009), 332–34.

20. Ibid., 341.

shuttle, the width of the loom would not exceed comfortable arm span, which might vary from thirty-six to forty-five inches or so. Wider looms are possible but would need to be operated by multiple weavers standing (warp-weighted) or sitting side by side (two-beam)[21] and weaving in tandem.[22] Standard widths for machine-manufactured cloth today include widths of thirty-six and forty-five inches, with some fabrics for draperies and other applications woven at fifty-four inches, so working with a bolt of today's cloth would be roughly equivalent to working with cloth sizes in the ancient world. Further, one must assume that the five meters of cloth would be a standard quality of fabric without exceptional dyes or woven patterns and of medium weave or thread count (neither too coarse nor too fine).

Let's break here a moment. Is this sounding like a lot of detail about weaving? If so, it is evidence that we are sticking fairly close to the method of cultural history. After all, we have seen that a characteristic of that method is to pursue the smallest matters in great depth.

Now back to the subject at hand. Allen's formation of 16.4 feet of cloth does seem to be a logical amount of material, given both the climate considerations in Jerusalem and the typical styles or cut of clothing in the Mediterranean portion of the empire. Typical "outdoor" dress across the region consisted of a tunic and either a cloak or a toga,[23] as mosaics found in Palestine and dated to the second through sixth centuries confirm.[24] The tunic, or *chiton*, was essentially a wide, calf-length shirt that might be constructed in sleeveless fashion or have sleeves of any length either incorporated at weaving or woven separately and sewn on.[25] Tunics would

---

21. G. M. Crawfoot, "Linen Textiles from the Cave of Ain Feshkha in the Jordan Valley," *PEQ* 83 (1951): 29. A more current article notes that these materials actually from Qumran Cave 1, not precisely from Ain Feshka. See Joan E. Taylor et al., "Qumran Textiles in the Palestine Exploration Fund, London: Radiocarbon Dating Results," *PEQ* 137 (2005): 159.

22. Among the upper classes, a ceremonial toga in a style known as the imperial toga was woven in widths of fifteen to eighteen feet. See "The Toga: From National to Ceremonial Costume," in *The World of Roman Costume* (ed. Lynn Sebesta and Larissa Bonfante; Madison: University of Wisconsin Press, 1994), 17. See also Dupont, *Daily Life*, 259.

23. Dupont, *Daily Life*, 258. See also Bernard, "Graeco-Roman Dress in Syro-Mesopotamia," in Sebesta and Bonfante, *World of Roman Costume*, 163–81.

24. Jan MacDonald. "Palestinian Dress," *PEQ* 83 (1951): 56.

25. Liza Cleland, Glenys Davies, and Lloyd Llewellyn Jones, *Greek and Roman*

be belted and hitched up above the knees to provide free movement of legs during work, a practice also found in biblical lands, given the description of a laborer girding himself prior to serving supper in Luke 17:8. The primary outer garment for the more Romanized residents was the toga, shaped in a half circle from a single piece of cloth and draped around the body. For those retaining Hellenized preferences for style, a ἱμάτιον was a rectangular piece of cloth that might be worn toga-style or might also be donned across the shoulders like a shawl or cape. A cloak proper, by contrast, might be used for travel or inclement weather. Cloaks were constructed with or without a hood and would be worn cape-style and fastened in the front with toggles sideways and secured at the shoulder with a brooch, or even sewn up the front and drawn on like a poncho.

Given the dimensions and the cloth involved, Allen's determination that five meters of material would be the annual allotment typical for a person of modest means, an individual would have enough fabric for two new tunics (each four feet in length from shoulder to bottom hem) or, alternatively, one new ἱμάτιον plus a bit of excess cloth each year. It is likely that not all garments in a wardrobe would need to be replaced every twelve months, and older garments might be repurposed for household and other uses such as appears to be the case with the linen scraps that were used as packing materials for some of the Dead Sea Scrolls.[26]

Further, the odds that a ἱμάτιον would last longer than a tunic are fairly good, given Jerusalem's climate and the fact that it would not need to be donned year round. Jerusalem can be a quite brisk in January, with an average of thirty-nine-degree nights and fifty-three-degree days, but reaches quite comfortable daytime temperatures between seventy and eighty-five degrees for the months of April to October.

The lower subsistence level of three meters of cloth would provide only enough material for one new tunic and a bit of extra cloth. But, even

---

Dress from A to Z (New York: Routledge, 2007), 200–1. See Mary Huston on wearing tunics during rough work: *Ancient Greek, Roman and Byzantine Costume and Decoration* (2nd ed.; London: Adam & Charles Black, 1947), 97. Lucille Roussin's position that Jewish tunics differ from Greco-Roman in that they are woven in two pieces and sewn together at the shoulders is not accurate. Cleland, Davies, and Jones maintain that piecing tunics with sewing was a usual practice across the empire. See Lucille Roussin, "Costume in Roman Palestine: Archaeological Remains and the Evidence from the Mishna," in Sebesta and Bonfante, *World of Roman Costume*, 183.

26.Crawfoot, "Linen Textiles," 5.

at that, people may not have been cold. After all, consumption certainly varied by individual per year. And there was a thriving secondhand market that would take some of the pressure off of those with only the three yards of cloth. Furthermore, it was possible to redye cloth to brighten the colors and make it appear newer.[27] While there is no evidence of re-dying in Luke's Gospel, clothing theft is attested in the parable of the Good Samaritan, which is the tale of a man whom robbers strip ἐκδύσαντες and abandon by the roadside (Luke 10:30). Liza Cleland and her coauthors do make the practical observation that evidence of clothing theft in the empire "strongly indicates that there was a market for second hand textiles."[28] The point to be made here is that the comfort level of someone who might be able to afford the five meters of cloth per year would be measurably different from one who was existing at the lower three-meter standard of living, but no one need run around naked unless completely penniless.

Assuming that an individual at least a few steps from destitution possessed at least two tunics and a ἱμάτιον, the next logical step is to scour the Gospel to determine if the characters in its pages are clothed at that level or at a lesser standard. Before running too far ahead into that project, however, it is appropriate to pause and quickly summarize some of the known characteristics of the textile trade and manufacturing process in the ancient economy.

8.2. Textiles and the Ancient Economy

In a concise survey of the textile industry in his *Introduction to the New Testament*, Helmut Koester remarked,

> Textiles were ordinarily manufactured in individual households, mostly by women. Small workshops supplied local demand. Precious textiles and luxury clothing were produced in factories and exported. Manufacture of textiles relied on traditional methods that saw little change throughout antiquity. An exception was the invention of the vertical loom, originating in Egypt and introduced to Italy and Greece at the beginning of the Roman period.[29]

---

27. Cleland, Davies, and Jones, *Greek and Roman Dress*, 75.

28. Ibid., 167.

29. Helmut Koester, *Introduction to the New Testament: History, Culture, and Religion in the Hellenistic Age* (2nd ed.; Berlin: de Gruyter, 1995), 83.

For an introductory-level text penned in 1995, Koester's information is adequate. But some elaboration is necessary.

Moses Finley, whose influential work *The Ancient Economy* was published in 1973, had several observations to make about the clothing industry and trade which underscore the majority of Koester's assertions. Basically, Finley used literary evidence from Strabo (*Geogr.* 5.1.7.12) and Dio Chrysostom (*Or.* 31.21–23) and some limited archaeological evidence to assert that cities like Padua exported carpets and cloaks to Rome. Tarsus produced high-grade linen that was exported throughout the empire, but the industries "brought the weavers an apparently steady livelihood, but on so low a level that few could afford the 500-drachma fee required for the acquisition of local citizenship."[30] He observes that, while cities may have had textile industries, they did not grow because of them,[31] and there were no formal textile guilds as would have existed in the Middle Ages. He essentially dismisses evidence from Pompeii in the form of graffiti in which a man is identified as a weaver as well as a notice that fullers (who remove lanolin from wool and dye cloth) erected a statue to Eumachia as insufficient to support contentions of production on a scale that would promote the rise of a middle class of artisans comparable with the Middle Ages.[32]

Despite Findley and Koester's portrait of the cloth trade, however, workers themselves may not have been completely powerless. To illustrate, a papyrus letter dated to 116 C.E. from Hermopolis recounts difficulties with workers in a weaving shop where the employees staged a strike in order to obtain a raise and were blocking attempts to hire substitute laborers.[33] For his part, Andrew Wilson references the incident in Acts 19:23–41, where Paul's preaching appears to threaten the livelihood of silversmiths. It seems to be the case that workers in that industry understood the dynamics of supply and demand for their products. As a final observation, workers themselves appear to have taken pride in their occupations and banded together in social groups. Certainly by the second century

---

30. Finley, *Ancient Economy*, 136–37.

31. Ibid., 137.

32. Ibid., 139, 194 (the latter was an addendum to his original text penned in 1984).

33. Jean-Jacques Aubert, "The Fourth Factor: Managing Non-agricultural Production in the Roman World," in *Economies beyond Agriculture in the Classical World* (ed. David J. Mattingly and John Salmon; New York: Routledge, 2001), 107.

C.E., worshipers in Alexandria synagogue chose to sit according to their trade groups, and the weavers were represented as one such faction.[34]

Another point where Finley may have overstated his case is when he mentions that cities did not grow due to the textile industry. Wilson, by contrast, is clear that this particular stance may be the result either of limited archaeological data that have tended to employ keyhole investigations that do not adequately show whether or not there might be diversity of manufacturing in a given city, or of digs that focus only on the areas of the city where public buildings and temples might be found rather than the areas where people lived and worked. Further, he cautions that looking only for single factories, which may have been rare, may underestimate the modest impact of manufacturing undertaken by many household-sized units, each of which may have made their own very small contribution to the larger economy.[35] To get at this type of economic information, he recommends large-scale clearance work as the best approach to dig sites.[36]

In sum, then, contrary to Koester and Finley, the production of fabric and garments cannot be discounted as playing an insignificant role in the ancient economy. Instead, textile production may have contributed positively to the overall standard of living of residents in the empire. The Gospel of Luke does provide glimpses into what this standard might be. First, references to the clothing worn by Jesus and the disciples will be analyzed, and then attention will be turned briefly to the clues the text offers about the production of textiles at large.

8.3. EVERYDAY CLOTHING AND THE GOSPEL OF LUKE

Studies of clothing in the Gospel could generally veer off in two directions. On the one hand, focus might fall on passages like 16:19, in which a rich man is dressed in purple and fine linen (πορφύρα, βύσσος); 15:22, where the prodigal son receives from his wealthy father "the first or best" clothes (στολὴν τὴν πρώτην); or 7:25, in which "soft clothes" are associated with those who live in royal palaces. This is valuable. It would be wise to heed

---

34. Roussin, "Costume in Roman Palestine," 183.

35. Andrew Wilson, "Timgad and Textile Production," in *Economies beyond Agriculture in the Classical World* (ed. David J. Mattingly and John Salmon; New York: Routledge, 2001), 288, 291.

36. Andrew Wilson, "Urban Production in the Roman World: The View from North Africa," *Papers of the British School at Rome* 70 (2002): 336.

the words of Morely, however, when he cautions that, when it comes to matters of style, there is little difference between elite and popular—and in any case eventually the masses tend to imitate the elite.[37]

On the other hand, it is easy to "theologize" about clothing and the New Testament. Peter Atkins demonstrates this beautifully when he likens the naked and then clothed state of the Gerasene demoniac in Luke 8:35 to conversion and the act of being clothed with new garments in the ritual of baptism.[38] The theologizing tactic might be applied to other contexts as well, such as highlighting the fact that God's providential goodness is evident in the fact that Jesus never procures his own clothing in the Gospel.

From the time his mother wraps him in swaddling clothes (2:7) though the point at which Joseph of Arimethea provides the σινδών or fine linen cloth for Jesus' burial, others always present him with garments. Incidentally, Jesus' garments tend to be of fine quality, given that the bleaching process for to obtain white cloth rendered it more expensive than the beige or brownish colors inherent in unbleached or dyed wool. Thus when God provides Jesus with a lightning-bright white robe at the transfiguration or Herod supplies a shinning robe just prior to his crucifixion in 23:11, Jesus is outfitted in good-quality attire.

A more profitable approach that would steer away from both the theologizing tendencies and preoccupations with the attire of the very wealthy is to examine what the disciples and others who were "everyday, ordinary citizens" wore, according to Luke.

The first hint comes in verse 3:11, when John, who is addressing the "crowds"[39] adjures his listeners that if they have two tunics, they must share with anyone who has none. We have already seen with Allen's model that, even at the barest subsistence level, one could be able to afford enough cloth for two tunics per year. So presumably those whom John was addressing were at least at the subsistence level or higher and were being encouraged to share with the destitute.

A later mention of tunics in the Gospel may relate to the idea that several tunics might be worn on top of each other at home.[40] Perhaps this was for warmth. Possibly this tendency to layer may have been what Jesus

---

37. Morely, *Trade*, 48.

38. Peter Atkins, "More Than Outward Appearances: The Importance of 'Clothing' in Some New Testament Passages," *ExpTim* 113.11 (2002): 363.

39. On the demographics for crowds, see Oakman, *Jesus and the Peasants*, 46–52.

40. Dupont, *Daily Life*, 261.

had in mind when the Twelve are not permitted to take a second tunic with them on their mission in 9:4. The absence of the second shirt may be a reminder that they are to be warmed because they were engaged in labor on behalf of Jesus during the journey, not wearing layers as though lounging around at home during leisure.

For their part, the seventy are sent out without benefit of sandals (10:4),[41] no doubt a literary twist to dramatize the fact that by 10:19 they have the authority to step on scorpions—an action much more life threatening with bare feet! In any event, two points about these missions may be made. First, the passages read in their current setting as if those sent out did possess the items but were merely to leave them behind. In short, they were to go out as if they were at subsistence level rather than at a level of more modest comfort. Second, when asked by Jesus in 22:35 whether they lack anything during their missions, the answer is negative. Clearly, others whom the disciples encountered had surpluses and were able to share and provide whatever was necessary.

In addition to these passages that focus on tunics, there are pericopes in which the ἱμάτιον, or toga, also appears. In verse 6:30, those listening to Jesus are counseled that if someone takes away their ἱμάτια, they are not to withhold their tunics either. If they have layered tunics, as previously mentioned, that does not necessarily mean that they are naked at this point; they may be merely reduced to subsistence level. In other verses, Jesus is wearing a fringed ἱμάτιον[42] when he heals a woman with a hemorrhage (8:44), the disciples throw their ἱμάτια on the colt prior to allowing Jesus to ride it, and the crowds lining the streets are of similar economic status in that they cast their togas on the road to create a carpet upon which Jesus' mount may step (19:36). This last action may indicate that the readers of Luke's Gospel in general are slightly more affluent than those of Matthew and Mark. In those two Gospels only some of the parade spectators throw

---

41. John Dominic Crossan views the instructions in 10:4, particularly the advice to carry no knapsack, as a way to differentiate Jesus' missionaries from wandering Cynic missionaries who carried a bag on their journeys. See "The Historical Jesus in Earliest Christianity," in *Jesus and Faith: A Conversation on the Work of John Dominic Crossan* (ed. Jeffrey Carlson and Robert A. Ludwig; Maryknoll, N.Y.: Orbis, 1994), 14–15. This interpretation is highly doubtful, given that his disciples were later told that it was time to take up purses and bags (Luke 22:36).

42. According to Cleland, Davies, and Jones (*Greek and Roman Dress*, 74), fringes were not typically part of Greek or Roman dress and were considered foreign.

cloaks on the ground in the tradition of 2 Kg 9:13 while others deposit tree branches, perhaps indicating the mixed economic status of crowd members, with some not quite a prosperous as others. The less well off either did not own overgarments or else did not have the luxury to submit what they did possess to such abuse.

The idea that Luke's community might have been more affluent than Matthew's or Mark's perhaps is also indicated by Luke's rendition of the parable about patching garments (5:36; Matt 9:16; Mark 2:18–22). While the other two Gospel authors worry about new, unshrunk cloth patches (likely obtained from one of the patch makers who had their own place and *collegia* within the garment industry)[43] puckering and tearing off of the torn garment during laundering, Luke's story has a completely different spin. He alone has the good fortune to possess two full togas, an older one and a newer one. His concern is that a piece borrowed from the newer to patch the old would devalue the newer while the patch itself would not match the old, maybe because the old garment was faded or of a different color.

The final example comes from Luke 22:35 and talks about pawning cloaks to obtain swords. The value of a toga, ἱμάτιον, cannot be doubted. After all, based on this conversation, it was equivalent to that of a weapon (22:36). Nonetheless, according to Luke's account, the disciples must have been of modest means rather than impoverished because they ultimately possessed two swords among their group. These were weapons that they had the wherewithal to buy without needing to resort to selling their togas. Rather than having to choose between clothes or weapons, they managed to afford both, an indication of their solvency.

Taken altogether, this parade of references from Luke's Gospel creates a picture of Jesus' followers from the population. Some of them, including the disciples themselves, may have been modestly comfortable, at least as much as can be determined by looking at references to clothing.

8.4. Evidence for Textile Manufacturing in the Gospel of Luke

In comparison with the number of verses that mention garments, passages in Luke's Gospel regarding the textile industry are rare. In this it

---

43. Judith Lynn Sebesta, "Tunica Ralla, Tunica Spissa: The Colors and Textiles of Roman Costume," in Sebesta and Bonfante, *World of Roman Costume*, 65.

differs from its companion book, Acts, which evidences knowledge of finished textiles and trade as represented by Lydia, who was a merchant of finished purple colored cloth (16:14), and Dorcas, who made her living sewing clothing and robes for others (9:39). Not counting Luke's casual mention that the shepherds were present at Jesus' birth (2:8–16), where they presumably had the economic means to hire others or impose on family members to watch their wool on the hoof while they traveled to the town, the Gospel itself has only three passages that provide significant information about textile production. All three of these center on the very early stages of cloth manufacturing.

The first occurs in 12:27 when, in an injunction not to be anxious about the basic needs of life, Jesus points out that the lilies of the field neither "labor" nor "spin" (οὐ κοπιᾷ οὐδὲ νήθει), with some texts containing the variant "spin nor weave" (ὑφαίνει). In basic wool production, after the fleece has been sheared from the sheep and the tags (manure-laden parts) removed—a process in the modern industry known as skirting— the grease wool is washed to eliminate some of the lanolin, picked (teased to help open the fibers), carded to begin the process of having the fibers adhere to one another (at which point additional burrs are removed), roved (divided into strips and loaded onto a spool), and finally spun into thread or yarn by adding twist.[44] In short, there is a significant amount of labor involved just in preparing the wool for spinning. Once sufficient yarn has been spun, it may either be dyed or used plain on a loom.

The weaving itself also involves hard work. First there is planning a design, if any, then stringing the loom with the warp threads and, depending on the type of loom (warp-weighted or two-beam), attaching the weights. Alternate strands of the warp (the vertical threads) are separated by strips of wood known as heddles and sheds before the weft begins to be passed through the threads via a shuttle. In all, the full process of spinning and weaving is time consuming. Yet Luke clearly implies that each individual need not "labor and spin" to provide cloth sufficient for their own use, as might be expected in a subsistence-level economy. Rather, God would provide. What appears to be the case here is not that clothing will miraculously materialize but rather that the economy has developed to the point where there is division of labor. The disciples need not worry about weav-

---

44. On the full process, from shearing to yarn, an excellent summary may be found on the Blackberry Ridge Woolen Mill site, Mt. Horeb, Wisconsin. See http:// www.blackberry=riddge.com/prosdscr.htm [cited 11 November 2010].

ing because others in the economy will step up to do those tasks, freeing the disciples to proceed with their mission.

Furthermore, not only does a division of labor exist but the Gospel's author envisions an economy where, rather than everyone being at a subsistence level, some individuals have a surplus of either funds or possessions. This is demonstrated in 8:2–3, the second, though indirect, evidence of textile manufacturing. In this passage a number of women—including Mary Magdalene; Joanna, the wife of Herod's steward; and Susanna, among others—provide either for Jesus alone or the ministry at large (depending on the textual variant), ἐκ ὑπαρχόντων, from their own resources (either monetary means or possessions such as clothes). In essence, Jesus' ministry is able to flourish only because the economy had enough flexibility that there were at least some Judeans who had means in excess of what was needed for their own survival.

The third passage that alludes to the textile industry also is one in which the level of production exceeds the quantity of demand that would be entailed by mere subsistence. In the parable of the lost sheep (15:3), which Luke indicates was addressed to the Pharisees and scribes, a man has a flock of one hundred sheep grazing in the wilderness and loses one, which he successfully locates after searching. Do one hundred sheep constitute a large herd? For perspective, the obscenely wealthy Varro, who lived in the late second century B.C.E., recorded that his own livestock holdings included eight hundred sheep. He knew of no other with flocks of that exact size, but he was aware of at least one with seven hundred.[45] Peter Garnsey and Richard Saller point out, however, that even seven to eight hundred head of sheep is pasturage on a modest scale in comparison to the millions of sheep of the "Aragonese Dogana of the medieval and early modern period."[46] Yet, before dismissing one hundred sheep as insignificant in comparison with the medieval era, it is a worthwhile exercise to estimate how much land would be required for raising one hundred sheep and how much wool a flock of that size might produce.

Garnsey and Saller lament a lack of data on the sheep industry during the Principate; nonetheless, it is possible to don the hat of an economic historian engaged in a quantitative exercise and posit a hypothetical model rooted in modern agronomy. Data from the current era may be subse-

45. Peter Garnsey and Richard Saller, *The Roman Empire: Economy, Society and Culture* (Berkeley: University of California Press, 1987), 68.

46. Ibid.

quently adjusted for variations in soil conditions, rainfall, and the ancient lack of livestock dietary supplements and modern pasture fertilizers. Such a model will not be precise but should give a rough idea of the resources required for raising one hundred sheep in rural Judea as well as their potential wool output.

In the United States, the average fleece weight upon yearly shearing is 7.5 pounds after washing. This is sufficient to provide three to four sweaters, which are generally constructed using three quarters to one and one-half pounds of yarn.[47] So one may posit that a modern flock of one hundred sheep would provide raw materials for three hundred sweaters or, given the dimensions of an ancient tunic, approximately two hundred tunics. Assuming that Palestinian sheep, not benefiting from the generations of animal husbandry, produced at a rate of seventy-five percent of their modern equivalents, the resulting amount would be 150 tunics. At our extrapolation from Allen's figures, that would be sufficient to clothe seventy-five people at the subsistence level or forty to fifty if some of the wool was converted into togas, ἱμάτια. In any event, it would appear to be a quantity of wool exceeding the need of an individual owner and his or her immediate family and dependents.

Lest one think that one hundred sheep would require immense estates for grazing, that number of sheep in a fairly fertile area like the state of Indiana would require only thirty acres. And, generally, sheep would be moved every twenty-one days from ten-acre subdivisions of within that plot of land.[48] If one hundred Palestinian sheep in the time of Jesus required grazing of a very generous 160 acres due to lack of rainfall and poor soils, that only amounts to one-half of a square mile. More research for this particular model needs to be conducted on arable land in Palestine, yet it is reasonable to assume that some livestock owners may not have held titles to the property upon which their sheep grazed but made use of commonly owned public lands like those of which the Bedouin tribes in the Middle

---

47. Data on wool weights are readily available in general Internet searches. Individual farms and cooperative extension offices provide this information on numerous sites. Sweater weight was extrapolated from yarn-skein labels and crochet instructions for number of skeins required for sweaters.

48. J. B. Outhouse, K. D. Johnson, and C. L. Rhykerd, "Managing and Utilizing Pasture and Harvested Forages for Sheep" [cited 9 November 2010]; online: http://www.agry.perdue.edu/ext/forages/publications/ID-153.htm.

East avail themselves today.[49] In short, a lot of wool can be produced on a reasonable amount of privately or publicly available land. Thus it is logical to assume that first-century residents of modest means might, with just a small handful of sheep, produce sufficient wool for both their own needs and a bit for sale to others.

8.5. Observations and Thoughts

At the conclusion of this study on clothing, there are three points to highlight. First, one must be careful to check one's assumptions about terms like *poverty* and *wealth* in the classical era. Greg Woolf speaks out on this issue when he laments that "ancient historians and archaeologists working on Mediterranean societies sometimes write as if all ancient agriculturalists were living in conditions of economic marginality."[50] Fortunately, the last decade has seen a more moderate approach, with historians advocating for careful use of language and the creation of models that portray subtleties and gradations of economic resources rather than assuming strict dichotomies between the "poor" and the "rich." As biblical scholars continue to explore ancient economies, care should be taken to acknowledge this small paradigm shift in the cognate field of classical studies, lest older stances and viewpoints end up codified in biblical scholarship.[51]

Second, when the clothing references in Luke's Gospel are examined for hints as to the economic context that gave rise to final form of the Gospel or that reflect the economic status of its audience, it seems possible that Luke's own community was of modest means. Although not strictly middle class, as we would describe it today, in terms of clothing, they do not appear to have been in severe want. Third, economic history and cultural history are methods that may prove helpful when investigating the history of the New Testament. These methods may serve as vehicles for finding new insights about familiar first-century documents and the contexts in which they were originally written.

---

49. Rena Zaubi, "Land Use Planning and the Palestinian Minority in Israel: A Comparative Regional Study," *Prospect* (June 2011) [cited 15 July 2011]; online: http://prospectjournal.ucsd.edu/index.php/2011/06/land-use-planning-and-the-palestinian-minority-in-israel-a-comparative-regional-study/.

50. Greg Woolf, "Regional Productions in Early Roman Gaul," in Mattingly and Salmon, *Economies beyond Agriculture*, 59.

51. Longenecker's *Remember the Poor* should help to keep us on track.

9
A Scarlet Woman? John 4

When explicating the various modes of historical writing, as we have seen, revisionist historians attempt to identify biases in received texts because often documents are written by those who hold the presuppositions of those who belong to the privileged and power positions in a society. They seek to tease out evidence from the past that actually represents groups and interests that are not dominant in the culture and thus barely discernible in the histories and documents that have been left behind. Thus revisionist historians call for new interpretations of material that relates to groups marginalized or even maligned in prior histories. This essay is written in this mode and is focused on the Samaritan woman, a character in John 4.

The female in this pericope has a marital history that, at first glance, seems to be beyond the pale. But is that really the case? The project turns on the issue of whether or not contemporary Western views of morality and marriage are being projected back onto the woman's first-century Roman context. This serves as a cautionary tale about how easily fallacies related to anachronism and ethnocentrism can crop up in works of history. Anachronism and ethnocentrism were both discussed in detail in chapter 4 and represent the kind of missteps to which those who read history should be attuned.

Beyond the revisionist agenda, though, setting out a sketch of the institution of marriage in the first-century world requires extensive use of secondary sources written by social historians. Marriage is, after all, a social convention. And, in true social-history fashion, rather than focusing on one particular marriage ceremony or one element, which would be more in the mode of cultural history—or on the emotional consequences of being involved in so many marriages, as would be typical of psychohistory—in this essay we will focus on the institution more widely. In other words, we will be seeking the overarching patterns and conventions that typify ancient relationships in society at large. Furthermore, while the prior chapter regarding clothing in Luke's Gospel was informed by economic concerns, the type of history that plays a role in portions of this analysis is legal history. As with economics, to recap a point made above (§2.2), legal concerns may be considered by historians to be a force that heavily influences events from the past. In the case of the Samaritan woman, we will want to know what the law books say about when marriages are designated "official" and how legal prescriptions might have impacted how, when, and how often marriages were contracted in ancient society.

It is also important to note that, like the prior chapter, this one is not a piece of "pure history" but is exegesis. Thus there are references to first-century readers of the Gospel, which would not be characteristic of essays written in the field of history. But, nevertheless, the heart of the argument is historical so far as it involves bringing what is known about first-century customs of marriage and divorce to bear on the New Testament text in order to produce a new interpretation about the character of a woman from the past. So, onward to the analysis itself, the first step of which is to set out why Roman marriage customs and conventions rather than Jewish, Greek, or some other should be considered as part of the background for understanding the woman at the well.

9.1. ROMAN CONTEXTS AND NEW TESTAMENT TEXTS

In *The River of God*, Gregory Riley envisions a paradigmatic shift in the field of New Testament studies in which scholars take seriously not only Jewish backgrounds and influences on New Testament texts but also Greco-Roman antecedents.[1] Greek strands, usually identified by the designation *Hellenistic*, are easy to accept on the surface. After all, the New Testament itself was written in Greek. Roman contributions to the early Christian milieu, though, are more difficult to pinpoint. Riley himself, as a glance at his index will confirm, refers to Greek influences on New Testament texts three times as often as he does Roman. Generally, when scholars do delve into Roman contexts, their focus is on a set number of elements, such as Paul's citizenship, the institution of slavery in relation to Onesimus in Philemon, and the realities of Roman political domi-

---

1. Gregory J. Riley, *River of God* (San Francisco: HarperCollins, 2001), especially 5–7.

nance as a background for the book of Revelation.[2] More recently, under the influence of postcolonial studies, it has become fashionable to examine the tensions inherent in Palestine's being subjugated to Rome in other early Christian literature like the Gospels, too.[3]

Relating aspects of the New Testament to the Roman milieu other than considerations directly stemming from conflicts inherent in Roman dominance and provincial administration, however, depends on the pervasiveness of Roman culture during the first century. So both classicists and biblical scholars are currently debating how Roman the ancient eastern provinces might have been. Ramsay MacMullen, for instance, though acknowledging both Greek and Jewish cultural strands in first-century Palestine, describes Herod as one of the primary proponents of Romanization of the East. For instance, Herod built buildings in grand Roman style, frequently employing the Roman construction method of pouring cement in forms.[4] And while Herod did put on Greek-style musicals and athletic competitions in his theatres, he also made certain to present entertainments featuring "gladiators and wild beasts," which were in vogue in Rome.[5] Onno Van Nijf, in studying the relationship of Greek culture and Roman imperial power in the East, concludes that elements from both civilizations were blended together. For instance, Greek-style athletic competitions were held during the Roman period, but they were frequently sponsored by Roman dignitaries, if not the emperors themselves.[6]

Even though all of this dialogue has been raging, Roman social history remains a largely untapped sphere of investigation in Johannine studies. [7] That presents a challenge that is hard to surmount. Now, all this talk about

---

2. On the issue of Paul's citizenship, see A. N. Sherwin-White, *Roman Law and Roman Society in the New Testament* (Oxford: Oxford University Press, 1963).

3. For work in this vein on the Fourth Gospel, see Tom Thatcher, *Greater Than Caesar: Christology and Empire in the Fourth Gospel* (Minneapolis: Fortress, 2009).

4. Ramsay MacMullen, *Romanization in the Time of Augustus* (New Haven: Yale University Press, 2000), 22.

5. Ibid.

6. Adaptations to these public events included the performance of imperial sacrifices and the renaming of the festivals themselves to honor specific emperors. See Onno Van Nijf, "Local Heroes: Athletics, Festivals, and Elite Self-Fashioning in the Roman East," in *Being Greek under Rome* (ed. Simon Goldhill; Cambridge: Cambridge University Press, 2001), 318–19.

7. For example, Sjef Van Tilborg, *Reading John in Ephesus* (Leiden: Brill, 1996); Richard J. Cassidy, *John's Gospel in New Perspective* (Maryknoll, N.Y.: Orbis, 1992), 16.

Romanization is not to deny that Jewish influences on the text exist. One must concede that the conversation at the well does echo the betrothal stories of the Jewish patriarchs, for instance,[8] and the existence of multiple husbands may also bring to mind the story of Sarah, who had eight husbands in total when Tobias is added in the book of Tobit (6:14). Rather, the goal is to investigate how the text might have resonated with Gentile converts to Christianity or Roman audiences. This is logical, given that, while some readers of the Gospel may have been Jewish,[9] the evangelist's careful translation of Hebrew terms into Greek (1:17, 40, 42) provides a clue that the Gospel may have been intended for circulation within a mixed audience.[10] Thus we come to the crux of our query. How might the Samaritan woman appear against the backdrop of Roman marital conventions?

9.2. Too Many Marriages and One Peculiar Relationship?

A vast majority of biblical scholars look askance at the Samaritan woman because of her marital history, a history revealed in verses 16–18. At that juncture in her conversation with Jesus, the woman is adjured to call her husband to join her at the well. The woman responds that she has no husband (ἄνδρα), and Jesus counters her assertion by revealing to her that, while she is literally correct in stating that she is not married, she has had five husbands and that she currently "has a man" who is not her husband. Based on this exchange, a variety of colorful descriptions have been ascribed to her. For instance, she has been identified as

---

8. See, for instance, J. Bligh, "Jesus in Samaria," *HeyJ* 3 (1962): 336. See also Jeffrey Lloyd Staley, *The Print's First Kiss: A Rhetorical Investigation of the Implied Reader in the Fourth Gospel* (SBLDS 82; Atlanta: Scholars Press, 1988), 98–103; Calum Carmichael, "Marriage and the Samaritan Woman," *NTS* 26 (1980): 332–46; Andrew E. Arterbury, "Breaking the Betrothal Bonds: Hospitality in John 4," *CBQ* 72 (2010): 63–83.

9. Attention was drawn to the synagogue expulsion as a possible context for the Johannine Community by J. Louis Martyn, *History and Theology in the Fourth Gospel* (New York: Harper & Row, 1968).

10. If this is true, then, as Richard Bauckham observes, although knowledge of Jewish symbols and images would be recognized by some readers of the Johannine text, non-Jewish readers as well as those with "only minimal knowledge of Christian belief" would still find the Gospel comprehensible ("The Audience of the Fourth Gospel," in Fortna and Thatcher, *Jesus in Johannine Tradition*, 110).

a "notorious sinner,"[11] as a "moral outcast,"[12] as "socially deviant,"[13] and even with the quite imaginative sobriquet of a "specimen of matrimonial maladjustment."[14] Sometimes the idea that she is of questionable character is linked to the idea that she is a moral outcast because she draws water at noon, an unusual hour, given that women came to socialize and obtain water in the early morning. As one scholar puts it, "Respectable women made their trips to the well in the morning, when they could greet one another and talk about the news. But this woman was one of the people they talked about, and the fact that she showed up at noon was a sure sign that she was not welcome."[15] This, however, is an example of a variation of the *post hoc ergo propter hoc* fallacy discussed in chapter 4—the trap of imputing false correlations between two separate events. The midday trip to the well may have been precipitated just as easily by some other reason, such as a request for water coming from the sixth man in this woman's life, extreme thirst related to an illness, or simply extreme warmth that caused her to want to add some extra water to a wilting garden. A day with a high heat index, one might conjecture, would also explain why the disciples were concerned for Jesus and why he needed to rest at the well.

Problems of logic aside, at times scholars who attempt to avoid fallacies and pass no moral judgments still cannot resist the occasional sly comment concerning her various relationships. For instance, Van Tilborg offers an implied criticism when he ruminates, "Could she have something of Ohola, the adulterous and oversexed woman from Ezekiel 23 who symbolizes Samaria?"[16] Similarly, Herman C. Waetjen hypothesizes that her story parallels that of Gomer, "who after an adulterous affair ... was redeemed by Hosea."[17] Even a bit more subtle are Lois Malcolm and Janet Ramsey. In their psychohistorical treatment, they only imply her fallen

---

11. D. Moody Smith, *John* (Nashville: Abingdon, 1999), 113.

12. D. A. Carson, *The Gospel according to John* (Grand Rapids: Eerdmans, 1991), 216. Carson maintains that the fact that she comes to the well alone rather than with a group of women indicates that her marital situation has led to her "public shame" (217).

13. Malina and Rohrbaugh, *Social-Science Commentary*, 98.

14. Leon Morris, *The Gospel according to John* (rev. ed.; Grand Rapids: Eerdmans, 1995), 225.

15. Barbara Brown Taylor, "Reflections on the Lectionary" *ChrCent* (12 February 2008): 19.

16. Sjef Van Tilborg, *Imaginative Love in John* (Leiden: Brill, 1993), 185.

17. Herman C. Waetjen, *The Gospel of the Beloved Disciple: A Work in Two Editions* (New York: T&T Clark, 2005), 163.

status when they discuss her need for forgiveness and how, in the course of her conversation with Jesus, her problem is externalized through the same tactic that psychologists employ to enable victims to better define their issues. The upshot of her conversation with Jesus, according to these two authors is that, "not merely a 'fallen' Samaritan woman, she now was revealed as someone who also worshipped God and was now ready for a new, healthy, and more complex identity."[18] It is no wonder that, by conflating her "fallen state" and the troubles with Samaria, allegorical interpretations abound,[19] though it is not clear that readers from the wider world might have grasped parallels between the woman's personal life and supposed elements of Samaria's rock-strewn relationship with the Jews.

A key objective in this essay is to determine whether or not, based on Roman customs of the period, it is accurate to describe the woman as "fallen" or to condemn her for a lack of morality due to her marital record, as the scholars mentioned here have done. Reexamining old questions in new ways, as is being proposed here, is a technique found in revisionist history. And so we will embark on an exploration of first-century marital conventions.

Studies concerning marriage in the Roman world, though, must be liberally peppered by caveats. First, it is virtually impossible to speak of Jewish, Roman, or even Christian marriages as if monogamous relationships in the ancient world might be easily categorized.[20] Wide ranges of regional variations were characteristic of the marital structures of each of these cultures. For example, rabbinic law permitted remarriage three times, though levirate marriage within Samaritan practice might not have had any restrictions in terms of numbers.[21] In any case, Michael Satlow cautions that there was no single concept of Jewish marriage in antiquity. Rather, "Jews understood marriage, and married, much like their non-Jewish neighbors," though they did attempt to add "Jewish" flavoring to

---

18. Lois Malcolm and Janet Ramsey, "On Forgiveness and Healing: Narrative Therapy and the Gospel Story," *WW* 31 (2010): 27.

19. Waetjen calls her "Lady Samaria" (*Gospel of the Beloved Disciple*, 163).

20. In 1985, Bernadette Brooten bemoaned the fact that classical studies were emerging on women in Rome but did not include discussions of Jewish and Christian women. See "Early Christian Women in Their cultural Context," in *Feminist Perspectives on Biblical Scholarship* (ed. Adela Yarbro Collins; Chico, Calif.: Scholars Press, 1985), 71.

21. Teresa Okure, "Jesus and the Samaritan Woman (Jn 4:1–42) in Africa," *TS* 70 (2009): 407.

local practices.[22] Likewise, even Roman marriage customs were adapted to various provincial contexts. For example, Roman law prohibited marriage between siblings, a practice condoned in Egypt.[23] In Roman Egypt, however, third-century divorce agreements and census returns indicate that sibling marriages were occurring side by side with Roman-style divorce regardless of normal Roman ideals.[24]

One other difficulty in studying matrimonial understandings relates to the fact that epigraphic evidence concerning Christian marriages before the third century is virtually nonexistent.[25] Further, what evidence is present, at least for Roman unions, pertains to the upper classes. The procedures among the lower echelons of society can only be inferred. For the purpose of this study, however, it is assumed that most residents of the Roman Empire, apart from their own social status or location in the provinces, would have at least a basic knowledge of the matrimonial habits of some Romans. Either they may have heard news about particular elite Romans or been aware of the customs practiced by those Roman officials who occupied and governed the provinces. In light of this presupposition and the "blending of traditions" cited above, it is reasonable to examine the pericope of the Samaritan woman against the backdrop of Roman connubial conventions.

---

22. Michael Satlow, *Jewish Marriage in Antiquity* (Princeton: Princeton University Press, 2001), xiii.

23. Justinian, *Digest* 23.2.17.

24. Donald C. Barker, "The Place of Residence of the Divorced Wife in Roman Egypt," in *Akten des 21. internationalen Papyrologenkongresses, Berlin, 13.–19.8.1995* (ed. Bärbel Kramer et al.; Stuttgart: Teubner, 1997), 59–66. Identifying the elements of "Christian marriages" is also a daunting task. As James Jeffers hypothesizes (*The Greco-Roman World of the New Testament Era* [Downers Grove, Ill.: InterVarsity Press, 1999], 240), Christian families in all likelihood resembled either Jewish or pagan families since the early Christians were converts from those groups.. Halvor Moxnes also acknowledges that among early Christian groups there were Christians married to nonbelievers, presumably in Roman- or pagan-style arrangements. See "What Is Family? Problems in Constructing Early Christian Families," in *Constructing Early Christian Families* (ed. Halvor Moxnes; New York: Routledge, 1997), 30. The issue of identifying the "Christian family" is further complicated by the fact that the "family as an institution is not an issue that is treated in a systematic way by New Testament authors" (18).

25. Geoffrey S. Nathan, *The Family in Late Antiquity: The Rise of Christianity and the Endurance of Tradition* (New York: Routledge, 2000), 38.

Marriage during the first century was legally recognized only for Roman citizens. Neither slaves nor those provincials or foreigners who did not possess citizenship could engage in relationships that were, by Roman standards, legal unions. Thus, in a very literal sense, most women of Palestine during the first century, including the Samaritan woman, were not married, no matter the relationships that they had formed. Particularities of the law aside, noncitizens and even slaves did enter relationships that the partners themselves considered to be long-term monogamous unions and had perhaps gone through ceremonies to begin those associations. Residents in the provinces would recognize these as analogous to legal marriages, though such relationships were without the benefits that accrued to legal alliances through the law.[26]

Legal Roman marriage was an honorable estate for the purpose of begetting children and merely required the agreement of those involved to achieve validity. Any ceremonies were incidental.[27] As J. A. Crook explains, marriage "was not sacramental, not 'holy' matrimony; it was not thought to be maintained or sanctioned by anything beyond the will of those who were parties to it.... The opposite of *iustae nuptiae* was not 'living in sin'" or immorality.[28] In essence, then, marriage was a simple contract, and adultery was a charge that only applied to those who had agreed to live under such a contract.[29] With the exception of outright prostitution, other

---

26. For instance, legal marriages enabled children to belong to their father. They took their father's name and social status. Generally, according to Thomas A. J. McGinn ("The Augustan Marriage Legislation and Social Practice: Elite Endogamy versus Male Marrying Down," in *Speculum Iuris: Roman Law as a Reflection of Social and Economic Life in Antiquity* [ed. Jean-Jacques Aubert and Boudewyn Sirks; Ann Arbor: University of Michigan Press, 2002], 46–93), the social status of fathers was higher than that of mothers. In addition to these benefits, children of legal marital arrangements had rights of inheritance should their fathers die intestate. Children born outside of legal marriage belonged to the mother and took her social status (Beryl Rawson, *Marriage, Divorce, and Children in Ancient Rome* [Oxford: Clarendon, 1991], 26).

27. The necessity of a priest's approval to legitimize marriage was established by the Fourth Synod of Carthage (Nathan, *Family*, 83).

28. J. A. Crook, *Law and Life of Rome 90 B.C.–A.D. 212* (Ithaca, N.Y.: Cornell University Press, 1967), 99.

29. The *Lex Julia adulteries coercendis*, the Julian Law concerning adultery, which was passed by Augustus in 18 B.C.E., made *adulterium* a criminal offense. Augustus also provided that financial considerations might be paid to a wife who sued her husband for divorce after catching him *in flagrante* (Nathan, *Family*, 21).

conjugal alliances were exempt from the censure associated with adultery.[30] So, was the woman of Samaria an adulteress? This is doubtful, given that she testifies concerning Jesus' knowledge of her life in verse 39. The word *testify* is imbued with legal associations. While women were permitted to offer testimony in Roman courts,[31] a privilege not accorded to females in Jewish jurisprudence,[32] those women convicted of adultery were prohibited from serving as witnesses. Since the Johannine text is clear that the woman at the well does testify and that her witness successfully persuades the residents of Sychar to learn more about Jesus, one may therefore infer that a Roman reader would assume she was not an adulteress.

Further evidence that she is not engaged in a scandalous extramarital affair is supplied by Jesus himself, who affirms that she was not currently in a formal marriage (v. 17, Καλῶς ἐιπας ὅτι Ἄωδρα οὐκ ἔχω). If she was not married to the sixth man, by definition she is not engaged in adultery, and, within the context of Roman relationship arrangements, her behavior is not necessarily unseemly nor a source of shame.[33]

Although she may not have been legally married to her last companion, there were a variety of socially acceptable, though only quasi-legal, alternatives to marriage that also might illuminate the woman's relationship to the sixth man, none of which would occasion the necessity of labeling her as a scarlet woman. Many of these arrangements involved persons of widely disparate social status or persons who might not possess the requisite citizenship status for legal unions. For instance, *contubernia*, an arrangement that was established by the *Senatusconsultum Claudianum* in 52 C.E. was a legally contracted relationship, although considered to be inferior to *matrimonium*. In this arrangement, women who were citizens were permitted to enter into long-term monogamous relationships with

---

30. According to Thomas McGinn, though, upper-class males were prohibited from marrying procuresses, actresses, women who had been caught in adultery, women condemned in criminal courts, or individuals whose parents fell into one of those categories by the *Lex Iulia et Papia* ("Augustan Marriage Legislation," 50). If a woman was married, though, and committed adultery, her husband was required to divorce her, and shame was imputed to the woman. If a woman was unmarried, though, she would not be labeled as an adulteress even if her congress was with a married man.

31. Justinian, *Digest* 22.5.18.

32. C. K. Barrett, *The Gospel according to St. John* (2nd ed.; London: SPCK), 240.

33. Justinian, *Digest* 23.2.43. Only women convicted of adultery were branded with *infamia*.

slaves, even though slaves did not have the right to pursue wedlock.[34] The institution of concubinage, *concubinatus*, was similar to *contubernia*. This, however, was a legally and socially recognized relationship "just short of marriage" between two free citizens[35] who were usually of different economic classes.[36] For instance, a person of the senatorial or equestrian class, who might lose social standing by association with a plebian or who might be forbidden by law to marry persons of lower station,[37] might establish a relationship with a concubine.[38] Concubines could inherit, and Justinian's *Digest* includes a fair amount of material indicating that they were not considered adulteresses or prostitutes since statute law made provisions for such relationships.[39] As was the case with marriage, no formal celebration was required to initiate the association. The intention of the parties alone was sufficient to enter this status. The ease with which concubinage might be transformed into legal marriage also is a clue that such relationships were not disgraceful. According to Susan Treggiari, "if a couple lived in concubinage and then began to regard each other as husband and wife, their legal marriage dated from the beginning of their new attitude."[40] Given the wide variety of alternatives to marriage and the simplicity by which some might be converted into legal arrangements, it would be no wonder that the Samaritan woman thought that Jesus' identification of her current marital status was astonishing.

Before leaving the discussion of alternatives to legal marriage, it is important to note one prohibition concerning legal marriages that was particular to soldiers, presumably even those stationed in the provinces.

---

34. Nathan, *Family*, 59.

35. So defined by Alan Watson in the glossary of his English translation of the Mommsen edition of Justinian's *Institutes*.

36. Nathan, *Family*, 22–23.

37. Justinian, *Digest* 23.2.49: "Note that the lower orders can marry certain women where those of higher rank cannot legally do so, because of their superior position."

38. It appears that Christian women of high status as late as the third century were choosing to engage in concubinage rather than marriage in cases where they were unable to find Christian husbands of appropriate social rank. This was criticized by some of the church fathers, but McGinn comments that to the Christian women, this would be preferable to losing social status by marrying Christian men from the lower social orders ("Augustan Marriage Legislation," 77).

39. Justinian, *Digest* 25.7.3.

40. Susan Treggiari, "Divorce Roman Style: How Easy and How Frequent Was It?" in Rawson, *Marriage, Divorce, and Children*, 33.

Augustus introduced a ban to forbid serving soldiers below a certain rank to wed.[41] Thus, soldiers presumably were not permitted to marry local women, even if those women had been granted Roman citizenship. Marriage might, though, take place after the term of service had elapsed. Perhaps the Samaritan woman might be imagined in a scenario where she was betrothed to a Roman solider but temporarily unable to marry him, a situation that would explain Jesus' observation ὅν ἔχεις οὐκ ἔστιν σου, "the one whom who have is not your husband" (v. 18). From a Roman perspective, she would not be condemned as immoral in such a situation.

With the wide variety of quasi-legal relationships available to couples in the Roman world, labeling the woman of Sychar as a person of loose morals based on her association with a man who is not her husband may miss the mark. In other words, imposing non-Roman standards of morality upon the woman may be doing her an injustice. Despite this, questions concerning the peculiar fact that she has had five husbands may be raised, given that it might appear to be a high number. Attention will now turn to the dissolution of marriages and then subsequently to remarriages by divorcees and widows in the Roman era in order to explore what the norms might have been.

Divorce may only be understood within the context of how and why Roman marital unions were formed. The initiation of a Roman marriage was dependent upon the consent of each partner and the *paterfamilias*. The *paterfamilias* was generally either the grandfather or, if he was no longer alive, the father to whom was ascribed the status "head of the household," a title that was held even if the married parties would be living in their own domicile. At any time during the course of the marriage, divorce was easy to obtain and depended only on the desire of either the husband or wife to dissolve the union. Divorce would result whether cohabitation continued or not. No cause need be given to dissolve the relationship and divorce was unilateral. At some points in Roman history, the rupture of the mari-

---

41. This ban was in effect until the reign of Septimius Severus at the inception of the third century (Adolf Berger, et al., "Marriage Law," in *The Oxford Companion to Classical Civilization* [ed. Simon Hornblower and Antony Spawforth; Oxford: Oxford University Press, 1998], 446–47). According to Iulius Paulus, a jurist in the late second and early third centuries, this prohibition was extended to encompass even those holding office in a province. An official could not marry a woman who was born in or lived under his jurisdiction, although betrothal (*sponsare*) was not prohibited (Justinian, *Digest* 23.2.38; see also 23.2.63).

tal union could also be initiated by a *paterfamilias*. In this last instance, divorce might take place apart from the desires of the couple.[42] Eva Marie Lassen observes that it was not until the second half of the second century C.E. that a *paterfamilias* was finally legally forbidden to break up a marriage in which the couple was living in harmony, otherwise known as *bene concordans*.[43] In addition, formal notice of divorce need not be given to the other party in the case of a marriage's dissolution. For instance, a man, simply by the act marrying a second woman, was considered to be divorced from his first wife on the grounds that he obviously had determined the first relationship to be at an end. Notifying his first wife of the fact was not requisite.[44] Treggiari lists two other characteristics of Roman divorce procedure that might seem odd from the perspective of the complexity of present day laws and legal filings.

First, divorce could be accomplished without ratification by an outside authority, be it church or state. Second, neither public nor private records were kept. She also adds the comment that "whether a divorce had occurred might be privileged information, known only to the spouses."[45] Mirielle Corbier remarks that divorced women were not ostracized by society but would manage their own dowries and any inheritances from their fathers if the *paterfamilias* was no longer alive and the woman was *sui iuris*, independent.[46] Not only was there little or no censure for ending marriages but statistics have been produced in which there is a one in six chance of a first marriage being dissolved by divorce within its first decade.[47]

---

42. Susan Treggiari, "Divorce Roman Style," 34.

43. Eva Maria Lassen, "The Roman Family: Ideal and Metaphor," in Moxnes, *Constructing Early Christian Families*, 106. J. A. Crook notes that many tomb inscriptions bear the phrase *bene concordans matrimonium*. Presumably, if a woman's marriage was of the *manus* variety, in which she was transferred into the power of her husband's family, the *paterfamilias* of her birth family would no longer hold sway over her or have the ability to initiate divorce proceedings. In contrast to Lassen, Treggiari maintains that the *paterfamilias* may have no longer been able to dissolve marriages in his own right by the first century B.C.E. ("Divorce Roman Style," 34).

44. Treggiari, "Divorce Roman Style," 35. Augustus apparently attempted to add to the marriage legislation that there be witnesses present at a divorce, perhaps to make that easier to confirm (Nathan, *Family*, 20).

45. Treggiari, "Divorce Roman Style," 36.

46. Mireille Corbier, "Divorce and Adoption as Roman Familial Strategies," in Rawson, *Marriage, Divorce and Children*, 52.

47. Ibid., 45–46.

Beyond simple marital discord, typical reasons for divorce within the upper classes included one party having an opportunity to contract a more socially advantageous or lucrative marriage than the one in which he or she was already engaged or the fact that the current union had resulted in no children. This latter cause for divorce was linked to the idea that one of the primary reasons for entering a marriage contract was the production of legitimate descendants. In a rather bizarre twist on the idea of a woman being divorced because she did *not* bear children, Augusto Fraschetti refers to an episode recorded by Plutarch in which a woman was divorced precisely because she *had* proven her fertility. Apparently, a man who had no children convinced a friend to divorce his fertile wife so that the childless man might marry her and father an heir.[48] Faschetti concludes that it may not have been uncommon, at least in the upper classes for a "fertile woman to be circulated among a series of different husbands in order to produce offspring."[49]

But what was driving this need to have legitimate children? Ostensibly, bearing legal children within marriages was connected with financial and social privileges from the time of Augustus. The *lex Julia de maritandis ordinibus* of 18 B.C.E. and the *lex Papia Poppaea* of 9 B.C.E. imposed sanctions against unmarried persons, including widows and divorcees, and those with few or no children. In essence, those who were without legal offspring in some cases could not inherit and in others had to forfeit portions of their legacies.[50] This legislation, designed to increase the Roman population, the numbers of which had been decimated through the civil wars at the end of the republic, spurred the phenomenon of serial marriages among the upper classes.

In such a climate, widows as well as divorcees were much sought out for matrimony. Although Roman culture valued the woman who had only had one husband, the *univira*, the Augustan legislation helped to promote

---

48. Augusto Fraschetti, *Roman Women* (trans. Linda Lappin; Chicago: University of Chicago Press, 2001), 5–6.

49. Ibid., 6. See also Corbier, "Divorce and Adoption," 57. Corbier indicates that there is some thought that having children by the same woman created a bond between the men who had been her spouses (59).

50. Lassen, "The Roman Family," 107. As Gaius indicates in his *Institutes* (2.144), even though one may be named as an heir in a will, one cannot accept the inheritance if one is unmarried. Childless individuals were penalized by losing half of any inheritance to which they might be entitled (2.286).

the idea that, for women, celibacy was not natural and that remarriage, even for a widow, was normal.[51] Consequently, there was no censure for widows who did choose to remarry during the first century.[52] To some extent, only when a woman had reached menopause was her widowhood viewed as "a worthy and laudable thing."[53] Even in Roman Egypt, "marriage was a contract which regulated property arrangements; once a woman had passed child-bearing age, formal marriage had little point and would only have complicated existing arrangements for children by a previous partner."[54] This state of affairs continued until Constantine the Great made it possible for widows to remain single without suffering financial penalties when he abolished the Augustan marriage legislation in the fourth century.[55]

While legislation encouraged serial marriages among the higher levels of society, one wonders whether the Samaritan woman's history of having five marriages is a bit over the top. Geoffrey Nathan weighs in on this issue and hypothesizes that nearly one-third of adult upper-class women could expect three marriages during their lifetime.[56] There are instances, though, where more than three have been attested. For example, during the era of Augustus, Vestilia was married six times.[57] Pompey and Sulla each had five spouses. Further evidence that serial monogamy was in fashion among the upper classes is provided by the satirists' tendency to lampoon the practice. Seneca, for instance, pokes fun of noble women for keeping track of the passing years by listing the names of their various husbands,[58] and Juvenal remarks that women tended to "boast of their great number of husbands

---

51. Corbier, "Divorce and Adoption," 56.

52. Jan Willem Drijvers, "Virginity and Asceticism in Late Roman Western Elites," in *Sexual Asymmetry* (ed. Josine Blok and Peter Mason; Amsterdam: Gieben, 1987), 242.

53. Nathan, *Family*, 107.

54. Dominic Rathbone, "Poverty and Population in Roman Egypt" in *Poverty in the Roman World* (ed. Margaret Atkins and Robin Osborne; Cambridge: Cambridge University Press, 2006), 105. He adds that in the era of Christian Egypt there was "moral pressure against remarriage and unmarried co-habitation."

55. Drijvers, "Virginity," 253.

56. Nathan, *Family*, 22.

57. Fraschetti, *Roman Women*, 7.

58. James Donaldson, *Woman: Her Position and Influence in Ancient Greece and Rome, and among the Early Christians* (London: Longmans, Green, 1907), 119. Incidentally, Donaldson may be among the first to set the situation the Samaritan woman against the backdrop of Roman marital conventions (119).

and make that a source of pride."[59] Within such a context, is it appropriate to censure the Samaritan woman for having had too many spouses?

9.3. CONCLUSION

While commentators in the current era may be tempted to depict Jesus' conversation partner as a scarlet woman or a person of dubious morals, one must take care not to anachronistically impose later codes of conduct or social strictures upon the first century. Through use of revisionist history spiced with a dash of social history and a touch of legal history, various points about marriage and relationships in the ancient world were made that go far toward rehabilitating the woman's reputation.

Some of this evidence included the discovery that, during the time when the Evangelist was writing, sequential marriages were the norm within the Roman upper classes, a circumstance encouraged both by the Augustan legislation and the ease by which divorce might be secured. Both widows and divorcees frequently remarried. Thus, the Samaritan woman's marital history of five husbands may not actually represent licentious behavior. In addition, criticisms for her association with a sixth man without the benefit of a matrimonial bond overlook the complexity of the various quasi-legal institutions to which Romans had recourse in establishing relationships. The existence of institutions like concubinage, *contubernia*, or even lengthy betrothals to soldiers where legal marriages were prohibited may indicate that the grounds for questioning the woman's morality are not as clear cut as might previously have been supposed.

Further, one might call to mind that the intended readership of this Gospel may include those not steeped in the Jewish tradition. In that case, the story of the Samaritan woman may function to invite not only Samaritans but others of the wider Roman Empire to accept the identity of Jesus. The woman at the well is the person through whom it became known that Jesus was the "savior of the world" (v. 42), and the Evangelist was no doubt aware that, at the time in which the Gospel was written, the known civilized world belonged to Rome.

---

59. Juvenal, *Sat.* 6.224.

10

Drinking the Spirit:
Ancient Medicine and Paul's Corinth

To some extent, an examination of the Holy Spirit in 1 Corinthians against the backdrop of medical treatises written in Greek in the eastern part of the empire is just another "sociological interpretation" of a biblical text. But a challenge leveled by late-twentieth century historiography, as was mentioned in chapter 2 above, was that historians should look for new sources and apply them in new ways. The object was to avoid a "canon of sources," or a select group of resources upon which one frequently draws. Here that call is taken to heart and an entirely different depth of inquiry is plumbed that has not received attention so far in this book—medical history. The "new" primary sources that are brought to bear on Paul's epistle are the medical treatises written in Greek in the eastern part of the empire, and the secondary resources will be heavily weighted to favor texts written by classicists and medical historians. Medical history appeared briefly in our discussion of the types of forces that can drive events from the past. A medical historian is convinced not only that big breakthroughs like the discovery of penicillin, the invention of x-rays, and learning that mosquitoes cause yellow fever change the course of human history but that concerns and knowledge about basic human health and the body likely have greater impact on events then is often given credit. The medical historian always has an eye open for places where this might be true.

Thus, in this chapter we will demonstrate that the boundaries between the disciplines of New Testament studies, history, medical history, and classics are fluid. The choice of medical history is not arbitrary. Paul's use of medical motifs provides the grounding for this cross-disciplinary exercise. So, even while not every text would readily lend itself to an explication based on medical elements, this one does.

In the twelfth chapter of 1 Corinthians, Paul launches into a famous and much-studied metaphor in which the individual members of a congregation are likened to the various disparate parts of the physical body, each contributing to the overall vigorous function of the whole. This image itself is fairly common in antiquity and appears in a wide range of classical sources, from Dionysius of Halicarnassus, a rhetorician who prospered during the reign of Octavian during the first century c.e.[1] and employed this illustration to explicate the workings of a city, to the historians Livy and Josephus,[2] and even by an author of Midrash Tehillim, who utilized it while explicating Ps 39:2 for a Jewish audience.[3] Yet verse 13, which is sandwiched between Paul's introduction of the body metaphor and his exposition of how individual anatomical parts relate to the whole, contains an element that is atypical of these noncanonical parallels from the classical world. Indeed, Paul affirms that we are all made to "drink of one Spirit," a sentiment not readily linked to other Greco-Roman literature.

10.1. The Difficulty with 1 Corinthians 12:13b

In his "comprehensive" listing of parallels to Pauline passages, Walter Wilson only manages to associate verse 12:13, which includes the reference to drinking the one Spirit, with another passage within the Corinthian correspondence itself, verse 1:13. In that verse, a rhetorical question is posed about whether Christ has been divided and whether individuals were baptized in the name of Paul or other leaders. Wilson, however, does not actually connect 12:13 to any text in ancient literature that mentions drinking. Charles Talbert also finds a relationship between this verse and the wider New Testament, perceiving the phrase that believers are made to drink the spirit to have a passing affinity with John 7:37–39 and John 4:14. In these Fourth Gospel passages, Jesus serves as the source of thirst-quenching living water.[4]

---

1. Dionysius Halicarnassensis, *Ant. rom.* 6.86.1–3. For this and other parallels, see Walter T. Wilson, *Pauline Parallels: A Comprehensive Guide* (Louisville: Westminster John Knox, 2009).

2. Josephus's *J.W.* 4.406 and Livy's *Early History of Rome* 2.32 are referenced in Bruce N. Fisk, *First Corinthians* (Interpretation Bible Studies; Louisville: Westminster John Knox, 2000), 78.

3. Charles H. Talbert, "Paul's Understanding of the Holy Spirit: The Evidence of 1 Corinthians 12–14" *PRSt* 11.4 (1984): 98. Talbert includes references to other ancient texts in which this metaphor is used as well.

4. Ibid., 99.

In any event, the first portion of 12:13, "For in one Spirit we were all baptized into one body," receives the most attention in contemporary studies and commentaries, with many exegetes simply skimming completely over the last part of the verse with its troublesome phrase about sipping the Spirit.[5] This is natural because the opening portion of the Paul's statement is anchored within the Judeo-Christian tradition. First, Paul's argument in 12:13a that everyone is granted the Spirit and that Jew and Greek, slave and free are equal beneficiaries of a variety of gifts that range from the utterance of wisdom to the interpretation of tongues (12:8–10) is evocative of images and language in Joel 2:28–29 (LXX Joel 3:1–2). According to the minor prophet, God says ἐκχεῶ ἀπὸ τοῦ πνεύματός μου ἐπὶ πᾶσαν σάρκα, "I will pour out my spirit of prophesying, seeing visions and dreaming dreams upon all flesh," not only upon the elders and the younger generation, the men and the women but also upon the slaves and the free. Yet there is an ironic twist to Paul's allusion to this passage from Joel. While the remainder of Joel 3 concerns judgment against those nations who had subjugated the Jews, Paul, within his context of an ethnically mixed Corinthian church, modifies his allusion so that instead of non-Jewish groups being given judgment, both Jews and Gentiles receive the baptism of the Spirit. In any event, the first portion of 1 Cor 12:13 resonates with the tradition as expressed in the Hebrew Scriptures and is expertly applied by Paul to the Corinthian community. Joel, however, says not a word about drinking God's Spirit. Thus, that portion of Paul's verse remains opaque.

A second reason why the initial portion of verse 12:13 snags the attention of interpreters while the latter part does not is that the lead phrase's image of Spirit baptism, being immersed in the Spirit, resonates with Christian praxis relating to the basic initiation ceremony of the faith. The concept of being made to *drink* the one Spirit in the last few words of the verse, however, does not have a similar corollary. Indeed, attempts to link imbibing the πνεῦμα with an earlier verse in 1 Corinthians concerning communion where participants are instructed to "drink" the cup of the new covenant (1 Cor 11:25) are stymied by Paul's choice of verb.

---

5. A typical treatment would be that of Oscar J. F. Seitz, who, in an effort to explore biblical warrants for church unity, repeatedly quotes the verse and even comments upon the first portion of 1 Cor 12:13 but never engages the motif of being made to drink the Spirit. See *One Body and One Spirit: A Study of the Church in the New Testament* (Greenwich, Conn.: Seabury, 1960), 72, 95, 105.

To be specific, in chapter 11 the instructions for partaking the sacred cup make use of the Greek word πίνω, while in chapter 12 the passive form of the verb ποτίζω is drawn upon to convey the idea of believers being induced to swallow the liquid Spirit.[6] J. W. McGarvey, a half century ago, writes the type of banal comment typical of scholars who do attempt to engage this puzzling Pauline phrase without alluding to communion but end up doing little more than restating the verse about quaffing the Spirit. He remarks by way of circular pseudologic or the fallacy of begging the question about which we have already learned in chapter 4 of this textbook: "The term 'drink' certainly expresses the idea of receiving within us what is drunk, and when used of the Holy Spirit refers to the reception of the Spirit within us."[7] A different tack is taken by Ronald Cottle, who digs into the full range of meanings for ποτίζω and prefers that the verb be translated not *drink* but in a way that emphasizes the sense of flooding or irrigating. He then concludes that the difficulty experienced by the congregation in Corinth is an inundation of the Spirit with which the church fails to cope in the type of orderly fashion that would edify the entire church membership.[8] Certainly, within the range of potential renderings for ποτίζω, "watering" is the logical translation when this verb appears within 3:6–8, in the context of a garden analogy where Apollos and others cultivated the congregation. The sense of a flood, of overflow, or of watering, however, is nonsensical when applied to other Pauline passages. For example, to use flood connotations for ποτίζω in 1 Cor 3:2, wherein Paul gives the members of the congregation milk to drink (ἐπότισα) would make little sense.

Ultimately, though, the literary setting of verse 12:13 within a series of images and discussions in both the proceeding and following chapters of 1 Corinthians that resonate with terms, thoughts, and practices related to medicine and healing help to confirm the plausibility of translating καὶ πάντες ἕν πνεῦ μα ἐποτίσθημεν as "all are made to swallow one spirit." The Spirit is divine medicine that heals the wounds of a divided congregation. Before proceeding to an exposition of the therapeutic praxis and theory of the first- and second-century Corinthian milieu as a possible backdrop

---

6. Care must be taken not to draw too firm a conclusion from this. Ancient authors were known to use synonyms, as John famously does with "love" in John 21:15–17.

7. J. W. McGarvey, "A Note on 1 Cor. 12:13," *ResQ* 1 (1958): 47.

8. Ronald E. Cottle, "All Were Baptized," *JETS* 17 (1974): 77, 80.

for Paul's text, it is necessary to briefly introduce the primary sources for knowledge about Greco-Roman healing in the period.

10.2. Some Basics of Greco-Roman Medicine

Roman medicine was Greek medicine, wholly transplanted from the eastern to the western area of the empire. It was a process begun as early as 293 B.C.E., when, in an effort to end a plague in Rome, consultation of the Sibylline books revealed that the Senate should invite Asclepius, one of the Greek gods of healing, to Rome, where the deity subsequently took up residence in a temple on Tiber Island. During the course of expansion of the Roman Empire, ever-larger numbers of eastern doctors made their way to the west, typically within the bounds of slavery. This influx of medical practitioners reached such a point, as recorded by Vivian Nutton, that "by the middle of the first century BC it had become almost *de rigueur* to employ a Greek physician." This practice was extraordinarily persistent. Nutton notes that even as late as 100 C.E., over seventy-five percent of the doctors in the western part of the empire were slaves or former slaves.[9]

Limiting the time span from the first century C.E. to the late second century C.E. results in a fair number of authors who have a contribution to make to the discussion of Roman medicine. This study draws only on five, three of whom, like Paul, were born in Asia Minor and possessed Roman citizenship. Cornelius Celsus is the earliest source within the specified time frame. Writing during the rule of Tiberius in the early first century, he completed an encyclopedia of arts, the medical portion of which is the only surviving section. It provides a systematic treatment of the history of Greek medicine. Neither Celsus's hometown nor province are known. Likewise, it is impossible to confirm whether he actually served as a physician himself. By contrast, much more is known about the next source for Roman medicine, Pliny the Elder.

Pliny, rather than focusing on the medical arts at large, is an excellent source for pharmacology. A cavalry officer trained in law, when he wrote his massive *Naturalis Historia*, he detailed many plants that were used either as remedies or contained toxic properties.[10] Pliny was born in the

---

9. Vivian Nutton, *Ancient Medicine* (New York: Routledge, 2004), 157, 164, 165.

10. Two other sources—Dioscorides (64 C.E.), a surgeon for Nero's army, and Soranus, a medic during the rules of Trajan and Hadrian, whose main works were lost—were not consulted in this study.

20s and died in 79 upon inhaling poisonous fumes from Vesuvius. The next two authors, Aelius Artistides and Marcus Antonius Polemon, had public-speaking careers that overlapped. Aristides worked as a rhetor; Polemon, a sophist. These two contemporaries stumped in Asia Minor, both frequenting Smyrna. Polemon, despite being granted the honor of delivering the inaugural speech for Emperor Hadrian in 130, is also known for a treatise on physiognomy, the technique of observing individual physical characteristics or body parts to make inferences about a person's character or psychology. Tamsyn S. Barton observes that there was significant cross-over between the disciplines of healing and physiognomics in the Roman Empire because both fields were prone to "establish lists of signs or symptoms, from which they infer the state of mind or body. (And) both often rely on common causes, either the humors or blood."[11]

In contrast with Polemon, Aristides's contribution to the body of knowledge is not that of a medical practitioner or historian of medicine but rather that of a patient. A devotee of both Sarapis and Asclepius, deities known for their healing powers, his *Sacred Tales* cover a period from the 140s to the 180s. These writings have been described as "the mental processes of a deeply neurotic, deeply superstitious, vainglorious man,"[12] but in any case they provide insight into the myriad of potions, ritual acts, bloodletting surgeries, and other curatives that were dispensed or thought to be efficacious in the era.

The final source is Galen. An extraordinarily prolific physician whose writings reveal a persuasive showman who "was invariably the hero" in the events he portrays in his own writings,[13] he was born in 129 in Pergamum, a center for the worship of Asclepius. Indeed, it was the deity himself who inspired Galen's father to encourage his son's career path. Galen lived well into his eighties, which puts him at the outer limit of the specified time period for sources of medical knowledge, but his rich writings build upon the findings of his predecessors and thus are of value for the decades associated with Paul's Corinthian correspondence. Galen's profession ultimately took him to Rome, where he became the personal doctor of Marcus Aure-

---

11. Tamsyn S. Barton, *Power and Knowledge: Astrology, Pysiognomics, and Medicine under the Roman Empire* (Ann Arbor: University of Michigan Press, 1994), 98.

12. C. A. Behr, *Aelius Aristides and the Sacred Tales* (Chicago: Argonaut, 1968), 110.

13. R. J. Hankinson, *The Cambridge Companion to Galen* (Cambridge: Cambridge University Press, 2008), 9.

lius. He received his extensive medical training first in Pergamum, then Smyrna, and then ultimately traveled to Corinth and Alexandria, hoping to catch up with Numisianus, who was the leading anatomist of that day.[14]

That Corinth, as late as the middle of the second century, had the reputation of being a center of medical knowledge capable of drawing experts in anatomy, tempts one to speculate as to whether or not physicians skilled in the scientific understanding of the human body were also present in Corinth in Paul's decades, providing a handy source for Paul's body analogy. A paucity of sources, however, does not provide for an easy link between any of the known anatomists from the first century and Paul's congregation in Corinth. A more profitable approach is merely to explicate ancient medical practice in general as a backdrop against which the action of "being made to drink the Spirit" may be interpreted as the administration of a medical antidote for the "ills" of the Corinthian congregation.

Rather than diving right into the literary evidence alone, it is necessary to mention scholarship that has also taken into account archeological discoveries concerning the temple of Asclepius in the city and related them to various passages within the epistle. Peter Gooch, in his investigation of chapters 8–10, in which Paul expounds on the dangers relating to consuming food given to idols, explores in detail Corinth's pagan temple to the healing god and its physical location near Lerna, a "public resort" that contained three dining rooms.[15] He noted that in other cities the Asclepia held banqueting facilities and eating rooms and that food played an integral role in the cult. Gooch concludes that eating was intimately related to healing and medicine in the cult of Asclepius. Jerome Murphy-O'Connor, looking at the same archeological evidence, conjectured,

> It is entirely probable that the wealthier members of Paul's flock had been wont to repair to the Asclepion for recreation. It was probably the closest the city had to a country club with facilities for dining and swimming. It would have been natural to continue going there after conversion, because even though the converts no longer believed in the healing god, they still would have seen the value of the site.[16]

---

14. Ibid., 4.

15. Peter D. Gooch, *Dangerous Food: 1 Corinthians 8–10 in Its Context* (Waterloo, Ont.: Wilfred Laurier University Press, 1993), 16.

16. Jerome Murphy-O'Connor, *St. Paul's Corinth: Texts and Archaeology* (Collegeville, Minn.: Liturgical Press, 1983), 190.

Gooch does not stop with merely linking food, idol worship, and recreation but points out that, within the context of the temple of this healing deity, the food offered to idols had medical associations. He lists three ways in which cultic food was employed for healing. First, it was used in the temple rites themselves; second, it was eaten by priests and worshippers; and, last, food was prescribed in cures.[17] The first two uses are borne out by Emma and Ludwig Edelstein, in whose massive study on the cult of Asclepius there is an account of a ritual in thanks for the god's miraculous healing, which involved sacrificial animals as well as breads. The Edelsteins assert that, no matter the location of the particular temple, "everywhere, it seems, the devout feasted with the god. In the Asclepius cult the ancient concept of the sacrifice as a communion between god and man was upheld tenaciously."[18]

In addition to the role of food in the worship ritual, the curative nature of food was integral to Roman medicine as a whole. To that end, healing cuisine might be consumed either in the temple or at home. Celsus reports that medicine was divided into three major strategies, which included diet, drugs, and surgery—diet was the first line of defense.[19] Regarding diet, in particular, the British classicist Helen King goes so far as to remark that it was difficult to draw the line between foods and medicines.[20] This blurring between ritual, food, and curatives is aptly illustrated by Aristides, who recounts a prescribed treatment that he himself underwent at the direction of the god:

> Then we were ordered to do many strange things. Of what I remember, there was a race, which it was necessary to run unshod in winter time. And again horseback riding, a most difficult matter. And I also remember…when the harbor was stormy from a south west wind and the boats were being tossed about, I had to sail across to the opposite side, and having eaten honey and acorns, to vomit, and the purge was complete. All these things were done while the inflamed tumor was at its worst. (*Sacred Tales* 1.65; trans. here and elsewhere by Behr)

---

17. Ibid., 21.

18. Emma J. Edelstein and Ludwig Edelstein, *Asclepius: Collection and Interpretation of the Testimonies* (Baltimore: Johns Hopkins University Press, 1998), 189.

19. Helen King, *Greek and Roman Medicine* (London: Bristol Classical Press, 2001), 44.

20. Ibid., 45.

The directions for this peculiar remedy for Aristides' growth likely were received in the temple of Asclepius in Pergamum, where Aristides lived for many years as a part of incubation. During incubation, a patient slept in a part of the temple known as the *abaton* with the hopes of receiving inspired medicinal advice from the divine son of Apollo in dreams. These sleep-related visions were interpreted with the assistance of temple functionaries within the sacred precincts. The application of the remedies, though, which often involved various foods, might then be administered either inside or outside the shrine. In this particular case, as accounted by Aristides, not only was food used in an attempt to affect a balance of the bodily humors, achieved when Aristides vomited, but vigorous exercise was also undertaken in the form of races and a boat journey.

Other cures experienced by Aristides and involving food, however, were executed within the temple. For instance, in 2.27 he records, "After this (I was ordered) to go to the Temple and make a full sacrifice to Asclepius, and to have sacred bowls set up, and to distribute the sacred portions of the sacrifice to all my fellow pilgrims."

In another account, a healing meal taken within the temple sounds eerily like the Christian Eucharist. Aristides writes, "Again he ordered me to drink this same drug with bread, and I ate it at the Sacred Tripod, and made this a start for my health" (*Sacred Tales* 3.27). The "drug" may have been wine, as elsewhere Aristides records, "When this also had been performed he took me off water and assigned me a measure of wine, the word was 'a demiroyal'.... I used this and it sufficed" (*Sacred Tales* 3.32) Whether this curative sacred meal was ingested in the Asclepion or before a household shrine is not clear, as the *Sacred Tales* are recounted without larger context and often out of order. Nevertheless, the various images of a healing repast of bread and drink, the partaking of curative foods to balance the humors, and the sponsoring of temple sacrifices to effect cures provide an interesting backdrop for Paul's concerns both about not eating food offered to idols as recorded in chapters 8–10 in the epistle and the proper processes for engaging in communion as laid out in chapter 11. Gooch, under the influence of this interpretive framework, draws on the medical imagery that pervades 1 Corinthians when he asserts that "the Lord's meal immunizes the believer against death."[21] In the city of Corinth, located in the shadow of the Asclepion, eating and drinking may have been not

---

21. Gooch, *Dangerous Food*, 59.

merely a convivial repast but evocative of the gracious healing powers of the pagan deity. Within this context, Paul's use of the passive voice of the verb ποτίζω, "we are all made to swallow the same Spirit," may well have evoked images of divine tonics rather than of farming and irrigation.

10.3. In the Shadow of a Healing Cult:
Health and 1 Corinthians

Three sections of 1 Corinthians, in addition to the discussion of idol food, may resonate with ancient healing therapies and help to promote reading the phrase "drink the Spirit" within the context of Greco-Roman curatives. These include the use of votives in Asclepian worship as a possible source of inspiration for the body analogy in 12:14–26, the concept of substitutionary healing, which may be related to Paul's discussion of the resurrection in chapter 15, and finally the relationship between healing and phenomena such as prophecy, divination, and oracles as relevant to the discussion of spiritual gifts.

The healing arts, when successful, generated expressions of gratitude on behalf of the faithful. Within the context of the cults of Asclepius and other healing gods, this sentiment often took the form of purchasing and dedicating replicas of the diseased body part. Andrew Hill, in a brief article that appeared in the *Journal of Biblical Literature* in the early 1980s, noted that the Asclepium at Corinth was the site of active cult activity from the fifth century B.C.E. to the fourth century C.E. and that excavations at the site have uncovered terra-cotta representations of hands, feet, arms, legs, breasts, genitalia, eyes, ears, and even heads. He comments that, contrary to Paul's formulation of the analogy in chapter 12, which views the body holistically, the presence of individual dismembered parts indicates that believers who participated in these cults were focused on not the whole newly healed person but rather the disparate organs and extremities.[22] Hill proposes that this scene from daily life within Corinth may have "provided the catalyst responsible for the formation of this specific body illustration" in Paul's correspondence.[23]

Another point of contact between the cult of Asclepius in Corinth and Paul's letter may also be found. Healing shrines across the Roman Empire

---

22. Andrew E. Hill, "The Temple of Asclepius: An Alternative Source for Paul's Body Theology?" *JBL* 99 (1980): 438.

23. Ibid., 439.

contained not only mass-produced clay figures but also custom-made body parts that vividly portray the details of the illness and are sometimes used in modern times by historians of medicine to attempt to infer the types of diseases and afflictions that might have been present in the ancient world. By studying these details about the replicas, they have discovered that residents in the classical world suffered a wide variety of maladies, from varicose veins, as depicted on marble legs, to koilonychias, or iron deficiency, which was apparent from the concave nails featured on votive hands.[24] At Corinth, a large number of votives representing male genitalia have led some scholars to conclude that, due to a nearby temple of Aphrodite that was crowded with professional prostitutes, the city may have had a specific medical specialty: Corinth may been a center for those seeking cures for impotence or who required sex therapy.[25] If this were really the case, it would leave Pauline scholars to look for connections between this particular healing forte and the Corinthians' concerns about sexual immorality in 7:2. Potential links concerning votives and both Paul's body metaphor and his concerns with sexual morality in chapter 7 aside, still one more aspect of ancient medicine might be related to 1 Corinthians. Specifically, there are glimmers of what I have chosen to term "substitutionary healing."

It is possible that figures of body parts were not only left as offerings of thanks, but also functioned as pleas to induce the god to heal the afflicted organ. In those scenarios, the statuettes substituted for the afflicted body parts and served as a sort of sympathetic magic proxy to encourage the desired action. For instance, archaeologists in Bath, England, in the temple of Minerva Medica unearthed a pair of second-century flat ivory breasts, which classicists have concluded may have been left by a poorly endowed young woman who desired divine assistance to improve her figure.[26] Aristides himself appears to take the idea of substituting a token or even body part as an inducement to the god to effect the healing of an affliction to extremes. He writes, "Also it was necessary to cut off some part of my body for the sake of the well being of the whole. But since this was difficult, he (the god) remitted it for me. Instead of this (I was) to remove the ring which I wore and dedicate it to Telesphorus (the son of Asclepius)—for

---

24. Gerald David Hart, *Asclepius: The God of Medicine* (London: Royal Society of Medicine, 2000), 97.

25. Ibid., 101–2.

26. Ibid., 96–97.

this had the same effect, as if I should give up my finger" (*Sacred Tales* 2.27–28).

With regard to what I am calling this "substitutionary theory of healing," Aristides goes so far as to theorize that not only the substitution of a part of his own body but the actual death of another individual might bring about healing. In this vein, he attributes two deaths of foster relatives from his household to the extension of his own life or healing. In one case, he was experiencing a fever that was not completely healed through taking an enema of Attic honey. The fever did not finally abate, Aristides records, "until the most valued of my foster children died. He died, as I later learned, on the same day as my disease ended. Thus I had my life up to this time as a bounty from the gods, and after this, I was given a new life through the gods, and as it were, this exchange occurred" (*Sacred Tales* 2.43–45).

In another instance a foster sister falls ill, and, though he sends his physician to attend her, the concerned hypochondriac himself is not well enough to travel to her bedside but remains at the temple. At the moment that his foster sister dies, Aristides receives a vision from the god in which this household member is dissected in the same manner that occurs when seeking an oracle from animals. In the dream, Aristides's name was found inscribed upon her intestines, from which he infers that this woman died to give him a safe journey. He sums up his interpretation of the dream, "Philumene had given a soul for a soul and a body for a body, hers for mine" (*Sacred Tales* 4.22–25). To find this substitutionary-death philosophy in Aristides provides an interesting lens through which to read Paul's words in 1 Cor 21:21–22, "For since death came through a human being, the resurrection of the dead has also come through a human being; for as all die in Adam, so all will be made alive in Christ." This account of the dream concerning Philumene's death is of interest both for its echoes of concepts found in Christian theology and for the way medicine, divination, and oracles were linked.

10.4. The Link between Healing and Prophecy

The idea inherent in this example from Aristides—that the art of medicine might be intimately connected with nonscientific practices and magics ranging from divination to prophecy—may sound odd in the modern era because patients are accustomed to objective diagnoses from their doctors. In the age of the Empire, though, medicine and pseudosciences were often inseparable. Within *On Prognosis*, Galen records an instance in which one of his patients announced to everyone that the Pythian Apollo, a famous oracle, had deigned to prophesy to the sick through the mouth of Galen.[27] And Aristides, in his speech *In Defense of Oratory*, gives remarks on the Pythia that make a connection between her prophetic activity and healing:

> What art do these priestesses know, who are incapable of preserving and memorizing their predictions? Medicine which has studied all human science and which is greater than cookery, is feeble, I think, in contrast to the cures from Delphi, which privately and publicly have been revealed to men for all diseases and sufferings. (2.35)[28]

The pagan association of doctors with the two healing gods Apollo, who communicated via the Pythia, and Asclepius, who through incubation provided healing oracles, certainly earns healers their place with those who prophesy or do miracles. As David Ackerman observes, "Often disease was viewed as pollution that needed to be purified. Purification came through prescribed action made known through super-human knowledge gained from oracles."[29] Thus healers do have their place on Paul's list of recipients of spiritual gifts and, both in 12:9 and in 12:28 and 30, healing is cataloged along with miracles, prophecy, and tongues.

Much of 1 Cor 12–14, and even the order in which spiritual gifts are listed by Paul, hints at issues stemming from rivalries that are touched off because some blessings of the Spirit were thought to be more important than others—or perhaps the idea that those from the community possessing particular gifts were more particularly favored by God over those granted other talents.[30] Clearly, Paul's desire was for the gifts to be used for the edification of the entire community. But why would healing be placed

---

27. Referenced by T. S. Barton, *Power and Knowledge*, 140.

28. P. W. Van der Horst identifies Aristides's full passage concerning the Pythia in *In Defence of Oratory* (34–43) as "remotely parallel to chapters 13 and 14 of 1st Corinthians" (*Aelius Aristides and the New Testament* [Leiden: Brill, 1980], 54). David A. Ackerman links the spiritual gifts not only with the Pythia but also the ecstatic rituals performed with the cult of Dionysus ("Fighting Fire with Fire: Community Formation in 1 Corinthians 12–14," *ERT* 29 [2005]: 354–55).

29. Ackerman, "Fighting Fire with Fire," 354–55.

30. Daniel G. Boyd, "Spirit and Church in 1 Corinthians 12–14 and the Acts of the Apostles," in *Spirit within Structure: Essays in Honor of George Johnston* (ed. E. J. Furcha; Allison Park, Pa.: Pickwick, 1983), 56.

on Paul's list of spiritual gifts and occupy, at best, a central or ambivalent position on the hierarchy? Aristides has already linked healing with miracles, oracles, and prophecies, but that would not explain, in and of itself, the source of jealousy and contention. One contributing factor might involve how highly ancient physicians esteemed themselves. Because medicine in our contemporary society is prized for the good it does for community members, with laws like HIPAA enforcing patient confidentiality, today's physicians are consequently not the accomplished showmen that their Greco-Roman counterparts were. Indeed, in the Empire, gifted healers performed public surgeries to drum up patients, received acclaim by debating rival physicians, and, like the sophists, engaged in open quarrels and competitions.[31] Among ancient healers, the tendency toward self-aggrandizement and self-promotion while hawking their businesses would make them a natural target for inclusion on lists of those whose talents might be deemed superior to others within a community.

So far in this chapter, several possible points of contact between medical practice and phraseology or content within 1 Corinthians have been covered. These have included:

▶   the evidence of votives possibly providing background for both the body metaphor in chapter 12 and for Paul's comments regarding sexuality in chapter 7
▶   Aristides's literary evidence of "substitutionary healing betraying," a similar thought-matrix to concepts in 1 Cor 15
▶   the dining rooms in the Asclepia perhaps providing context for the discussion of food offered to idols
▶   the observation that ancient doctors, both by dint of association with the inspiration of the gods and by their own self promotion, may have caused conflict in a community concerned with hierarchies of gifts and blessings

Considered individually, these points might not justify imputing a medical connotation for the phrase in 12:13 that Christian believers are "made to drink the one Spirit," but taken together they help to make a compelling case for understanding sipping the Spirit and letting it enter one's body as an antidote for the ailing community. Before closing, however, it is neces-

---

31. T. S. Barton, *Power and Knowledge*, 148.

sary to make a few more comments pertinent directly to 12:13b and medical terminology and practice.

10.5. *Pneuma* and Ancient Medicine

In a recent intriguing article, Clint Tibbs points out that "there are good reasons to argue that the earliest Christian pneumatology reflected a spirit world populated with many holy and evil spirits, not one Holy Spirit, as is so commonly assumed today."[32] As a consequence, he puts forth the interpretation that the one spirit mentioned in verses 9, 11, and 13 does not represent a single entity but a unified spirit world committed to Jesus and the heavenly Father.[33] This reading is intriguing, for it cautions exegetes against imposing preconceived notions and theologies upon the text.

In the attitude of such openness, we can take this as license to point out that the word πνεῦμα had a different connotation altogether in medical practice. Specifically, it was the technical term for "a refined airy element that held together a cosmos" of hot and cold, wet and dry.[34] This, in turn, might be related to the four humors that, when balanced, were the hallmark of health. There was even a name for the school of medical practitioners that were flourishing by the year 50 C.E. and held that this πνεῦμα was the controlling factor in death and disease: Pneumatists.[35] Galen, for his part, critiqued the Pneumatists but, in the course of doing so, remarked that Athenaeus, their founder, "eagerly explored the parallels between the microcosm of the body and the macrocosm. Just as a living being could not exist without taking in *pneuma*, so too the universe was a living entity imbued with all-permeating *pneuma*."[36]

The Pneumatists, like another ancient medical sect known as the Methodists—closely related on account of their systematized process of diagnoses—had a tendency to look beyond the individual to grasp the commonalities of illness or health.[37] In fact, the Methodists asserted that, in the case of illness, the entire body, not only the affected appendage,

---

32. Clint Tibbs, "The Spirit (World) and the (Holy) Spirits among the Earliest Christians: 1 Corinthians 12 and 14 as a Test Case," *CBQ* 70 (2008): 314.

33. Ibid., 329.

34. Nutton, *Ancient Medicine*, 202.

35. Ibid.

36. As summarized by Nutton, *Ancient Medicine*, 203.

37. Nutton, *Ancient Medicine*, 201.

must be attended. Here too we have echoes of Paul's body analogy in relating individual parts to the whole. The key issue of contention between the Pneumatists and Galen, however, involved a debate about blood. Venisection was a common medical practice in the Greek East. In fact, Aristides recounts that, to cure one of his illnesses, the god "commanded that I have blood drawn from my elbow, and he added, as far as I remember 'sixty pints.' This was to show that there would be need of not a few phlebotomies" (*Sacred Tales* 2.46–47). The purpose of bloodletting surgeries was to help adjust the balance of yellow bile, black bile, phlegm, and blood in the body to a healthful ratio, but the debate between the Pneumatists and Galen centered on the elusive *pneuma* that was also involved in the process. In a treatise entitled "Concerning Venesection against Erasistratus," Galen argued against the theory that that the arteries are filled with *pneuma* on the grounds that, when punctured, they emit blood. The pneumatists, however, rejoined that "since the *pneuma* escapes (first) on the puncturing, the vacuum must be filled and the only available source is the supply of blood."[38] With this background concerning Greco-Roman medicine at the time of Paul and the prevalence of the idea of *pneuma* as an agent in the healing process, the possibility that in 1 Cor 12:13 Paul envisioned a healer administering the potion of the Holy Spirit, or one spirit, to a wounded congregation takes on a slightly different character.

Furthermore, the idea that a healing agent would be included in a potion that is drunk and is actually necessary in the Corinthian context may also be indicated by Paul's use of the verb πάσχω in 12:26. Hill observes in a footnote that this particular word was found in classical and Koine sources to "signify any kind of physical distress, whether an illness or an injury inflicted by violence."[39] Clearly, Paul's congregation, the broken body, was in need of healing. And healing, according to Celsus is accomplished through not only diet and surgery but also the administration of drugs, as was previously mentioned. Despite a number of odd medicines, the effectiveness of which are doubtful, the Romans did have a number of herbal remedies that, when administered in potion form, were successful. Guido Majano, a historian of medicine, remarked after studying Pliny that the pharmacologist sometimes scores a bull's-eye.[40] Majano

38. T. S. Barton, *Power and Knowledge*, 149.

39. Hill, "The Temple of Asclepius," 438 n. 8.

40. Guido Majano, *The Healing Hand: Man and Wound in the Ancient World* (Cambridge: Harvard University Press, 1975), 349.

is astonished to find not only a number of widely known effective herbal medicines but also the plant ephedron, known even today for its power to stop hemorrhages and to cure coughs when administered in sweet wine.[41] Surely, then, the idea that the congregation, as a broken body, is given a potion imbued with *pneuma* and herbs to effect its healing is a vivid and reasonable image by which 12:13 may be understood.

10.6. CONCLUSION

In conclusion, although interpreters sometimes ignore 12:13b or relate it to communion or baptism, a reading in which the Pauline 1 Corinthians is interpreted vis-à-vis ancient medical practices, as recounted by ancient sources and modern treatises on Greco-Roman medical history, is helpful. The ancient world was an environment in which healing gods, votives, medicinal diets, prophetic oracles of healing, boastful physicians, and herbal concoctions for drinking all play a part. The existence of these cures and medical practices helps to explain the phrase "all are made to swallow one Spirit" as the administration of a divine healing antidote. It is, perhaps, a Pauline wordplay on the medical *pneuma* of his day and the extremely effective therapeutic potion of love administered by the Christian God to the unified body of believers.

---

41. Ibid.

Epilogue

Even though a work may be intended to be more informative than argumentative, sometimes along the way points emerge that are worth a bit of reflection. In the conclusion of his hefty and very provocative book, *The Resurrection of Jesus: A New Historiographical Approach*, Michael R. Licona writes,

> I discovered that historians and biblical scholars give little attention to the philosophy of history and important aspects of historical method. In fact, there appear to be no canons of history. Yet biblical scholars have much they can learn from discussions among philosophers of history. Informing themselves of these discussions will help them avoid repeating the work of others and allow them to focus on new areas.[1]

To this statement I am compelled to respond, "Amen." But I want to add two points. First, Licona's formulation appears to assume that New Testament historians should learn from professional historians outside the field but not necessarily engage them or invite them into the ensuing dialogue when the methods are applied to the subject of early Christianity. There is a vast difference between borrowing from one another and actually working together. If the first of these is what is commonly described as an interdisciplinary frame of mind and is what Licona indicates, then perhaps it is time to be deliberate about taking the next steps into what may be designated cross-disciplinary work. The social historians have taught us that boundaries between disciplines are fluid. There is nothing wrong with wading across the increasingly shallow stream between classical history and New Testament studies to work on collaborative projects. That is not to say that this isn't happening on a small scale. From time to time, classicists do show up in the lists of contributors in texts published by bib-

---

1. Licona, *Resurrection of Jesus*, 620.

lical-studies presses.[2] Even cross-disciplinary work with other disciplines besides classics would be of value. There is already much fruitful team-work between psychologists and New Testament scholars who are exploring psychohistorical issues related to our field. This type of collaboration, however, needs to move from the margins to center stage (to borrow language from the revisionist historians).

Second, Licona envisions New Testament historians focusing on new areas. I hope I have shown that, for virtually every historical method that has made an appearance in the last one hundred years, someone in our discipline knows the method and has employed it, even if they have been reluctant to state upfront what the method is actually called, as was noted in the case of the Marxist New Testament historians. What we could wish, however, is that some of the approaches would become more popular. A good dose of studies that use quantitative methods, including but not limited to economic history, which already has a few strong advocates, would stimulate conversation; an avalanche of works that delve into new and specialized areas of cultural history would be eye opening; a few more psychohistorical treatments by those who have the specialty knowledge to pull them off correctly would not be remiss; and even a small smattering of counterfactual or imaginative histories would pave the way for us to gain some new perspectives on topics that other methods have cudgeled nearly to death.

But this point raises a question. If at least a few studies representing the wide variety of historical methodologies are present in our field, why aren't they being emulated on a wide scale? Licona hypothesizes that the reason for this is the deleterious effect of the near monopoly of historicism (historical positivism) on our field, combined with a lacuna in students' education in historiography. He states, "When writing on the resurrection of Jesus, biblical scholars are engaged in historical research. Are they doing so without adequate or appropriate training? How many have completed so much as a single undergraduate course pertaining to how to investigate the past?"[3]

Granted, for a method that has been long branded "outmoded" in the field of history, historicism has hung on in biblical studies as a major

---

2. For example, Susan Treggiari, a classicist, contributed to *Marriage and Family in the Biblical World* (ed. Ken M. Campbell; Downers Grove, Ill.: InterVarsity Press, 2003), 132–82.

3. Licona, *Resurrection of Jesus*, 18–19.

influential force long past its "best by" date. And although at the outset of writing this book I may have agreed with Licona that the real problem is educational and that every advanced student needs to be run through a course on historiography, I'm no longer certain that is the real issue. I now contend that the heart of the problem is that the field of New Testament studies by and large (though not necessarily every individual or institution within it) has fallen into the fallacy of reification. It has a problem of language and definition because the terms it uses for the task of conducting historical investigations in relation to the Bible are abstractions that have shifted or lost their meaning.

Essentially, my fear is that, when the term *historical criticism* is used, novices assume it encompasses anything that has to do with looking at the Bible as history or history in the Bible. That was likely what it meant when it was first coined generations ago. What it actually denotes now in mainline practice is philological approaches with a touch of historicism. In short, I wonder if, when teaching and learning "historical criticism" in basic survey classes on biblical-interpretation methods, scholars and students may be under the mistaken impression that they *are* engaged in learning about modern historiography of the sort taught in history classes in universities. A partial corrective has come with the increasingly popular use of the term *social-science interpretations*. This is an attempt to put a Band-Aid over the old "historical criticism" to highlight trends in professional historiography in the late twentieth century. But this also is a broad catchall category that verges on reification itself. Even though its use does remind the field that twentieth-century historiography at large borrowed heavily from the various disciplines of economics, psychology, sociology, anthropology, and so forth, to say that one is taking a social-scientific approach in a given research project raises the question of which one? Or, which combination? (Yes, it is possible to combine methods from the various houses of history.) Nor is it the case that imaginative or counterfactual history fits neatly under the label *social-science interpretation*. In sum, historical criticism as an abstract category has taken on a life of its own and may mean different things to different scholars, while *social-science interpretation* obscures the variety of methodological presuppositions associated with the individual approaches for which it is an umbrella term. It lacks precision.

Rather than reinventing the wheel, it is time to take stock of the labels that we are using and if they are now too broad or too baggage laden to serve as useful categories, then borrowing terminology already in vogue in the field of professional history may be a reasonable strategy. This would have the added benefit of facilitating communication and providing a common vocabulary for collaborative projects.

The final observation leaves the thorny issue of historical positivism and how to overcome it aside and tackles a different topic entirely.

Good history is all about sources. And history since the middle of the twentieth century has been bold to make use of all sorts of materials in a myriad of formats. Throughout this project alone, public-domain Internet sites, e-books, newspapers, anecdotes involving personal conversations and interviews, a working paper from an online discussion forum at a major research university, and even a mass-market paperback novel joined the ranks of traditionally published scholarly books and journal articles in the bibliography. Oddly enough, the style manuals in our guild[4] offer little guidance about these alternate types of sources. The cultural historians have important lessons to teach us about the value of the sea of materials that have become available as the information age begins to reach its zenith. Is it time to evaluate anew presuppositions about online and multimedia resources? Professional papers that are captured on video and posted on YouTube, interviews given by historians and prominent members of our own field on the History Channel, and other materials besides are just waiting "out there" to enrich our scholarly conversations. At the beginning of last year, Amazon reported that sales of e-books had overtaken the sales of paperback by 15 percent.[5] Are the ways in which we are researching and the libraries (however they may now be defined) that we are using to author works in biblical studies keeping pace with these transformations?

Change is inevitable. Methods come and go. Terminology may require updating. Not every change is good, nor will everyone adopt innovations at the same pace. But the past itself is immutable. It merely waits for us to learn new things about it.

---

4. My personal copy of the *SBL Handbook of Style for Ancient Near Eastern, Biblical, and Early Christian Studies* (ed. Patrick H. Alexander et al.; Peabody, Mass.: Hendrickson, 2002) is older and contains only brief information on Internet resources in 7.3.12–14.

5. Julianne Pepitone, "Amazon Sales Pop as Kindle Books Overtake Paperbacks" [cited 15 July 2011]; online: http://money.cnn.com/2011/01/27/technology/amazon_earnings/index.htm.

Bibliography

Ackerman, David A. "Fighting Fire with Fire: Community Formation in 1 Corinthians 12:14." *ERT* 29 (2005): 347–62.

Agosto, Efraín. "Forward." Pages xiii–xvi in *The Colonized Apostle: Paul through Postcolonial Eyes*. Edited by Christopher D. Stanley. Paul in Critical Contexts. Minneapolis: Augsburg Fortress, 2011.

Albertz, Rainer. "Secondary Sources Also Deserve to Be Historically Evaluated: The Case of the United Monarchy." Pages 31–45 in *The Historian and the Bible: Essays in Honour of Lester L. Grabbe*. Edited by Philip R. Davies and Diana V. Edelman. LHBOTS 530. New York: T & T Clark, 2010.

Allen, Robert C. "How Prosperous Were the Romans? Evidence from Diocletian's Price Edict (AD 301)." Pages 327–45 in *Quantifying the Roman Economy: Methods and Problems*. Edited by Alan Bowman and Andrew Wilson. Oxford: Oxford University Press, 2009.

Appleby, Joyce, Lynn Hunt, and Margaret Jacob. *Telling the Truth about* History. New York: Norton, 1994.

Arterbury, Andrew E. "Breaking the Betrothal Bonds: Hospitality in John 4." *CBQ* 72 (2010): 63–83.

Ashton, John. *Understanding the Fourth Gospel*. Oxford: Clarendon, 1991.

Atkins, Peter. "More than Outward Appearances: The Importance of 'Clothing' in Some New Testament Passages." *ExpTim* 113.11 (2002): 363–64.

Aubert, Jean-Jacques. "The Fourth Factor: Managing Non-agricultural Production in the Roman World." Pages 90–111 in *Economies beyond Agriculture in the Classical World*. Edited by David J. Mattingly and John Salmon. New York: Routledge, 2001.

Augustine. *The City of God*. Translated by Marcus Dods. New York: The Modern Library, 1950.

Barker, Donald C. "The Place of Residence of the Divorced Wife in Roman Egypt." Pages 59–66 in *Akten des 21. Internationalen Papyrologenkongresses, Berlin, 13.–19.8.1995*. Edited by Bärbel Kramer, Wolfgang Luppe, Herwig Maehler, and Günter Poethke. Stuttgart: Teubner, 1997.

Barr, James. *The Semantics of Biblical Language*. 1961. Repr., London: SCM, 1991.

Barrett, C. K. *The Gospel according to St. John*. 2nd ed. London: SPCK, 1978.

Barton, Stephen C. "Money Matters: Economic Relations and the Transformation of Value in Early Christianity." Pages 37–59 in *Engaging Economics: New Testament*

Scenarios and Early Christian Reception. Edited by Bruce W. Longenecker and Kelly D. Liebengood. Grand Rapids: Eerdmans, 2009.

Barton, Tamsyn S. *Power and Knowledge: Astrology, Pysiognomics, and Medicine under the Roman Empire.* Ann Arbor: University of Michigan Press, 1994.

Baukham, Richard. "The Audience of the Fourth Gospel. Pages 101–11 in *Jesus in Johannine Tradition.* Edited by Robert Fortna and Tom Thatcher. Louisville: Westminster John Knox, 2001.

———. *Jesus and the Eyewitnesses: The Gospels as Eyewitness Testimony.* Grand Rapids: Eerdmans, 2006.

Behr, C. A. *Aelius Aristides and the Sacred Tales.* Chicago: Argonaut, 1968.

Beker, J. Christiaan. *Paul the Apostle: The Triumph of God in Life and Thought.* Philadelphia: Fortress, 1980.

Berger, Adolf, et al. "Marriage Law." Pages 446–47 in *The Oxford Companion to Classical Civilization.* Edited by Simon Hornblower and Antony Spawforth. Oxford: Oxford University Press, 1998.

Bligh, J. "Jesus in Samaria." *HeyJ* 3 (1962): 329–46.

Bonavita, Helen Vella. "Key to Christendom: The 1565 Siege of Malta, Its Histories and Their Use in Reformation Polemic." *Sixteenth Century Journal* 33 (2002): 1021–43.

Bornkamm, Günther. *Jesus of Nazareth.* Translated by Irene McLuskey, Fraser McLuskey, and James M. Robinson. San Francisco: Harper & Row, 1960.

Boyd, Daniel G. "Spirit and Church in 1 Corinthians 12–14 and the Acts of the Apostles." Pages 55–66 in *Spirit within Structure: Essays in Honor of George Johnston.* Edited by E. J. Furcha. Allison Park, Pa.: Pickwick, 1983.

Braaten, Carl E. *New Directions in Theology Today: Volume II, History and Hermeneutics.* Philadelphia: Westminster, 1966.

Bradley, Keith R. *Discovering the Roman Family: Studies in Roman Social History.* Oxford: Oxford University Press, 1991.

Breisach, Ernst. *Historiography: Ancient, Medieval and Modern.* 3rd ed. Chicago: University of Chicago Press, 2007.

Brooke, George J. *The Dead Sea Scrolls and the New Testament.* Minneapolis: Fortress, 2005.

Brooten, Bernadette. "Early Christian Women in Their Cultural Context." Pages 65–91 in *Feminist Perspectives on Biblical Scholarship.* Edited by Adela Yarbro Collins. Chico, Calif.: Scholars Press, 1985.

Bruce, F. F. *Paul: Apostle of the Heart Set Free.* Grand Rapids: Eerdmans, 1977.

Bultmann, Rudolf. *The Gospel of John.* Translated by G. R. Beasley-Murray, R. W. N. Hoare, and J. K. Riches. Philadelphia: Westminster, 1971.

Burke, Peter, ed. *New Perspectives on Historical Writing.* 2nd ed. University Park: Pennsylvania State University Press, 2001.

Burridge, Richard A. *What Are the Gospels? A Comparison with Graeco-Roman Biography.* SNTSMS 70. Cambridge: Cambridge University Press, 1992.

Campbell, Ken M., ed. *Marriage and Family in the Biblical World.* Downers Grove, Ill.: InterVarsity Press, 2003.

Cancik, Hubert. "The History of Culture, Religion and Institutions in Ancient Historiography: Philological Observations concerning Luke's History." *JBL* 116 (1997): 673–95.

Carlson, Jeffrey, and Robert A. Ludwig, eds. *Jesus and Faith: A Conversation on the Works of John Dominic Crossan*. Maryknoll, N.Y.: Orbis, 1994.

Carmichael, Calum. "Marriage and the Samaritan Woman." *NTS* 26 (1980): 332–46.

Carroll, Michael P. "Moses and Monotheism and the Psychoanalytic Study of Early Christian Mythology." *JPsychohist* 15 (1988): 295–310.

Carson, D. A. *Exegetical Fallacies*. 2nd ed. Grand Rapids: Baker, 1996.

———. *The Gospel according to John*. Grand Rapids: Eerdmans, 1991.

Cassidy, Richard J. *John's Gospel in New Perspective*. Maryknoll, N.Y.: Orbis, 1992.

Chavalas, Mark W. "Recent Trends in the Study of Israelite Historiography." *JETS* 38 (1995): 161–69.

Chilton, Bruce D. "Historical Jesus." Pages 159–62 in *Dictionary of Biblical Criticism and Interpretation*. Edited by Stanley E. Porter. New York: Routledge, 2007.

Cicero. *De Oratore*. Translated by E. W. Sutton and H. Rauckham. 2 vols. LCL. Cambridge: Harvard University Press, 1988.

———. *De re Publica, De Legibus*. Translated by Clinton W. Keyes. LCL. Cambridge: Harvard University Press, 1928.

Clareno, Angelo. *A Chronicle or History of the Seven Tribulations of the Order of Brothers Minor*. Translated by David Burr and E. Randolph Daniel. St. Bonaventure, N.Y.: Franciscan Institute, 2005.

Cleland, Liza, Glenys Davies, and Lloyd Llewellyn Jones. *Greek and Roman Dress from A to Z*. New York: Routledge, 2007.

Collins, John J. "The 'Historical Character' of the Old Testament." Pages 150–69 in *Israel's Past in Present Research: Essays on Ancient Israelite Historiography*. Edited by V. Phillips Long. Winona Lake, Ind.: Eisenbrauns, 1999.

———. *The Scepter and the Star: Messianism in Light of the Dead Sea Scrolls*. 2nd ed. Grand Rapids: Eerdmans, 2010.

Corbier, Mireille. "Divorce and Adoption as Roman Familial Strategies." Pages 47–78 in *Marriage, Divorce and Children in Ancient Rome*. Edited by Beryl Rawson. Oxford: Clarendon, 1991.

Cottle, Ronald E. "All Were Baptized." *JETS* 17 (1974): 75–80.

Cowan, Steven B., and James S. Spiegel. *The Love of Wisdom: A Christian Introduction to Philosophy*. Nashville: B&H Academic, 2009.

Cowley, Robert, ed. *What If? The World's Foremost Military Historians Imagine What Might Have Been*. New York: Berkley Books, 1999.

———, ed. *What If? 2: Eminent Historians Imagine What Might Have Been*. New York: Berkley Books, 2001.

———. "When Do Counterfactuals Work?" Pages 115–19 in *Recent Themes in Historical Thinking: Historians in Conversation*. Edited by Donald A. Yerxa. Columbia: University of South Carolina Press, 2008.

Craddock, Paul. *Scientific Investigation of Copies, Fakes and Forgeries*. Oxford: Butterworth-Heinemann, 2009.

Craffert, Pieter F. "Multiple Realities and Historiography: Rethinking Historical Jesus Research." Pages 87–116 in *The New Testament Interpreted: Essays in Honour of Bernard C. Lategan*. Edited by Cilliers Breytenbach, Johan C. Thom, and Jeremy Punt. NovTSup 124. Leiden: Brill, 2006.

Crawfoot, G. M. "Linen Textiles from the Cave of Ain Feshkha in the Jordan Valley." *PEQ* 83 (1951): 5–31.

Crook, J. A. *Law and Life of Rome 90 B.C.–A.D. 212*. Ithaca, N.Y.: Cornell University Press, 1967.

Crosby, Michael H. *House of Disciples: Church, Economics and Justice in Matthew*. Maryknoll, N.Y.: Orbis, 1988.

Crossan, John Dominic. "The Historical Jesus in Earliest Christianity." Pages 1–21 in *Jesus and Faith: A Conversation on the Works of John Dominic Crossan*. Edited by Jeffrey Carlson and Robert A. Ludwig. Maryknoll, N.Y.: Orbis, 1994.

Curran, John. "Flavius Josephus in Rome." Pages 65–86 in *Flavius Josephus: Interpretation and History*. Edited by Jack Pastor, Pnina Stern, and Menahem Mor. JSJSup 146. Leiden: Brill, 2011.

Danker, Frederick William. Introduction to BDAG. Chicago: University of Chicago Press, 2000.

Davies, Margaret. *Matthew*. Readings a New Biblical Commentary. Sheffield: JSOT Press, 1993.

Davies, Philip R., and Diana V. Edelman, eds. *The Historian and the Bible. Essays in Honour of Lester L. Grabbe*. LHBOTS 530. New York: T&T Clark, 2010.

Dewey, Arthur J. "The Eyewitness of History: Visionary Consciousness in the Fourth Gospel." Pages 59–70 in *Jesus in Johannine Tradition*. Edited by Robert T. Fortna and Tom Thatcher. Louisville: Westminster John Knox, 2001.

Donaldson, James. *Woman: Her Position and Influence in Ancient Greece and Rome and among the Early Christians*. London: Longman, Green, 1907.

Dray, William H. *Philosophy of History*. Englewood Cliffs, N.J.: Prentice-Hall, 1964.

Drijvers, Jan Willem. "Virginity and Asceticism in Late Roman Western Elites." Pages 241–73 in *Sexual Asymmetry: Studies in Ancient Society*. Edited by Josine Blok and Peter Mason. Amsterdam: Geiben, 1987.

Dupont, Francis. *Daily Life in Ancient Rome*. Translated by Christopher Woodall. Oxford: Blackwell, 1989.

Edelstein, Emma J., and Ludwig Edelstein. *Asclepius: Collection and Interpretation of the Testimonies*. Baltimore: Johns Hopkins University Press, 1998.

Ehrman, Bart D. *The New Testament: A Historical Introduction to the Early Christian Writings*. 4th ed. Oxford: Oxford University Press, 2008.

Elliott, Neil. "Marxism and the Postcolonial Study of Paul." Pages 34–50 in *The Colonized Apostle: Paul though Postcolonial Eyes*. Edited by Christopher D. Stanley. Minneapolis: Augsburg Fortress, 2011.

Erickson, Erik. *Young Man Luther: A Study in Psychoanalysis and History*. 1962. Austen Riggs Monograph 4. New York: Norton, 1993.

Evans, Richard J. "Response." Pages 120–30 in *Recent Themes in Historical Thinking: Historians in Conversation*. Edited by Donald A. Yerxa. Columbia: University of South Carolina Press, 2008.

———. "Telling It Like It Wasn't." Pages 77–84 in *Recent Themes in Historical Thinking: Historians in Conversation*. Edited by Donald A. Yerxa. Columbia: University of South Carolina Press, 2008.

Fass, Paula S. "Cultural History/Social History: Some Reflections on a Continuing Dialogue." *JSH* 37 (2003): 39–46.

Fee, Gordon D. *New Testament Exegesis*. Rev. ed. Louisville: Westminster John Knox, 1993.

Finger, Reta Halteman. *Of Widows and Meals: Communal Meals in the Book of Acts*. Grand Rapids: Eerdmans, 2007.

Finley, M. I. *The Ancient Economy*. Berkeley: University of California Press, 1999.

Fischer, David Hackett. *Historians' Fallacies: Toward a Logic of Historical Thought*. New York: Harper & Row, 1970.

Fisk, Bruce N. *First Corinthians*. Interpretation Bible Studies Series. Louisville: Westminster John Knox, 2000.

Fortna, Robert T. *The Fourth Gospel and Its Predecessor*. Edinburgh: T&T Clark, 1988.

Fortna, Robert T., and Tom Thatcher, eds. *Jesus in Johannine Tradition*. Louisville: Westminster John Knox, 2001.

Fraschetti, Augusto. *Roman Women*. Translated by Linda Lappin. Chicago: University of Chicago Press, 2001.

Freud, Sigmund. *Moses and Monotheism*. New York: Vintage, 1967.

Friesen, Steven J. "Poverty in Pauline Studies: Beyond the So-Called New Consensus." *JSNT* 26 (2004): 232–61.

Fukuyama, Francis. *The End of History and the Last Man*. New York: Free Press, 2006.

Funk, Robert, and the Jesus Seminar. *The Gospel of Mark: Red Letter Edition*. Sonoma, Calif.: Polebridge, 1991.

Furnish, Victor P. "On Putting Paul in His Place." *JBL* 113 (1994): 3–17.

Gagarin, Michael, and Elaine Fantham, eds. *Oxford Encyclopedia of Greece and Rome*. Oxford: Oxford University Press, 2010.

Garnsey, Peter, and Richard Saller. *The Roman Empire: Economy, Society and Culture*. Berkeley: University of California Press, 1987.

Gilderhus, Mark T. *History and Historians: A Historical Introduction*. 6th ed. Upper Saddle River, N.J.: Pearson/Prentice Hall, 2007.

Gingrich, F. Wilbur. "New Testament Lexicography and the Future." *JR* 25 (1945): 179–82.

Goldman, Bernard. "Graeco-Roman Dress in Syro-Mesopotamia." Pages 163–81 in *The World of Roman Costume*. Edited by Judith Lynn Sebesta and Larissa Bonfante. Madison: University of Wisconsin Press.

Gooch, Peter D. *Dangerous Food: 1 Corinthians 8–10 in Its Context*. Waterloo, Ont.: Wilfred Laurier University Press, 1993.

Gowler, David B. *What Are They Saying about the Historical Jesus?* Mahwah, N.J.: Paulist, 2007.

Green, Anna, and Troup, Kathleen. *The Houses of History: A Critical Reader in Twentieth-Century History and Theory*. New York: New York University Press, 1999.

Gregory, Dick, and Robert Lipsyte. *Nigger: An Autobiography*. New York: Simon & Schuster, 1964.

Hankinson, R. J. *The Cambridge Companion to Galen*. Cambridge: Cambridge University Press, 2008.

Hanson, K. C., and Douglas Oakman. *Palestine in the Time of Jesus: Social Structures and Social Conflict*. Minneapolis: Fortress Press, 1998.

Harrell, J. Albert. "Cannibalistic Language in the Fourth Gospel and Greco-Roman Polemics of Factionalism: John 6:53–56." *JBL* 127 (2008): 133–58.

Harris, William V. *Ancient Literacy*. Cambridge: Harvard University Press, 1989.

Harsgar, Michael. "Total History: The *Annales* School." *JCH* 13 (1978): 1–13.

Hart, Gerald David. *Asclepius: The God of Medicine*. London: Royal Society of Medicine, 2000.

Hartog, Francis. "The Invention of History: The Pre-history of a Concept from Homer to Herodotus." *History and Theory* 39 (2000): 384–95.

Hens-Piazza, Gina. *The New Historicism*. Guides to Biblical Scholarship. Minneapolis: Fortress, 2002.

Herman, Peter C. "Rastell's *Pastyme of People*: Early Monarchy and the Law in Early Modern Historiography." *Journal of Medieval and Early Modern Studies* 30 (2000): 275–308.

Herodotus. *Histories*. Translated by A. D. Goodley. 4 vols. LCL. Cambridge: Harvard University Press, 1920–1926.

Hill, Andrew E. "The Temple of Asclepius: An Alternative Source for Paul's Body Theology?" *JBL* 99 (1980): 437–39.

Hofstadter, Richard. *The Progressive Historians: Turner, Beard, Parrington*. New York: Knopf, 1969.

Homer. *The Iliad*. Translated by E. V. Rieu. London: Penguin, 1950.

Horrell, David G. "Aliens and Strangers? The Socioeconimc Location of the Addressees of 1 Peter." Pages 176–202 in *Engaging Economics: New Testament Scenarios and Early Christian Reception*. Edited by Bruce W. Longenecker and Kelly D. Liebengood. Grand Rapids: Eerdmans, 2009.

Horsley, Richard A. *Paul and the Roman Imperial Order*. Harrisburg, Pa.: Trinity Press International, 2004.

———, ed. *Paul and Empires: Religion and Power in Roman Imperial Society*. Valley Forge, Pa.: Trinity Press International, 1997.

Horsley, Richard A., with John S. Hanson. *Bandits, Prophets and Messiahs: Popular Movements at the Time of Jesus*. New Voices in Biblical Studies. San Francisco: Harper & Row, 1985.

Howell, Martha, and Walter Prevenier. *From Reliable Sources: An Introduction to Historical Methods*. Ithaca, N.Y.: Cornell University Press, 2001.

Hull, Robert F., Jr. *The Story of the New Testament Text: Movers, Materials, Motives, Methods and Models*. SBLRBS 58. Atlanta: Society of Biblical Literature, 2010.

Huston, Mary. *Ancient Greek, Roman and Byzantine Costume and Decoration*. 2nd ed. London: Black, 1947.

Iggers, Georg G. *Historiography in the Twentieth Century: From Scientific Objectivity to the Postmodern Challenge*. Middletown, Conn.: Wesleyan University Press, 2005.

Jeffers, James S. *The Greco-Roman World of the New Testament Era: Exploring the Background of Early Christianity*. Downer's Grove, Ill.: InterVarsity Press, 1999.

Jefferson, Charles Edward. *The Character of Jesus*. New York: Crowell, 1908.

Jones, Timothy Paul. *Misquoting Truth: A Guide to the Fallacies of Bart Ehrman's Misquoting Jesus*. Downer's Grove, Ill: InterVarsity Press, 2007.

Jongman, Willem M. "The Early Roman Empire: Consumption." Pages 592–618 in *The Cambridge Economic History of the Greco-Roman World*. Edited by Walter Scheidel, Ian Morris, and Richard Saller. Cambridge: Cambridge University Press, 2007.

Josephus. Translated by H. St. J. Thackeray et al. 10 vols. LCL. Cambridge: Harvard University Press, 1926–1965.

Joynes, Christine E., and Christopher C. Rowland, eds. *From the Margins 2: Women of the New Testament and Their Afterlives*. BMW 27. Sheffield: Sheffield Phoenix, 2009.

Kähler, Martin. *The So-Called Historical Jesus and the Historic Biblical Christ*. Translated by Carl E. Braaten. Philadelphia: Fortress, 1988.

Kennedy, D. James, and Jerry Newcombe. *What If Jesus Had Never Been Born?* Rev. ed. Nashville: Nelson, 2001.

King, Helen. *Greek and Roman Medicine*. London: Bristol Classical Press, 2001.

Kirkpatrick, Patricia G., and Timothy Goltz eds. *The Function of Ancient Historiography in Biblical and Cognate Studies*. LHBOTS 489. New York: T&T Clark, 2008.

Kloppenborg, John S., Marvin W. Meyer, Stephen J. Patterson, and Michael G. Steinhauser. *Q-Thomas Reader*. Sonoma, Calif.: Polebrige, 1990.

Knox, John. *Jesus Lord and Christ*. New York: Harper & Brothers, 1958.

Kock, Leon de. "Interview with Gayatri Chakravorty Spivak: New Nation Writers Conference in South Africa." *ARIEL: A Review of International English Literature* 23 (1992): 29–47.

Koester, Helmut. *Introduction to the New Testament: History, Culture, and Religion in the Hellenistic Age*. 2nd ed. Berlin: de Gruyter, 1995.

———, ed. *Ephesos: Metropolis of Asia: An Interdisciplinary Approach to its Archaeology, Religion and Culture*. HTS 41. Valley Forge, Pa.: Trinity Press International, 1995.

Koontz, Dean. *Winter Moon*. Mass market ed., 2011. New York: Bantam, 1993.

Krippendorf, Klaus. *Content Analysis: An Introduction to Its Methodology*. 2nd ed. Thousand Oaks, Calif.: Sage, 2004.

Lassen, Eva Marie. "The Roman Family: Ideal and Metaphor." Pages 103–20 in *Constructing Early Christian Families*. Edited by Halvor Moxnes. New York: Routledge, 1997.

Ledbow, Richard Ned. "Good History Needs Counterfactuals." Pages 91–97 in *Recent Themes in Historical Thinking: Historians in Conversation*. Edited by Donald A. Yerxa. Columbia: University of South Carolina Press, 2008.

Levine, Joseph M. *The Autonomy of History: Truth and Method from Erasmus to Gibbon*. Chicago: University of Chicago Press, 1999.

Licona, Michael R. *The Resurrection of Jesus: A New Historiographical Approach*. Downers Grove, Ill.: InterVarsity Press, 2010.

Liverani, Mario. "The Chronology of the Biblical Fairy-Tale." Pages 73–88 in *The Historian and the Bible: Essays in Honour of Lester L. Grabbe*. Edited by Philip R. Davies and Diana V. Edelman. LHBOTS 530. New York: T&T Clark, 2010.

Loader, James Alfred, and Oda Wischmeyer. "Twentieth Century Interpretation." Pages 371–83 in *Dictionary of Biblical Criticism and Interpretation*. Edited by Stanley E. Porter. New York: Routledge, 2007.

Longenecker, Bruce W. *Remember the Poor: Paul, Poverty, and the Greco-Roman World*. Grand Rapids: Eerdmans, 2010.

Longenecker, Bruce W., and Kelly D. Liebengood, eds. *Engaging Economics: New Testament Scenarios and Early Christian Reception*. Grand Rapids: Eerdmans, 2009.

Lucian of Samosata. *Herodotus and Aëtion*. Pages 90–93 in *The Works of Lucian*. H. W. Fowler and F. G. Fowler. Vol. 2. Oxford: Clarendon, 1905.

MacDonald, Jan. "Palestinian Dress." *PEQ* 83 (1951): 55–68 and plates.

MacMillan, Margaret. *Dangerous Games: The Uses and Abuses of History*. New York: Modern Library, 2008.

MacMullen, Ramsay. *Romanization in the Time of Augustus*. New Haven: Yale University Press, 2000.

MacMullen, Ramsay, and Eugene N. Lane, eds. *Paganism and Christianity 100–425 C.E.: A Sourcebook*. Minneapolis: Fortress, 1992.

Maier, Gerhard. *The End of the Historical Critical Method*. Translated by Edwin W. Leverenz and Rudolph F. Norden. St. Louis: Concordia, 1977.

Majano, Guido. *The Healing Hand: Man and Wound in the Ancient World*. Cambridge: Harvard University Press, 1975.

Malcolm, Lois, and Janet Ramsey. "On Forgiveness and Healing: Narrative Therapy and the Gospel Story." *WW* 30 (2010): 23–32.

Malina, Bruce J., and Richard L. Rohrbaugh. *Social-Science Commentary on the Gospel of John*. Minneapolis: Fortress, 1998.

Martinez, Florentino Garcia, ed. *Echoes from the Caves: Qumran and the New Testament*. STDJ 85. Leiden: Brill, 2009.

Martyn, J. Louis. *History and Theology in the Fourth Gospel*. New York: Harper & Row, 1968.

Marx, Karl, with Friedrich Engels. *The German Ideology*. Great Books in Philosophy. Amherst, N.Y.: Prometheus, 1998.

McGarvey, J. W. "A Note on 1 Cor. 12:13." *ResQ* 1(1958): 45–47.

McGinn, Thomas A. J. "The Augustan Marriage Legislation and Social Practice: Elite Endogamy versus the Male Marrying Down." Pages 46–93 in *Speculum Iuris: Roman Law as a Reflection of Social and Economic Life in Antiquity*. Edited by Jean-Jacques Aubert and Boudewyn Sirks. Ann Arbor: University of Michigan Press, 2002.

McKitterick, Rosamund. *Perceptions of the Past in the Early Middle Ages*. Conway Lectures in Medieval Studies. Notre Dame: University of Notre Dame Press, 2006.

Megill, Allan. "Memory." Pages 797–99 in *Encyclopedia of Historians and Historical Writing*. Edited by Kelly Boyd. New York: Routledge, 1999.

———. "The New Counterfactuals." Pages 101–6 in *Recent Themes in Historical Thinking: Historians in Conversation*. Edited by Donald A. Yerxa. Columbia: University of South Carolina Press, 2008.

Mellor, Ronald. "Roman Historiography and Biography." Pages 1541–62 in vol. 3 of

Civilization of the Ancient Mediterranean: Greece and Rome. Edited by Michael Grant and Rachel Kitzinger. New York: Charles Scribner's Sons, 1988.

Merrill, Michael. "Introduction." *RHR* 9/10 (1975): 1–4.

Miller, J. W. *Jesus at Thirty: A Psychohistorical Inquiry.* Minneapolis: Fortress, 1997.

Minear, Paul S. *The Bible and the Historian: Breaking the Silence about God in Biblical Studies.* Nashville: Abingdon, 2002.

Moore, Stephen D. *Empire and Apocalypse: Postcolonialism and the New Testament.* BMW 12. Sheffield: Sheffield Phoenix, 2006.

———. "Paul after Empire." Pages 9–23 in *The Colonized Apostle: Paul through Postcolonial Eyes.* Edited by Christopher D. Stanley. Minneapolis: Augsburg Fortress, 2011.

Morely, Neville. *Trade in Classical Antiquity.* Cambridge: Cambridge University Press, 2007.

———. "The Poor in the City of Rome." Pages 21–39 in *Poverty in the Roman World.* Edited by Margaret Atkins and Robin Osborne. Cambridge: Cambridge University Press, 2006.

Morris, Ian. Introduction to *The Ancient Economy* by M. I. Finley. Berkeley: University of California Press, 1999.

Morris, Leon. *The Gospel according to John.* Rev. ed. Grand Rapids: Eerdmans, 1995.

Moxnes, Halvor, ed. *Constructing Early Christian Families.* New York: Routledge, 1997.

Mukherjee, Siddhartha. *The Emperor of All Maladies: A Biography of Cancer.* New York: Scribner, 2010.

Murphy-O'Connor, Jerome. *St. Paul's Corinth: Texts and Archaeology.* Collegeville, Minn.: Liturgical Press, 1983.

Nathan, Geoffrey S. *The Family in Late Antiquity: The Rise of Christianity and the Endurance of Tradition.* New York: Routledge, 2000.

Nietzsche, Friedrich. *The Use and Abuse of History.* Translated by Adrian Collins. Indianapolis: Bobbs-Merrill, 1957.

Noll, K. L. "The Evolution of Genre in the Book of Kings: The Story of Sennacherib and Hezekiah as Example." Pages 30–56 in *The Function of Ancient Historiography in Biblical and Cognate Studies.* Edited by Patricia G. Kirkpatrick and Timothy Goltz. LHBOTS 489. T&T Clark, 2008.

Noll, Mark A. "History." Pages 295–99 in *Dictionary for Theological Interpretation of the Bible.* Edited by Kevin J. Vanhoozer. Grand Rapids: Baker Academic, 2005.

Novick, Peter. *That Noble Dream: The 'Objectivity Question' and the American Historical Profession.* Cambridge: Cambridge University Press, 1998.

Nutton, Vivian. *Ancient Medicine.* New York: Routledge, 2004.

Oakman, Douglas E. *Jesus and the Peasants.* Matrix: The Bible in Mediterranean Context 4. Eugene, Ore.: Cascade, 2008.

Okure, Teresa. "Jesus and the Samaritan Woman (Jn 4:1–42) in Africa." *TS* 70 (2009): 401–18.

Outhouse, J. B., K. D. Johnson, and C. L. Rhykerd. "Managing and Utilizing Pasture and Harvested Forages for Sheep." Online: http://www.agry.perdue.edu/ext/forages/publications/ID-153.htm.

Padilla, Osvaldo. *The Speeches of Outsiders in Acts: Poetics, Theology, and Historiography.* SNTSMS 144. Cambridge: Cambridge University Press, 2008.

Palmer, Darryl. "Historiographical Literature." Pages 162–64 in *Dictionary of Biblical Criticism and Interpretation.* Edited by Stanley E. Porter. New York: Routledge, 2007.

Patzia, Arthur, G. *The Making of the New Testament: Origin, Collection, Text and Canon.* 2nd ed. Downers Grove, Ill.: InterVarsity Press, 2011.

Pepitone, Julianne. "Amazon Sales Pop as Kindle Books Overtake Paperbacks." *CNNMoney,* 27 January 2011. Online: http://money.cnn.com/2011/01/27/technology/amazon_earnings/index. htm?source=cnn_bin&hpt=Sbin

Pieters, Jürgen. "New Historicism: Postmodern Historiography between Narrativism and Heterology." *History and Theory* 39 (2000): 21–38.

"Population." *Encyclopædia Britannica. Cited 1 April 2012.* Online: http://www.britannica.com.turing.library.northwestern.edu/EBchecked/topic/470303/population.

Porter, Stanley E. "Thycydides 1.22.1 and Speeches in Acts: Is there a Thucydidean View?" *NovT* 32 (1990): 121–42.

Rathbone, Dominic. "Poverty and Population in Roman Egypt." Pages 100–14 in *Poverty in the Roman World.* Edited by Margaret Atkins and Robin Osborne. Cambridge: Cambridge University Press, 2006.

Rawson, Beryl. "Adult-Child Relationships in Roman Society." Pages 7–30 in *Marriage, Divorce, and Children in Ancient Rome.* Edited by Beryl Rawson. Oxford: Clarendon, 1991.

Reed, Randall W. *A Clash of Ideologies: Marxism, Liberation Theology, and Apocalypticism in New Testament Studies.* Princeton Theological Monograph Series 136. Eugene, Ore.: Pickwick, 2010.

Reeves, Marjorie. *The Prophetic Sense of History in Medieval and Renaissance Europe.* Variorum Collected Studies Series. Aldershot: Ashgate, 1999.

Rempel, Morgan H. "Daybreak 68: Nietzsche's Psychohistory of the Pre-Damascus Paul." *Journal of Nietzsche Studies* 15 (Spring 1998): 50–58.

Riley, Gregory J. *The River of God: A New History of Christian Origins.* San Francisco: Harper, 2003.

Rorty, Richard. "The Historiography of Philosophy: Four Genres." Pages 49–75 in *Philosophy of History.* Edited by Richard Rorty, J. B. Schneewind, and Quentin Skinner. Cambridge: Cambridge University Press, 1984.

Roussin, Lucille. "Costume in Roman Palestine: Archaeological Remains and the Evidence from the Mishna." Pages 182–90 in *The World of Roman Costume.* Edited by Judith Lynn Sebesta and Larissa Bonfante. Madison: University of Wisconsin Press.

Sanders, E. P. *Judaism: Practice and Belief 63 BCE–66 CE.* Philadelphia: SCM, 1992.

———. *Paul and Palestinian Judaism.* Minneapolis: Fortress, 1992.

Sandnes, Karl Olav. *The Challenge of Homer: School, Pagan Poets and Early Christianity.* LNTS 400. London: T&T Clark, 2009.

———. *The Gospel 'According to Homer and Virgil' Cento and Canon.* NovTSup 138. Leiden: Brill, 2011.

Satlow, Michael. *Jewish Marriage in Antiquity.* Princeton: Princeton University Press, 2001.

Scheidel, Walter. "Epigraphy and Demography: Birth, Marriage, Family and Death." *Princeton/Stanford Working Papers in Classics.* Cited June 2007. Online: http://www.princeton.edu/~pswpc/pdfs/scheidel/060701.pdf.

———. *Measuring Sex, Age and Death in the Roman Empire: Explorations in Roman Demography.* JRASup 21. Ann Arbor: Journal of Roman Archaeology, 1996.

———. "Stratification, Deprivation, and Quality of Life." Pages 40–59 in *Poverty in the Roman World.* Edited by Margaret Atkins and Robin Osborne. Cambridge: Cambridge University Press, 2006.

Schneiders, Sandra M. " 'Because of the Woman's Testimony…': Reexamining the Issue of Authorship in the Fourth Gospel." *NTS* 44 (1998): 513–35.

Schrecker, Ellen, ed. *Cold War Triumphalism: The Misuse of History after the Fall of Communism.* New York: New Press, 2004.

Schüssler Fiorenza, Elisabeth. *Jesus and the Politics of Interpretation.* New York: Continuum, 2000.

Schweitzer, Albert. *The Quest of the Historical Jesus.* Translated by W. Montgomery. New York: Collier /Macmillan, 1968.

Scott, Bernard Brandon. "To Impose Is Not to Discover: Methodology in John Dominic Crossan's *Historical Jesus.*" Pages 22–30 in *Jesus and Faith: A Conversation on the Work of John Dominic Crossan.* Edited by Jeffrey Carlson and Robert A. Ludwig. Maryknoll, N.Y.: Orbis, 1994.

Sebesta, Judith Lynn, and Larissa Bonfante, eds. *The World of Roman Costume.* Madison: University of Wisconsin Press, 1994.

Seitz, Oscar J. F. *One Body and One Spirit: A Study of the Church in the New Testament.* Greenwich, Conn.: Seabury, 1960.

Sheppard, Beth M. "The Rise of Rome: The Emergence of a New Mode for Exploring the Fourth Gospel." *American Theological Library Association Summary of Proceedings* 57 (2003): 175–87.

Sherwin-White, A. N. *Roman Law and Roman Society in the New Testament.* Oxford: Oxford University Press, 1963.

Smith, D. Moody. *John.* Nashville: Abingdon, 1999.

Smith, Jonathan Z. *Drudgery Divine: On the Comparison of Early Christianities and the Religions of Late Antiquity.* Chicago: University of Chicago Press, 1990.

Spalding, Roger, and Christopher Parker. *Historiography: An Introduction.* Manchester: Manchester University Press, 2007.

Staley, Jeffrey Lloyd. *The Print's First Kiss: A Rhetorical Investigation of the Implied Reader in the Fourth Gospel.* SBLDS 82. Atlanta: Scholars Press, 1988.

Stearns, Peter N. "Social History Present and Future." *Journal of Social History* 37 (2003): 9–19.

Stendahl, Krister, ed. *The Scrolls and the New Testament.* London: SCM, 1957.

Stern, Fritz, ed. *The Varieties of History: From Voltaire to the Present.* New York: Meridian, 1956.

Stone, Shelly. "The Toga: From National to Ceremonial Costume." Pages 13–45 in *The*

World of Roman Costume. Edited by Judith Lynn Sebesta and Larissa Bonfante. Madison: University of Wisconsin Press.

Swedenborg, Emanuel. *Secrets of Heaven.* Translated by Lisa Hyatt Cooper. West Chester, Pa.: The Swedenborg Foundation, 2008

Talbert, Charles H. "Paul's Understanding of the Holy Spirit: The Evidence of 1 Corinthians 12–14." *PRSt* 11.4 (1984): 95–108.

———. *What Is a Gospel? The Genre of the Canonical Gospels.* Philadelphia: Fortress, 1997. Repr., Macon, Ga.: Mercer University Press, 1985.

Taylor, Barbara Brown. "Reflections on the Lectionary: Sunday, February 24." *ChrCent* (February 12, 2008): 19.

Taylor, Joan E., Kaare L. Rasmussen, Gregory Doudna, Johannes Van der Plict, Helge Egsgaard. "Qumran Textiles in the Palestine Exploration Fund, London: Radiocarbon Dating Results." *PEQ* 137 (2005): 159–67.

Teeple, Howard M. *The Historical Approach to the Bible.* Evanston, Ill.: Religion and Ethics Institute, 1982.

Tetlock, Philip E., and Aaron Belkin, eds. *Counterfactual Thought Experiments in World Politics: Logical, Methodological, and Psychological Perspectives.* Princeton: Princeton University Press, 1996.

Thatcher, Tom. *Greater Than Caesar: Christology and Empire in the Fourth Gospel.* Minneapolis: Fortress, 2009.

Theissen, Gerd. *The Social Setting of Pauline Christianity: Essays on Corinth.* Translated by John H. Schütz. Philadelphia: Fortress, 1982.

Thompson, Thomas L. "Reiterative Narratives of Exile and Return: Virtual Memories of Abraham in the Persian and Hellenistic Periods." Pages 46–54 in *The Historian and the Bible: Essays in Honour of Lester L. Grabbe.* Edited by Philip R. Davies and Diana V. Edelman. LHBOTS 530. New York: T&T Clark, 2010.

Thucydides. *History of the Peloponnesian War.* Translated by Charles Forster Smith. 4 vols. LCL. Cambridge: Harvard University Press, 1975–1980.

Tibbs, Clint. "The Spirit (World) and the (Holy) Spirits among the Earliest Christians: 1 Corinthians 12 and 14 a Test Case." *CBQ* 70 (2008): 95–108.

Treggiari, Susan. "Divorce Roman Style: How Easy and How Frequent Was It?" Pages 31–46 in *Marriage, Divorce and Children in Ancient Rome.* Edited by Beryl Rawson. Oxford: Clarendon, 1991.

Tropper, Amram. "The Fate of Jewish Historiography after the Bible: A New Interpretation." *History and Theory* 43 (2004): 179–97.

Trueman, Carl R. *Histories and Fallacies: Problems Faced in the Writing of History.* Wheaton, Ill.: Crossway, 2010.

Usher, Stephen. "Greek Historiography and Biography." Pages 1525–40 in *Civilization of the Ancient Mediterranean: Greece and Rome.* Edited by Michael Grant and Rachel Kitzinger. New York: Charles Scribner's Sons, 1988.

Van der Horst, P. W. *Aelius Aristides and the New Testament.* Leiden: Brill, 1980.

Vanhoozer, Kevin J., ed. *Dictionary for Theological Interpretation of the Bible.* Grand Rapids: Baker Academic, 2005.

Van Nijf, Onno. "Local Heroes: Athletics, Festivals, and Elite Self-Fashioning in the

Roman East." Pages 306–34 in *Being Greek under Rome*. Edited by Simon Gold-hill. Cambridge: Cambridge University Press, 2001.

Van Seters, John. *In Search of History. Historiography in the Ancient World and the Origins of Biblical History*. New Haven: Yale University Press, 1983.

Van Tilborg, Sjef. *Imaginative Love in John*. Leiden: Brill, 1993.

———. *Reading John in Ephesus*. NovTSup. Leiden: Brill, 1996.

Waetjen, Herman C. *The Gospel of the Beloved Disciple: A Work in Two Editions*. New York: T&T Clark, 2005.

The Warring States Project. "The Discipline of History. Postmodernism Is Not the Only Problem." University of Massachusetts, Amherst. August 19, 2002. Online: http://www.umass.edu/wsp/methodology/difficulties/discipline.html

Watson, Francis. *Paul, Judaism and the Gentiles: Beyond the New Perspective*. Rev. and exp. ed. Grand Rapids: Eerdmans, 2007.

———. *Text and Truth: Redefining Biblical Theology*. Grand Rapids: Eerdmans, 1997.

Watts, Fraser, ed. *Jesus and Psychology*. Philadelphia: Templeton Foundation Press, 2007.

Wiesehöfer, Josef (Kiel). "Child Exposure." *Brill's New Pauly* (2012). Cited 1 April 2012. Online: http://referenceworks.brillonline.com/entries/brill-s-new-pauly/child-exposure-e613990.

Wilson, Andrew. "Timgad and Textile Production." Pages 271–96 in *Economies beyond Agriculture in the Classical World*. Edited by David J. Mattingly and John Salmon. New York: Routledge, 2001.

———. "Urban Production in the Roman World: The View from North Africa." *Papers of the British School at Rome* 70 (2002): 231–73.

Wilson, Walter T. *Pauline Parallels: A Comprehensive Guide*. Louisville: Westminster John Knox, 2009.

Winter, Bruce W. *Roman Wives, Roman Widows: The Appearance of New Women and the Pauline Communities*. Grand Rapids: Eerdmans, 2003.

Wire, Antoinette Clark. *The Corinthian Women Prophets: A Reconstruction through Paul's Rhetoric*. Minneapolis: Fortress, 1990.

Wit, Hans de, and Gerald O. West. *African and European Readers of the Bible in Dialogues: In Quest of Shared Meaning*. Studies of Religion in Africa 32. Leiden: Brill, 2008.

Witherington, Ben, III. *The Jesus Quest: The Third Search for the Jew of Nazareth*. Downers Grove, Ill.: InterVarsity Press, 1995.

———. *John's Wisdom: A Commentary on the Fourth Gospel*. Louisville: Westminster John Knox, 1995.

Woodman, A. J. *Rhetoric in Classical Historiography*. Portland, Ore.: Croom Helm and Areopagitica Press, 1988.

Woolf, Greg. "Regional Productions in Early Roman Gaul." Pages 49–69 in *Economies beyond Agriculture in the Classical World*. Edited by David J. Mattingly and John Salmon. New York: Routledge, 2001.

Yerxa, Donald A. "On the Current State of History: An Interview with Richard J. Evans." Pages 23–27 in *Recent Themes in Historical Thinking: Historians in Con-*

versation. Edited by Donald A. Yerxa. Columbia: University of South Carolina Press, 2008.

Zeldin, Theodore. "Social History and Total History." *JSH* 10 (1976): 237–45.

Zuabi, Rena. "Land Use Planning and the Palestinian Minority in Israel: A Comparative Regional Study." *Prospect* (June 2011). Online: http://prospectjournal.ucsd .edu/index.php/2011/06/land-use-planning-and-the-palestinian-minority-in-israel-a-comparative-regional-study/.

Index of Ancient and Medieval Texts and Persons

Index of Modern Persons

INDEX OF SUBJECTS